TIM BURTON

A Child's Garden of Nightmares

Edited by Paul A. Woods

Plexus, London

Copyright © 2002, 2007 by Plexus Publishing Limited
Published by Plexus Publishing Limited
25 Mallinson Road
London SW11 1BW
Tel: 020 7924 4662
Fax: 020 7924 5096
First printing 2007

A catalogue record for this book is available
from the British Library.

ISBN-10: 0-85965-401-X
ISBN-13: 978-0-85965-401-2

Cover design by Phil Gambrill
Book design by Bradley at White Light
Printed in Great Britain by Bell & Bain

CONTENTS

INTRODUCTION

Once upon a time, there was a lonely little boy who was ignored by the people around him. Instead of normal friends, he grew up to love monsters and dogs . . .

Born in Burbank, California on 25 August 1958, Timothy William Burton was a child of the end of the Baby Boom. In the Hollywood suburb where he grew up, every one of the endless houses and bungalows, lit up at night by the cathode-ray tube, was a sanctum of secrets. His overactive adolescent imagination re-interpreted everything it perceived, until Home Sweet Home became Bluebeard's Castle. This rampant imaginativeness, ground out of most of us by conformity, adulthood and responsibility, bred a world of dark daydream and bright pastel nightmare – the world we can all occasionally experience via the films of Tim Burton.

As an alienated suburban child, Burton's love of monster movies and cartoons – later expressed in his own strange drawings – coalesced into a love of artifice and the grotesque, manifested in incidents like the time he tore the heads from his toy soldiers and told the boy next door it was the work of invaders from outer space. Remembering the cheap-and-cheerful horrors he witnessed at Saturday-afternoon matinees, Burton has reflected how, 'A lot of the things you see as a child remain with you . . . you spend a lot of your life trying to recapture the experience.'

While his apparently hyper-normal parents were bemused by, and uncommunicative to, their misfit son, the young Tim Burton took refuge in the world of imagination that gave him succour. Like some suburban Colonel Kurtz, little Tim made a friend of horror. But, unlike its real-life counterpart, horror did not sit on a bloody throne atop a pile of war victims' bodies. Its grotesquerie was a comfort.

'When you don't have many friends,' Burton would recall much later of his formative years, 'and you don't have a social life . . . You're at a distance from the rest of society; you're kind of looking out of a window . . . But there's enough weird movies out there so you can go a long time without friends.' Black-and-white classic monster movies, 1950s science fiction, Saturday-morning TV cartoons, animated fairy tales – he drank all of it in.

'I grew up watching things like *The Brain that Wouldn't Die* on Saturday afternoon television,' Burton recalls of the disreputable Grade-Z features he loved just as well. 'There's a guy with his arm ripped off and blood smeared all over the wall. I was eight years old while watching this on TV. I never saw it as negative. I find that stuff, when it's not rooted in reality, to be cathartic.' So it was that Burton's gothic-infantile aesthetic began to form.

When he began making Super 8 short films at thirteen, he was in thrall to the classic horror movies of the 1930s and '40s: the first was inspired by *The Wolfman;* the second was based on the kind of mad-doctor movie Boris Karloff once specialised in; but the third was his first attempt at animation, a stop-motion short featuring model cavemen. After attending the California Institute of Arts, he developed this aspect further in his short animated film *Stalk of the Celery Monster* (1979), which brought him to the attention of the Disney Corporation.

Raised just down the road from Disney Studios, Burton, though he has sometimes dumped derision on the company name, is also a child of Uncle Walt. His several years working for Disney, while frustrating, began the gradual evolution of a cartoon-gothic aesthetic later recognised as uniquely his own. For Burton's internal Disneyland is one where the atmospheres of the Phantom Manor ride, with its joking, jeering corpses, and Snow White's enchanted forest – where beautiful women become old crones, and the fears of pre-pubescent children stare out from gnarled tree trunks – hold sway.

It was, perhaps, weirdly appropriate that his first personal project for Disney should adopt Vincent Price, the silken-voiced sadist of American gothic horror, as a spiritual father-figure. Price

himself lent his voice to the animated short *Vincent* (1982), about a neurotic young boy who pretends to be the Edgar Allan Poe characters formerly played by the veteran actor. Despite claiming that, 'Growing up as part of the television generation, I probably veer toward bad taste,' Burton acknowledges that he also tries 'to turn bad taste into good taste.' Thus, the Universal monster archetypes of his youth – the Frankenstein Monster, Count Dracula, the Wolfman – all the ultimate outsiders, were not transformed into the supernaturally-destructive serial killers of post-1970s horror movies. Instead, in Burton's gothic toytown, Karloff's retarded, otherworldly Monster became a loveable family dog – raised from the dead by familiar-looking electrode bolts through his neck – in *Frankenweenie* (1985), his second film to be suppressed by the Disney studios and widely discovered many years later. For Burton, the morbid sentimentalist, was given his sense of alienation by the vicious human race, and has invested much of his love in puppy dogs.

(One of his outright commercial failures in the 1990s was a 1991 cartoon show called *Family Dog*. Produced by Steven Spielberg and shelved for two years, it told its story purely from the viewpoint of the title mutt, which presumably must have seemed a good idea at the time. More recently, Burton appears to be considering burial alongside his late, lamented pet chihuahua Poppy – pet cemetery authorities permitting.)

Burton's post-Disney work retained its macabre cartoonishness and arrested emotional development. *Pee-wee's Big Adventure* (1985), his first directorial feature, is an enjoyably infantile romp around the universe of sweet/sinister kids' TV character Pee-wee Herman. Pee-wee was the creation of actor Paul Reubens, who would join a coterie of long-term Burton collaborators including production designer Rick Heinrichs, an old friend from Disney days, and soundtrack composer Danny Elfman. (Reubens' character's shrill asexuality was later undermined by his creator's arrest for masturbating in a porn cinema. No longer a staple of Saturday morning kids' TV, Reubens continues his career as a character actor – not least in the films of Tim Burton.) After the cult success of *Pee-wee* came the unanticipated commercial hit *Beetlejuice* (1987) – which treated the gory trappings of gothic horror like a lovingly crafted theme-park ride, its most likeable character being the eponymous degenerate zombie.

Burton was creating his own niche in gothic juvenilia. While initially credited to Pee-wee creator Reubens, the cheesy mock-up film studio that the title character passes through contained, among other things, a Godzilla movie pastiche in full roar. Long derided for the cheapness of their special effects, Japanese monster lover Burton knows the oneiric potency of crude stop-motion models and a man in a fire-breathing dinosaur suit. ('Because I was quiet,' testified Burton, 'because I was not demonstrative in any way, those [Godzilla] films were my form of release. I enjoyed the idea of venting anger on such a grand scale.' In tribute, he would later have the pyromaniac puppet aliens of *Mars Attacks!* take a break in their own destructiveness to watch Godzilla stomp on a model Tokyo on TV.)

The playground Hades of *Beetlejuice* was the most impressive of Burton's hermetically-sealed worlds – Michael Keaton's Betelgeuse popping in and out of the kitschly artificial afterlife at will. Patently phoney, but with a loving attention to miniature detail, it was a smallscale antecedent of the dark, *noir*-ish Gotham City where Batman dwells, the gothic nightmare hamlet of *Sleepy Hollow* (1999), and even the new 'enchanted forest' of the uneven *Planet of the Apes* (2001). (And,

Tim Burton directs Geena Davis and Alec Baldwin in a haunting scene from Beetlejuice. *Burton recycled the gothic gore of the horror movies he loved as a boy for laughs.*

given Burton's all-inclusive love of horror films, it can't only be this writer who sees a parallel between the netherworld the Maitlands enter in *Beetlejuice* and the limbo-world inside the painting in Lucio Fulci's surreal Italian splatter movie *The Beyond*.)

Little wonder, perhaps, that the keyholders of the popular imagination chose Burton to immortalise the USA's pop-mythology: *Batman* (1989) is an epic action movie in which atmosphere is everything and the action itself counts for very little – an easier film to admire than to love, though *Batman Returns* (1992) followed through on the earlier film's promise with grotesque characterisation and memorable imagery to match. *Ed Wood* (1994) grants the most comically inept of 1950s exploitation filmmakers a style of romantic monochrome biopic denied to any 'serious' director. Burton, who was enraptured in childhood by the surrealistic illogic of Wood's *Plan 9 from Outer Space*, made *Ed Wood* his masterpiece – reconciling the poetry of cheapo horror and science fiction to the quiet tragedy of human aspiration.

Mars Attacks! (1997) is a gleeful show of total destruction, based on Burton's fondly vague memory of early 1960s sci-fi trading cards that 'got yanked off the market fast, as they were deemed too controversial.' ('You ever see something that kind of disappears, and then you wonder if it was a dream, or something real?' Burton asked SF genre expert Bill Warren, as ensconced in his subconscious as ever.) *Sleepy Hollow* takes an American pseudo-folk tale, a short story by Washington Irving, and turns it into a bloody fairy tale – a simultaneous tribute to the gaudy English gothic of Hammer Films and the poetic irrationality of Italian horror filmmaker Mario Bava. (Readers will find a number of reviews and analyses herein by Kim Newman and J. Hoberman, two writers who understand American cinema's relationship with what horror genre historian David J. Skal calls 'monster culture', as well as introductions to the pop-cultural material Burton has interpreted.)

All have been subject to the criticism that Burton, who provides ideas for but does not write his own screenplays, lacks interest in narrative content, his films being a connected series of *mise-en-scenes* at best or structureless set-pieces at worst. Burton, however, invests sincere artistry into his supposedly frivolous core material. Child-like suspension of disbelief carries the day. We identify on the screen with sympathetic freaks, monsters or ghouls – and the Bat, at least in his sexually repressed dreams, lays down with the Cat. The caped crusader is a haunted man, almost as neurotically unbalanced as his grotesque enemies. ('He remains in the shadows,' said Burton of Batman. 'The power of that character is in his sadness and loneliness.' Many commentators claim this as an autobiographical trait, also manifest in *Vincent*, *Edward Scissorhands* and the oddball Ichabod in *Sleepy Hollow*. Burton begrudgingly accepts the analogies – though he clearly has a sense of fun that balances his melancholia.)

But darkness and frivolity walk hand in hand. The pagan demons that haunt Halloweentown are just naughty little moppets, and jerky animated puppets from Mars just want to have fun, albeit by trashing our planet and slaughtering us all – and, for the adolescent catharsis it provides, all we want to do is join in. As Frank Rose quotes *Edward Scissorhands* (1990) writer Caroline Thompson in 'Tim Cuts Up', 'Tim's are the obsessions of a twelve-year-old. And this is . . . a twelve-year-old's culture.'

Edward himself, as incarnated by a young Johnny Depp, is one of the most enduring images in Burton's garden of nightmares. Originating not in America's monster culture but in the young Burton's sketchbook, he is the filmmaker's oneiric image of himself – the monstrous misfit boy with a child's heart and an ancient soul. Like Pee-wee, Betelgeuse, Batman and all of Burton's animated characters, his soul is expressed via bizarre costume and make-up. 'When you cover up,' claims Burton, 'you can let something else weird leak through. It goes back to the original Greek theatre: it's all masks . . .'

An angelic Frankenstein Monster, Edward remains heart-rendingly innocent until he recalls the moral dictum of Mary Shelley's father, often used to describe the behaviour of her famous creation: 'Treat a person ill and he will become wicked.' 'Edward's painful story encompasses what I feel about life,' Burton would confirm, lending credence to the critics who saw it as veiled autobiography. 'It's a

Edward Scissorhands (Johnny Depp) is, like the Frankenstein Monster, an innocent child in a stitched-together body – but he briefly finds social acceptance.

mix of the good, the bad, the dark, the light, the funny and the sad.' Perhaps the ultimate expression of how Burton has conveyed genuine emotion via his gothic fairy-tale sensibilities, Burton admits, 'I burst out crying, myself,' at *Edward Scissorhands*. 'From that moment on, I didn't care what anyone else thought and I've never felt that way about anything else I've directed.'

The sentimentality of *Edward Scissorhands* is most explicit in its snowy Christmas scene – as with *Batman Returns* and, of course, *The Nightmare Before Christmas* (1993), cheekily prefixed 'Tim Burton's' after he handed over the directorial reins to fellow former Disney artist Henry Selick. But this is Christmas as a mix of gaudy consumerism and gothic imagery. 'I love fairy tales,' Burton has testified, 'but they've lost their meaning thanks to a guilty Disney sanitising them.' Still, Burton had slowly drip-fed elements of the Brothers Grimm and *Struwwelpeter* into the blood supply of the Disney corporation for years, until the gothic fairy tale sensibility of the long-suppressed *Vincent* and *Frankenweenie* grew into *The Nightmare Before Christmas*.

Unleashing a subtly marketed series of collectibles and toys, *The Nightmare Before Christmas* has become a seasonal favourite of children (and parents) who prefer the taste of saccharine with a hint of strychnine. Besides breeding a less creepy, more cuddly brood of monster – still surfacing in animated hits like *Shrek* and *Monsters, Inc.* – it also allowed Burton to indulge his penchant for macabre children's stories. His original poem *The Nightmare Before Christmas* was published in 1993 with his own artwork, heavily influenced by Charles Addams (creator of *The Addams Family*) and Edward Gorey, cult author/illustrator of many sardonically salutary tales about the demises of unfortunate children.

Tim Burton — A Child's Garden of Nightmares

The Gorey influence was brought more heavily to bear on *The Melancholy Death of Oyster Boy and Other Stories* (1997) – Burton's second book, a collection of 23 sad little self-penned surrealistic poems about misfit children, illustrations rendered in Burton's strangely affecting expressionistic scrawl. (Dedicated to Lisa Marie – his girlfriend and muse since the early 1990s, who appeared as Vampira in *Ed Wood* and the Queen of Outer Space in *Mars Attacks!* – who Burton's friends credit with all but saving his life. See Christine Spines' 'Men Are from Mars, Women Are from Venus'.) With a similar degree of black humour, but also with natural empathy for his freakish title character, Burton tells of a half-mollusc child born to parents who had been eating shellfish on their honeymoon. Protests his mother, 'He cannot be mine. / He smells of the ocean, of seaweed and brine.' Rendered impotent by their predicament, his father turns cannibalistic when a doctor advises him that eating his tragic little boy might cure his problem: 'Son, are you happy? / I don't mean to pry, but do you dream of Heaven? / Have you wanted to die?'

Less tragic characters include the Pin Cushion Queen ('Life isn't easy / for the Pin Cushion Queen. / When she sits on her throne / pins push through her spleen') and glutinous superhero Stain Boy ('He can't fly around tall buildings, / or outrun a speeding train, / the only talent he seems to have, / is to leave a nasty stain'). Unsurprisingly, perhaps, *The Melancholy Death of Oyster Boy* didn't make the best-seller lists. Published after the neglected *Mars Attacks!* and before the well received baroque-gothic *Sleepy Hollow*, it is, however, undiluted Tim Burton. Happily, Stain Boy, like his illustrious predecessor Batman, returned – on a series of short animated films on the internet, beginning in 2000 and no more than two minutes long, in which Burton pits his creation against Burbank supervillains Roy the Toxic Boy, Staring Girl and Bowling Ball Head.

But despite having claimed, at the time of *Ed Wood*'s release, 'No one will dare try anything new in Hollywood. Their lynch-mob mentality really disturbs me,' his helming of 20th Century Fox's $140 million 'reimagining' of *Planet of the Apes* produced his least Burtonian film so far. However remarkable the ape make-ups and mannerisms, and despite the atmospheric sets that maintain more interest than the predictable action sequences, the film lacks the sense of foreboding and alienation present in the 1968 original – an immense disappointment from someone as grounded in the 1960s monster culture as Burton, for whom the new millennium coincided with a state of flux.

His eight-year relationship with Lisa Marie, to whom he was engaged – and who was his muse, to the extent that he staged a photoshoot with her replicating the famous iron maiden scene with Barbara Steele from Bava's *Black Sunday/The Mask of Satan* – would be thrown over in favour of English actress Helena Bonham Carter. ('Love is a big mass of emotional conflicts,' Burton said in the early days of his relationship with Lisa Marie, 'they're never straightforward. Love will always be a complete abstraction in my mind.')

Ms. Bonham Carter became a subsequent fixture in her partner's films, with a vivid supporting role as a witch in *Big Fish* (2003) – despite giving birth shortly after, to the childlike artist's first child. As a welcome step sideways from the hollow *Apes* remake, *Big Fish* fails in its director's tongue-in-cheek ambition to become 'un-Burtonized'. An odyssey (the source novel by Danny Wallace is subtitled *A Story of Mythic Proportions*) through the American backwoods and byways, its tall tales of a circus-owning werewolf, a sheep-devouring giant, a glass-eyed witch and singing Siamese twins are reminiscent of George Pal's carnivalesque 1964 fantasy, *The Seven Faces of Dr Lao*.

But the element that lends this fantasy its humanity is a personal one. In 2000, while his semi-estranged son was scouting locations for the *Apes* remake, Bill Burton died; his wife, Rickie, followed him two years later.

As the younger Burton (who inherited the script from Spielberg) began production on *Big Fish*, he realised he'd hit on a very poignant concept. In an epic shaggy dog story, Ewan McGregor, as the younger self of the dying Albert Finney, lives out all the rich fantasies that drive his sceptically uptight son nuts.

'I went back to thinking about my father,' reminisced Burton, 'and as bad a relationship as I had, early on it was quite magical. He had false teeth, so he would pretend when the moon was full that he would turn into a werewolf. We loved it, and you realise he was quite a magical character . . . . I forgot that for too long.' But while *Big Fish* found big themes in modern folk tales, Burton would reinforce his flair for juvenile fantasy.

Charlie and the Chocolate Factory (2005) is Burton's first McDonald's Happy Meal tie-in since *Batman Returns*; like that film, it has a dark enough tone to give the youngest little junk-food junkies nightmares. But then, as new father Burton confessed of his own attitude to kiddietainment, 'I get nightmares watching Teletubbies . . .' For the adult audience, it's chiefly of interest to those who grew up on Roald Dahl's sardonically moralistic kid-lit novels, or have nostalgic memories of the first flawed attempt (with Gene Wilder as Willy Wonka) to film his chocolate factory novel.

Chocolate Factory was the big summer hit of its year, placing it alongside the filmmaker's other big moneymakers, *Batman* and (ironically) *Planet of the Apes*. Its huge appeal was helped by Johnny Depp, Burton's other muse, with a showstopping turn as Wonka. Effete, gently sinister, with androgynous shades of Michael Jackson, he even won plaudits from an initially aggrieved Wilder.

Along with the great star of Hammer and Euro-horror, Christopher Lee, and Helena Bonham Carter, Depp is now part of a regular Burton ensemble. They all moonlighted from the set of *Chocolate Factory* to lend their voices to Burton's smaller (but more interesting) PG-rated film of 2005, *Corpse Bride*.

Or *Tim Burton's Corpse Bride*, to give it its full title – for, like *The Nightmare Before Christmas*, Burton attached a proprietorial prefix to his pencil-drawn concept, brought to life by stop-motion animation. His use of this endlessly painstaking process (ultimately dropped from *Mars Attacks!* in favour of CGI) is a labour of love, apparently inspired as much by a 1960s animated oddity like *Mad Monster Party* as by mythic monster maker Ray Harryhausen – a personal hero to both Burton and Peter Jackson, his Antipodean soul brother.

Its main characters, Depp's Victor and Helena's Emily, are spindly, bug-eyed caricatures of the actors. (Emily, the title character, has a maggot in her eye socket that speaks like creepy character actor Peter Lorre.) Inspired by Russian-Jewish folklore, Ms. Bonham Carter's Victorian gothic character has been murdered on her wedding day but still seeks love in the land of the living.

But, points out Helena, 'I don't think it's that dark. It's a terribly romantic notion that we're going to meet the people that we miss . . .' Burton agrees with his muse: 'Tiny, tiny little kids come up and tell me that they loved the movie . . . it's us as adults as we near death, you know, we get terrified and we put fear on [them] . . .'

Corpse Bride stills falls short of its predecessor's manic inventiveness. If we take Burton's beloved Poe/Corman/Price movies as the apotheosis of his tastes, *Nightmare* is an infernally riotous *Masque of the Red Death* to *Corpse Bride*'s softly sepulchral *Tomb of Ligeia*.

So will Burton, the eternal child savant, ever be able to turn such gothic themes into more adult fare? The first test comes with *Sweeney Todd – The Demon Barber of Fleet Street* (2008). Darker in tone than anything else Burton has done, its story of a Victorian barber turned serial killer originated in the nineteenth-century 'penny dreadful' papers.

But this is Stephen Sondheim's Broadway musical version, its gore leavened with humour and archly satirical songs. With Johnny Depp as throat-slashing Sweeney, and Helena Bonham Carter as Mrs Lovett, the piemaker next door – ingredients supplied by Sweeney – the Burton ensemble will be bursting into tune, with misanthropic lyrics to make us sympathise with the legendary cutthroat.

As Burton hurtles towards 50, his creative adolescence should prove every bit as entertaining as his childhood.

PAUL A. WOODS

SHORTS

VINCENT

by David Coleman

Although it's not the most publicised film from the Walt Disney Studios, *Vincent* is certainly the most unusual. Designer/director Tim Burton and creative producer Rick Heinrichs made the animated short film for $60,000 from the studio.

The film concerns the anecdotes of a young boy who emulates his screen idol, Vincent Price. Rather than spending his time watching television, doing his homework or playing softball, the aptly-named Vincent would rather be reading Edgar Allan Poe's short stories, wiring electrodes to his dog for a diabolical experiment or fantasising about dipping his obese aunt in a tub of boiling wax. *Bambi* it ain't.

Besides its offbeat storyline, *Vincent* also has unusual animation. Instead of the typical cel animation people associate with Disney, Burton and Heinrichs used three-dimensional model animation.

'This is something that Disney hasn't experimented with too much,' said Heinrichs. 'Although they had toyed with the idea of doing a children's movie as a feature using dimensional animation in the past, they have shelved the idea due to their unfamiliarity with the process. We felt, however, that we could convince the hierarchy that a feature-length, model animated film with the Disney logo on it could be commercially feasible, and *Vincent* was our way of showing them.'

Once they had gotten the financial backing of Disney vice-president Tom Wilhite, Burton and Heinrichs began production, along with animator Stephen Chiodo and cameraman Victor Abdalov, both of the ill-fated *I Go Pogo* movie. Because the film was officially an 'off the lot' project (meaning Disney supplied the money while the two creators furnished the resources), Burton and Heinrichs rented space at Dave Allen's animation studio to shoot the black and white, 35mm film.

Burton based the storyboards for *Vincent* on a children's short story he had created earlier, from which Heinrichs cast the actual ball-and-socket models. The combination of the bizarre characters and the continually shifting expressionist backgrounds produces a film that might be termed '*The Cabinet of Dr Caligari* meets Ray Harryhausen'.

'One of the best things about making this film,' said Heinrichs, 'was getting to meet Vincent Price.' Price, who narrates the film in rhyme, met with the creators in December 1981, before the animation was developed. 'We were finished recording his dialogue within an hour. Vincent seemed quite pleased and flattered by the entire project.

'To be quite honest, it's something of a fluke that this film was made at all, because it's very unusual for a studio the size of Disney to invest in a short film such as *Vincent*. It shows that they *are* serious about expanding and cultivating a new image among filmgoers. I think the industry is going to see a really exciting growth period at the Disney Studio the next few years.'

'Vincent Malloy is seven years old. | He's always polite and does what he's told. | For a boy his age he's considerate and nice | but he wants to be just like Vincent Price' – Tim Burton, *Vincent.*

Tim Burton and Vincent Price

interview by Graham Fuller

PART ONE

In 1982, Tim Burton paid homage to Vincent Price, the cinema's king of exquisite pain and sweet dementia, with a black-and-white animated short about a wraithlike little boy who reads Edgar Allan Poe. This cartoon, *Vincent*, was narrated in a voice as syrupy as coagulating blood, by Price himself. The director and his muse are now reunited in *Edward Scissorhands*, the story of yet another shock-haired youth with a sense of mortal dread. Like Burton's *Beetlejuice* and *Batman*, this is a bright-hued modern myth resonant with longing. There is, accordingly, a bond between Burton's comically anguished heroes and those Price played in Roger Corman's Poe adaptations in the early sixties. It was in a Hollywood hotel, on an inappropriately sunny day, that I discussed these matters with Burton, sleepy-eyed and disheveled, and Price, a beautiful sage in his eightieth year – and where they reminded me more of Frodo and Gandalf than Igor and Roderick Usher.

I saw your film Vincent *recently. What interested me was that from the very first image, which is of a black cat crawling into a house, it's immersed in Poe, even before Poe is mentioned. Was this how you two got to know each other?*
Burton: Yes. I actually wanted to do it as a children's book first, and I did it in storyboard form. Then Disney gave me the opportunity to do it as a short film, and it was sent to Vincent, and by getting his investment we were able to make it. Obviously, the thing came from a very personal, strong, pure place for me. So it was kind of scary, sending it to him. Because you never know what somebody is *really* going to be like! And when it means a lot to you, it makes it all the more frightening.
Price: And of course for me, it was the most gratifying thing that had ever happened. It was immortality – better than a star on Hollywood Boulevard.
Burton: So when he looked at it and responded the way he did, it was the most amazing thing, and I imagine it will *always* be the most amazing thing that ever happened, because it was a real validation. It sounds sort of corny, but it made me feel good and continues to make me feel good about what life has to offer. And in terms of creativity and art, it was a very important thing for me. Because I can be quite negative. A lot of those feelings that were in Vincent's characters, some of the deep, dark, depressed things, are also there, but with the light. And that's what I would always get out of watching his films – a perfect balance of light and dark that has continued to help me.

Are you the little boy in that cartoon?
Price: To some degree, he is.
Burton: Without being too literal, there are aspects of me. *Vincent* actually helped me to understand it better. And again, it was a real form of therapy for me.

(to Price) What did you think of this young man who wanted to salute you in a cartoon?
Price: Well, the thing that I think tickled me the most was that he had caught what I had tried to do in those films, which was to send them up a little bit because they were so preposterous. I remember when Peter Lorre, Boris Karloff, and myself were sent *The Raven* by Roger Corman. We'd all been friends for a long time. We called each other up and said, 'It'll be great fun to play it, but how are they going to get a story? It's a poem – there's no plot.' And Roger, I think, realised

Burton talks with his friend and mentor Vincent Price on the set of Edward Scissorhands. *It was the horror veteran's last screen role, as Edward's gentle mad scientist creator.*

this. So when we geared up to play it, we just sent it up a little bit, because there was nothing else you could do. But we talked all the laughs out of it, because you have to get that part over with. The one thing that you must have in any kind of mystery or fairy tale film is logic. And the logic has to be in the actor – I'm sure of that.

Corman's Poe films are very funny, but they somehow leave you with this sense of unease.
Price: Yes, and that's exactly why they work.
Burton: I love the catharsis. What they gave me was, I'd sit there and watch him, and he'd be dealing with the most preposterous images and situations, but dealing with them with such passion and feeling. I responded to Vincent's sincerity. It's wonderfully heightened in *House of Usher*. In a weird way, those films are cartoon versions of Poe. I grew up feeling everything was odd and strange, and those films deal with that. They were like a symbolic version of *life*.
Price: They were symbolic, in a funny way. Roger had a *big* underlying thing about psycho-analysis. He'd talk about it, and we'd kid him and say, 'Oh, cut it out, Roger. Cut that bullshit out. Cut it out and let's get at it.' But we listened to it, and it made the films real.

I always think of that moment in The Masque of the Red Death ***when you turn around and confront this phantom image of yourself. It's like someone coming face-to-face with . . .***
Price: With his own ego. Yes, exactly.

Were you interested in Poe before you did those films?
Price: I was interested in him because I am an American, and I think Poe is the greatest writer we ever produced. His influence on the world of art is *incalculable*. Manet illustrated him. Dore and Redon illustrated him. Every great painter did something from Edgar Allan Poe. Every great poet. Baudelaire. French literature and English literature were all influenced by him. The detective novel comes out of 'The Gold Bug'. It fascinates people, though when he dedicated 'The Raven' to Elizabeth Barrett Browning, she thought it was crazy. Even people who don't know Poe, I think, are affected on some level by the same feeling – it's the closest thing to dreams.

Do you have a favourite of your Poe films, Vincent?
Price: I think *The Tomb of Ligeia* was the closest to what Poe wrote. Because it is a very strange story, a very unhealthy story. It's about *necrophilia*! And *cats* who become your *dead wife* and . . . ooohhh!

Tim's films have this same mood of suffering. **Beetlejuice,** *though, he's a comic character, is trapped in a kind of hell, and so are* **Batman** *and* **Edward Scissorhands.**
Burton: What I respond to are characters who are going through something. I think there is something that's very funny about tragedy . . . Again, it's a kind of catharsis that I think you need to go through, and I need to go through, to continue. But the line between what's absurd and what really makes up life becomes more and more blurred the older I get.
Price: I think the most persistent thing in life at any age is the nightmare, even if you're a perfectly happy person. It's so preposterous, this thing that happens to you in the middle of the night. Thank God that most of the time you forget them.

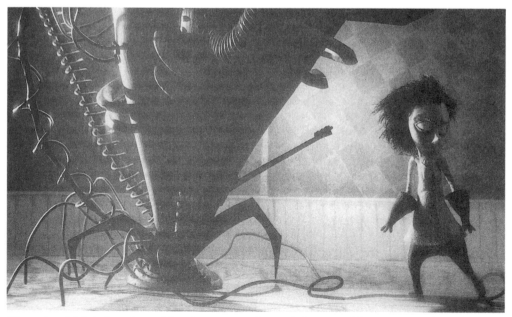

Vincent and his infernal machine. As a wanna-be mad doctor and horror movie fan, it's easy to see the autobiographical element in Burton's animated character.

HANSEL AND GRETEL

by Taylor L. White

Following *Vincent*, the team of Burton and Rick Heinrichs opted for a change of pace, having worked both in full-cel (on Disney's *The Black Cauldron*) and stop-motion animation. The result was *Hansel and Gretel*, their first full-fledged foray into live action produced for the Disney Channel, then still a young pay-cabler hungry for new products. Shot in 16mm on a budget of $116,000, this 45-minute re-telling of the classic Grimm fairy tale, complete with an all-oriental cast, is more bizarre and over-the-edge than even the otherworldly antics of Burton's *Beetlejuice*.

Scripted by executive producer Julie Hickson to follow the traditional fable, what separates this version from other filmed fairy tales – or anything else for that matter – is Burton's defiance of the mundane. Burton's cock-eyed vision scrambles the familiar elements in an ethnic blender, churning out what can best be described as 'The Brothers Grimm Meet Bruce Lee'.

In Burton's fable, the stepmother who abandons poor Hansel and Gretel is no mother at all, but a *man* played in full Kabuki garb by Michael Yama, who also essays the role of the evil witch. The father (Jim Ishida) is not a woodcutter, but a toymaker, which allows for the customary gadgetry found in all of the director's works, this time inspired by the Japanese Transformer toys, popular at the time. Sending the film completely over the edge is a hilarious karate duel pitting Yama as the witch against Hansel and Gretel at the climax. Imagine all of this accompanied by the tinkling piano music of John Costa of *Mister Rogers' Neighborhood* fame and you have Burton at his utmost crazed.

Like *Vincent*, the cable show was shot off the Disney lot in a small Hollywood studio to avoid conflict with studio unions. Despite its extreme budget limitations, a wide variety of ambitious special effects techniques were used, including front projection, forced perspective and a handful of impressive stop-motion shots, once again achieved by Stephen Chiodo working from models built by Heinrichs based on Burton's designs. Also impressive is a number of on-set gags, most notably the witch's house built from sweets and edibles, where the walls ooze like jelly donuts.

But the project sorely lacks the strong sense of character and dramatic content that lurks in the core of *Vincent*. The cast, all amateurs, either underplay or overplay their roles to the hilt, particularly Yama, whose mechanical acting style is matched by his outlandish get-up as the witch, complete with a white, pasty face, and a foot-long candy cane nose. Burton's awkward handling of the cast can perhaps be forgiven since his previous experience came only from working with actors fashioned from clay and steel armatures.

The main problem with *Hansel and Gretel* lies in its often plodding 45-minute running time. To his detriment, Burton was contracted by Disney to fill up a full one hour time slot with a yarn that should take no longer than fifteen minutes to tell. Most scenes are padded to run twice as long as they should. The lingering shots allow you to savour the brilliant artistry that went into the production, but with little else to hold your attention your eyes begin to glaze over well before the finish.

The reception to *Hansel and Gretel* at Disney was less than warm. It aired only once, on Halloween, and was then laid to rest on the shelf.

FRANKENWEENIE

by Michael Mayo

Probably the last studio on earth you'd expect to do yet another version of the Frankenstein legend is Walt Disney Studios, but the ever-changing World of Walt has done just that. The latest short film from the studio, *Frankenweenie*, is an affectionate tribute to the James Whale film starring Boris Karloff, designed and directed by mad genius Tim Burton with a sly but subtle eye for understated parody that may turn this 30-minute featurette into Disney's first modern cult classic.

Burton's rewrite of Whale's 1931 version of Mary Shelley's classic, with a script by Lenny Rips, turns the story into its gentlest version yet. Barret Oliver's beloved dog, Sparky, is killed in an accident. Oliver buries the dog, but believes he may have a chance to bring the dog back to life when his weird science teacher, played by Paul Bartel, shows him how you can make a frog's leg jump using electricity. Oliver decides to do his teacher one better and patches the dog back together, shooting it full of electricity in an attic laboratory jerryrigged with makeshift electrical equipment.

Miraculously, the equipment works and Sparky is brought back to life. Oliver then tries to keep the dog in the attic so his unknowing parents, played by Shelley Duvall and Daniel Stern, won't know what's going on. The dog manages to slip out though, and is briefly glimpsed by neighbours, who set the neighbourhood abuzz with stories of a monster that seems to be coming from the house. Despondent that he seems about to lose his dog again, Oliver retreats to the tattered windmill on an abandoned miniature golf course. Sparky goes out looking for him, and is followed by the angry neighbours to the golf course where they set the windmill ablaze unaware that Oliver is in it. Overcome by smoke, Oliver falls unconscious and is saved only when Sparky manages to drag him outside. The exertion is too much for the dog though, and Sparky dies again from the effort of rescuing his master. The neighbours, however, now see the error of their ways and make their own effort to rescue the dog. Gathering their automobiles in a circle, they get out their jumper cables, hook them all on Sparky's electrodes, and jump-start the dog back to life. Everyone lives happily ever after.

Frankenweenie is the first theatrical featurette for 25-year-old Tim Burton, who got the idea while watching the original Universal film. 'I had just seen *Frankenstein* again and started thinking – for some reason – about a dog I had when I was young. I started thinking just how incredible the whole idea of *Frankenstein* really is, of bringing something dead back to life. But all the versions of it so far have just dealt with the horrible aspects of the idea. At some point, the idea of my dog and *Frankenstein* just connected and we started developing it. I put the idea on storyboards and pitched it to Richard Berger [production chief at Walt Disney] and he liked it. We got a writer named Lenny Rips to write the script and continued to develop it from there.'

At this point, the more prosaic but vital talents of casting and deal-making were needed. For these Burton turned to Julie Hickson, a 35-year-old ex-executive from Disney's story department who discovered Burton and his talents while he was involved in designing an eventually aborted project for Disney called *Trick or Treat* [title later changed to *Nightmare Before Christmas*].

'I had been an executive in the story department about two years when I met Tim on the *Trick or Treat* project, and I was just amazed and intrigued by his work and talent,' said Hickson. 'When you go to the movies today, I think you're lucky if you see more than two real ideas on the screen; and I think that if you look at Tim's drawings, aside from the artistry involved, there's a lot of ideas there . . . they're really jam packed, and it's exciting to work for someone like that. I tried to help get

In Frankenweenie, *Burton overcomes the childhood trauma of losing a pet with a Frankenstein-style resurrection.*

Trick or Treat off the ground. That didn't work out, but we started working together, and after Tim got to do *Vincent* and started working on *Frankenweenie*, I left the story department and Richard Berger asked me to produce the film for Tim.'

At 25, Burton is yet another member of the Cal Arts mafia to make his home at Disney Studios, but there are few who have had their ambitions start so close to the studio. 'I was actually born here in Burbank,' said Burton, 'right across the street at St. Josephs. I'm sure there are a lot of people who dream of working at Disney, but growing up in Burbank with the studio right here really gets to you.

'I came here first when I was thirteen, just to visit and ask what I would have to do to work here,' continued Burton. 'They told me the standard stuff about going to school and they said a good place to go would be the California Institute of the Arts. I hate school, but Cal Arts isn't your basic college . . . it was a place where I could basically get away with a lot of stuff. So I went to Cal Arts for a couple of years, did some other stuff on the side during the summer, then came here. I don't know if it's the same now or not, but back then the program involved doing a film at the end of the year. The Disney people would come out and pick out a few people . . . the few, the proud, and that's how I got here. I started in animation, worked a year on *The Fox and the Hound*, then did some concept and development on about ten projects that never went anywhere. I met Julie Hickson at one meeting on *Trick or Treat* where I found that she was the only one who understood what I was doing, so we started working together.'

'We did a version of *Hansel and Gretel* for the Disney Channel that didn't turn out to be a big hit,' said Hickson, smiling about it. 'It was a candy-land martial arts version of the story with an all-oriental cast that didn't have a big budget but we had a lot of fun doing it. I think it showed all of one time, at Halloween.'

To develop *Frankenweenie* and make sure it showed more than one time, Hickson decided to try and get some 'name' actors. The first place she started was with Shelley Duval, who had once tried to sell Disney on the idea of her cable-TV series *Faerie Tale Theatre*.

'I really believe that you can get anybody you want if you just get the right kind of material that they can respond to,' said Hickson. 'I only knew Shelley a little, but I just had the feeling that she'd understand what we were trying to do because she had to fight to get *Faerie Tale Theatre* going with just her vision of it and hardly any money. So I thought that if I could just get to her directly, she'd respond to it. So I wrote her a letter and she read the stuff and a dialogue began and she was terrific about it. Once I had her, it was easier to get people like Daniel Stern, because he wanted to work with her. Paul Bartel was incredible too, because he loved the material and really believes in supporting short films. The project gained a momentum that was just magical because usually you don't get the actors you want for something, but here we did. Basically, we got this cast for no money because they all wanted to do it.'

More sharp-eyed aficionados will recognise the original Kenneth Strickfaden electrical equipment for Universal's *Frankenstein* integrated into the attic laboratory where Oliver brings the dog back to life. 'It was both Tim's and my idea to get the original Strickfaden equipment,' said Hickson. 'There was never any doubt in our minds that we wanted it, but it was hard to get. It was hard for Disney to understand why we wanted the equipment so badly until they saw it.'

'It's one of those things that's like a dream come true when you first see that stuff,' adds Burton.

The associate producer of *Frankenweenie* is Rick Heinrichs, who produced Burton's earlier award-winning short *Vincent*, also for Walt Disney Productions. It's the story of a boy who emulates his screen idol, Vincent Price, shot in stop-motion and black and white, and set to a rhyming narration by Price. One scene in the short, foreshadowing the concept of *Frankenweenie*, shows a Frankenstein-like Vincent wiring up his dog to electrodes in an imaginary attic laboratory.

Frankenweenie was originally slotted to begin production so it could go out with the summer 1984 re-release of *The Jungle Book*, but Disney decided to reschedule the $1 million production for a late summer shoot and put it out with the Christmas re-release of *Pinocchio*. Because it was officially an 'off the lot' production, shifting it onto the official schedule only gave the filmmakers two weeks of actual preproduction time.

'A lot of the rush is because Disney was trying to keep the production costs down,' said Hickson. 'There's an enormous overhead at the studio so we couldn't become official because then all these numbers start to be attached and we couldn't afford that. The actual production was a fifteen day shoot with a couple of months for post-production. We're really happy about being with *Pinocchio* because they'll be terrific together. They're both very primal stories. Ours is like a fairy tale, really.'

'We'll have a beautiful black and white film with one of the best colour movies ever made,' said Burton. '*Pinocchio* is Julie's and my favorite Disney movie, so we're real happy about this. It's basically been our first time working at a studio this way, and we love it. When I look at the stuff we asked them to make from the designs, I don't think we could have gotten it at any other studio. It's like Disneyland. When you look at Disneyland, there's a certain bent, it's subtle, but it really is different.

'It's been interesting in another sense too, in that shorts are harder to do than features, aside from marketing them, because with features, you have some idea of what your budget should be. But with shorts, it's hard for studios to know how much money they should give you or how much money they will make. The word around town a couple of years ago was that Spielberg was going to start a shorts unit, but we haven't heard anything since. Doing *Vincent* really gave me insight into the world of short films though, and it's amazing because they really can generate opportunities for you.'

But *Frankenweenie* did not come to life at Christmas 1984 after all, although it received a short theatrical run in Los Angeles in December to qualify for Academy Award consideration. Two marketing test screenings for mothers and young children (roughly ages six through nine) held in late September earned the short a PG rating. The film features no gore or on-screen violence (its sole bit of violence is the off-screen death of the dog in the beginning of the picture when it chases a ball into the street and is run over). But test marketing reportedly showed that mothers were worried about children possibly being led to try and play with electricity and concerned about the general 'intensity' of the piece. Studio executives deemed the featurette unsuitable for pairing with *Pinocchio* and planned to release it later in 1985.

Does Burton think his work is strange or too intense? 'I really don't look at it so much that way,' he said. 'I think of it more like the old *Silly Symphony* cartoons. What interests me is trying to give things like *Vincent* and *Frankenweenie* real feelings and emotions . . . not just make them funny all the time.

'We did *Frankenweenie* as if the original story had never existed,' continued Burton. 'This suburban family is the Frankenstein family and the little boy is Victor, but it's not a nudge in the ribs type of thing. We don't have the family watching the Universal original as a foreboding of things to come. At least to me, the more you went with a heh-heh-heh mad scientist kid, the less impact the film had. I don't think this is a dark or macabre story, and we didn't try to make the dog something horrible. He brings the dog back to life because he really loves the dog. We tried to make the film as straightforward as possible, and I think it takes on a whole new light. I think the parts that are funny are still funny, but that you can also make the leap to being serious, like those old *Silly Symphony* cartoons which are fun, but powerful and full of real feelings that stay with you a long time.

'It was amazing, to me, to be 25 and taken seriously with an idea like *Frankenweenie*,' summed up Burton. 'That's where Richard Berger came in because he really understood the idea and was great about it . . . very supportive, and for people like us, that's an amazing thing, especially since it hasn't always been that way in the past. It feels great. It really does.'

ALADDIN'S LAMP

by Taylor L. White

In 1985, Burton took his second dip into fairy tale territory with 'Aladdin and his Wonderful Lamp', a 47-minute episode of Showtime's *Fairie Tale Theatre*, shot on video and produced by *Frankenweenie* co-star Shelly Duvall, who also introduced each segment of the cable TV series.

Working on Duvall's series, Burton joined the ranks of a lengthy list of top-name directors signed on to film episodes, including Francis Ford Coppola and Nicholas Meyer. While those directors were forced to scale down their customary directorial ambitions to accommodate the series' lesser budgets, as a neophyte Burton adapted comfortably to the show's obvious limitations.

The episode was Burton's first opportunity to work with a number of big name actors, including James Earl Jones and Leonard Nimoy, each playing roles of the broadest proportions. Nimoy, doing the flipside of his sedate Mr Spock, zestfully chews the scenery as the evil Moroccan magician bent on gaining possession of the magic lamp. And Jones, playing three separate roles as narrator and two genies, gives a splendid, gargantuan performance, especially as the blue-faced, pointy-eared Genie of the Lamp. His bombastic delivery and booming laugh are a joy to behold as he steals the show in his every scene. Unfortunately, the titanic talents of these veteran actors largely overshadow the story's lead, Robert Carradine, painfully miscast as the young Aladdin. Likewise, Valerie Bertinelli leaves little impression in her role as the token princess and Aladdin's love interest, merely a helpless victim of Nimoy's dastardly deeds.

Thanks a to witty, aptly paced script by Mark Curtiss and Rod Ash, Burton is allowed to showcase his talents amidst a good humoured, well-told story, old as it is. Thankfully, Burton's offbeat design and quirky weirdness complement the tale rather than render it top heavy as in *Hansel and Gretel*.

The sequence most quintessentially Burton takes place early on when Nimoy, as the magician, sends Aladdin into a creepy underground cave, deep in the desert, to retrieve the magic lamp. The catacombs are filled with skeletons and other creepy-crawlies, and *Caligari*-inspired tunnels. One of the cave's corridors, embedded with cartoon skulls, is visually echoed later by Burton in the

Burton's Fairie Tale Theatre *version of* Aladdin. *James Earl Jones' booming, blue-faced Genie (left) pre-dates his Robin Williams-voiced counterpart in Disney's 1992 animated hit.*

dream sequence hospital hallway seen in his *Pee-wee's Big Adventure*.

When Aladdin finds the lamp, it is housed inside the gaping mouth of a bronze fish, with a hand holding the lamp poking out from inside. The fish is one of the many impressive props built for the episode by the Chiodo Brothers. When Aladdin lifts the lamp, the scene explodes into a virtual potpourri of Burtonisms, with a handful of blue beasties, silhouetted on a black background, diving onto view. Formed like spiders, dragons and demon heads, done dirt cheap, the shapes are signature Burton.

Also, regardless of the ancient era in which the episode takes place, Burton somehow manages to insert his trademark gimmicks, this time in the form of a series of toys owned by the Sultan. The best is an ancient Arabian TV set airing a show starring a batch of costumed, horned demons; a nice effect mounted by Ed Nunnery.

Of Burton's creative entourage, other members who also contributed high-styled touches included Rick Heinrichs, who designed and built a multi-spired miniature palace perched amid a desert vista at the opening, and *Frankenweenie* scorers David Newman and Michael Covertino, whose music embellished the proceedings.

OTHER WEIRDNESS

by Taylor L. White

In 1985, when NBC resurrected *Alfred Hitchcock Presents*, Burton signed on to direct an updated remake of 'The Jar', based on a short story by Ray Bradbury. The original episode, with a teleplay by James Bridges, starred Pat Buttram as country bumpkin who purchases a strange jar from a carnival sideshow whose eerie, amorphous contents have a mesmerising effect on its viewers, each of whom sees something completely different. Burton's remake adeptly shifts the rural setting to the highbrow world of art exhibition, with Griffin Dunne playing the jar's owner and Fiona Lewis filling the role of his shrewish wife whose timely demise ranks as one of the best of the series, old or new. The show also co-starred Laraine Newman and Paul Bartel and featured a number of future *Beetlejuice* alumni, including scripter Michael McDowell who penned the teleplay, scorer Danny Elfman and Rich Heinrichs, who created the misshapen form inside the jar.

The following season Burton contributed designs to the special animated episode of *Amazing Stories* entitled 'Family Dog', directed by Brad Bird. Burton and Bird had worked together at Disney in 1979 during the making of *The Fox and the Hound*. At the time, they put together a sample reel of their work which included Bird's 'Family Dog' presentation, an idea for a short that would show the world from a dog's-eye view. Burton contributed character designs for the sample reel and was called back to create new characters for additional sequences once Bird sold Steven Spielberg on the idea of expanding the short into a half-hour TV episode, one of the series' best.

One of Burton's most intriguing projects, as yet unproduced, is *The Nightmare Before Christmas*, a proposed stop-motion fantasy done in the same vein as *Vincent*. Although long in preparation, having been developed under the old regime at Disney, the property is still reportedly a pet project for Burton and is currently being considered by a number of producers, including Debra Hill and David Kirschner. If made, the film may become the first seasonal classic to surface during two holidays.

Another would-be Burton project that has since fallen by the wayside is *True Love*, written by *Hansel and Gretel* scripter Julie Hickson. Curiously described as 'a cross between *To Kill a Mockingbird* and a Japanese monster movie,' *True Love* is a cockeyed fantasy love story about two lovesick boys battling for the affections of the new girl on the block. Like *Hansel and Gretel,* much of the story contains that prevailing Oriental influence so dominant in the earlier short. For example, one of the lead boys is a Japanese Dr Wu-type whose bedroom houses a full laboratory where he busily concocts formulas allowing him to metamorphose into a series of weird, Transformer-type monsters. The project now occupies shelf space at Warner Brothers because Burton and the studio could not reach an agreement on the film's proposed budget, approximately $11 million.

Certainly the most obscure of Burton's past efforts is *Luau*, a short film directed by Burton with Jerry Reese and his fellow co-workers in the animation department at Disney during their stint on *The Black Cauldron*. *Luau* was perhaps Burton's first and last appearance in front of the camera, having cast himself in the role of the most powerful being in the universe, a disembodied head which, near the climax, competes in a surfing contest, minus his body.

Burton has proved himself a maverick visionary bent on pushing the boundaries of weirdness, whose appeal has stemmed from his keen ability to make the cheap and cheesy appealing. Now that his patented strangeness has received that all-important 'commercial' imprimatur, it will be interesting to see what path he follows. Will it be more popular, less personal, high-flying, high-budgeted fare like *Batman*? Or will he get back to major weirdness

PEE-WEE'S BIG ADVENTURE

by Taylor L. White

For his feature film debut, Burton, then 26, collaborated with infantile funnyman Pee-wee Herman on *Pee-wee's Big Adventure*, a dippy and irresistable laughfest which glowingly showcased the best of both talents involved. With its goofy gadgetry and wacky humour, the film is one of those rare occasions when the creative ingredients contributed by each party mesh perfectly. Rightfully so, since both Burton and Herman obviously grew up in the same weird neighbourhood of quirky artistry and wacky humour. Case in point, both are still permanently stuck in the throes of early adolescence, each shares a rabid affinity for toys and gimmicks, and neither is cut from a mold deemed 'normal' by today's world. That appeal also caught on with audiences who turned out in droves, making the film a surprise hit for Warner Brothers in the summer of 1985.

The jaunty, loosely structured script by Herman, Phil Hartman and Phil Varhol is purely an excuse to jam as much Pee-wee shtick into 90 minutes as possible. During Herman's comedic quest to retrieve his stolen bicycle he takes a cross country roadtrip, stopping at Burtonland almost every step of the way. Burton's trademark twistedness is especially apparent in a pair of dream sequences, one set in a nightmarish hospital highlighted by expressionistic sets leading to Hell itself, and the other starring a bike-chewing stop-motion tyrannosaurus rex animated by Rick Heinrichs.

Certainly the most memorable moment is the now legendary Large Marge gag in which Pee-wee, after being abandoned in the middle of nowhere, is picked up by ghostly truck driver Alice Nunn, who does a wonderful living dead impersonation. The hilariously startling stop-motion effect was achieved by *Vincent* animator Stephen Chiodo, who spent four weeks fabricating the clay visage molded from Nunn's face and then another eleven hours doing 36 frames of animation, seen as exactly one and a half seconds of screen time. To assure that the clay face maintained the actress's skin tone, facial makeup was applied to each movement to eliminate the clay pallor. Chiodo also used the same grey fright wig worn by Nunn to unite the live show with the animation. Although the scene is a throwaway like many others in the film, it is also the most unforgettable.

The film also lets Burton reflect his penchant for Japanese monster movies, when Herman blazes through the movie set where Godzilla and Ghidrah are battling it out amidst miniature tanks and explosives.

It also saw the start of the creative relationship between Burton and composer Danny Elfman, who has scored all of Burton's movies [with the sole exception of *Ed Wood*]. To stress the importance of Burton's contribution to *Pee-wee's Big Adventure* one only need look at *Big Top Pee-wee*, the dismal follow-up in which director Randall Kleiser clearly failed to jibe with Herman's sensibilities.

Pee-wee Herman, aka character actor Paul Reubens. The surreal, skewed world of his hit TV show Pee-wee's Playhouse *called for a similar sensibility to bring it to the big screen.*

IS AMERICA READY FOR A NUT WHO'S A GENIUS?

by David Elliott

Pee-wee's Big Adventure must be the goofiest movie since *Million Dollar Legs*, a 1932 aberration starring W. C. Fields as the potted president of Klopstokia. I can imagine Fields taking a look at Pee-wee Herman and reaching for a final, killing shot of booze – Pee-wee is his nightmare of the ultimate kid, the one you can't get rid of.

I am among the multitude that hasn't exactly been yearning for Pee-wee's debut as a movie star. Fifteen minutes of him on David Letterman's show, with his cartoon moves, Geeks-R-Us patter and constipated wimp's voice, seemed to be the full serving of his talent. But lo and behold, Pee-wee (and the savvy actor inside him, Paul Reubens) is the gas and motor of a delightful comedy. For those who can get into the right warp, this may be the funniest movie of the year.

As Pee-wee works himself in and out of jams while trying to find his lost, dearly beloved bicycle – that's the whole premise of his big adventure – one recalls the immortal words of conductor George Szell about pianist Glenn Gould: 'That nut's a genius.' Or maybe Pee-wee's only a nut. But like Gould, he's salted with inspiration.

Pee-wee lives in a world unlike mine or yours. His house is a kind of toy store kleptomaniac's paradise, crammed with beautifully inane appliances and gag-shop gewgaws. His yard is stocked with giant fake animals and one real one, a pee-wee mutt named Speck. It's a world of primary colours, baby wit ('That's my name – don't wear it out!') and perfectly moronic pleasures, like putting Scotch tape on your face and gleefully ripping it off.

Pee-wee adores his bright red fifties dream-bike, and when the fat, rich, greedy Francis (Mark Holton) steals it, he flips into an infantile rage. But for an obsessional nerd, he's also a cool guy – he always has a comeback line, a fast-stepping strategy and the plucky verve of a born adventurer. (In spirit, he's a throwback to the great silent film comedians.) I can't do the comedy justice. You really have to be there. When Pee-wee, cornered by a biker gang, saves himself with a hip dude's dance to 'Tequila', and when he makes innocently lewd remarks to a waitress inside the mouth of a giant ceramic dinosaur at a truck stop, and when he takes a tour of the Alamo conducted by the pertest, twangiest little gal in Texas, this comedy is like no other. I don't know if it will be a hit, but this fruitcake must be the surest cult movie ever made.

Director Tim Burton has a light, sure knack for visual wit, and his compositions trigger the fun in situations. The surreal episodes spring at us like pages in a pop-up book, full of twinkly colours and oddball dream touches. And composer Danny Elfman also rises to the occasion, in a score that neatly mimics the jaunty tunes of Nino Rota for Fellini films and Bernard Herrmann's tense music for Hitchcock.

There are a few dead spots, including some in the film's audience. This type of off-the-wall humour leaves some viewers in a permafrost of indifference, or even hostile. But more than movie lovers should relish the weird surprises and the whopper ending, when Pee-wee mounts his bike and tears around the Warner Bros. studio (shades of *Blazing Saddles*). The place is humming, cranking out sixties beach comedies, Japanese monster movies and Tarzan pictures.

The key to this hip kids' party is, of course, the ineffable Pee-wee Herman. Is America ready for a movie star who is like a mad mix of Harry Langdon, Pinky Lee, Wally Cox and wiseguy Groucho Marx? If we're not, it's our loss.

PEE-WEE'S BIG ADVENTURE

review by Alan Jones

Many of you won't even know who Pee-wee Herman is but this can be easily put right. Pee-wee started out as a character created by alternative improvisational performer Paul Reubens who in turn is the persona for 34-year-old Paul Rubenfeld. With his strange boy-like character, severe crew-cut, madeup face and slightly too small grey suit complete with red bow-tie, Pee-wee became a Los Angeles cult favourite when he wrote and starred in *The Pee-wee Herman Show* presented at the Roxy nightclub on Sunset Strip. The show proved so popular it was videotaped and shown on Home Box Office cable television.

The only way I can describe this one-off special is to ask you to imagine watching a *Carry On* film version of *Blue Peter*, as Pee-wee's brilliance lies in satirising American children's television shows like *Pinky Lee* and *Howdy Doody*. This description can't highlight the cleverness of the concept but, since the sleeper success of *Pee-wee's Big Adventure*, Pee-wee has become a national celebrity due mainly to his unique television show, *Pee-wee's Playhouse*.

Pee-wee's bedroom is a little boy's garden of delights. With hindsight, Big Adventure's *infantile surrealism shows Burton's hand (including a toy Godzilla on the windowsill).*

That obscure object of desire: infantile manchild Pee-wee regains his bicycle, the distance travelled on his **Big Adventure** *signified by a very literal North Pole.*

Packed with colourful characters and wildly inventive animated objects like a resident genie, a tiny dinosaur family that lives in a mouse-hole and a variety of sweet insects and animals that pop out of the refrigerator, the weekly series has been such a hit it is repeated in the evening for parents to catch up on what has been entrancing their children on Saturday mornings. And it is precisely this across the board appeal which has made Pee-wee Herman such a well-loved personality. The sexual innuendos, double-entendres and sharp humour can be appreciated by adult audiences and the weird computer graphics, non-stop activity and *Magic Roundabout* sensibility captures the imagination of kids.

Reubens has made a rap record, supplied voices for Freaky Frankenstone on *The Flintstones* and the alien in *Flight of the Navigator* and is at present planning a Hollywood theme park called Pee-weeland. And if all this doesn't tip you off as to where Pee-wee Herman is coming from, it isn't my fault.

Pee-wee's Big Adventure is an embarrassment of riches really. It contains ghostly truck drivers, minimalist cel animation, dinosaurs, Godzilla, Santa Claus, soap opera, pet shops and dream sequences. The story follows Pee-wee's desperate attempts to track down his beloved bicycle after it is stolen by a jealous bully. As Pee-wee travels to the Alamo and back he braves all kinds of dangers to find his most treasured possession. Along the way he encounters an escaped convict, hitches a ride with Large Marge, a character straight out of *The Twilight Zone*, befriends a truck-stop waitress who dreams of a new life in Paris, and gets involved with a group of rowdy Hell's Angels before the *Blazing Saddles* climax spearheads a film of his life starring Morgan Fairchild and James Brolin.

Enter Pee-wee's demented Disneyfied universe and you'll emerge at the end with a warmly funny reaffirmation of life's surrealist values.

Tim Burton, who previously directed the seven-minute short *Vincent* and the half-hour ode to the early Frankenstein films *Frankenweenie*, was the perfect choice to bring the kooky atmosphere of Pee-wee's world to the big screen. The pitting of child-like attitudes against the quirky realities of life is the constant he has brought to all his work to date. Making outlandish ideas believable in a cynical cartoonish atmosphere is his masterstroke in *Pee-wee's Big Adventure* and the reason why it is consistently wacky entertainment for the Filofax generation. There is more imagination, meticulous detailing and sharp observation packed into the first fifteen minutes of this film than anything seen for a long time, although the Pee-wee Herman cosmos is probably something of an acquired taste. But, for sheer lunacy, Pee-wee's hilarious tour of the Alamo and his outlandish attempts as a drag-artist to throw the police off the scent are spoilt-child theatrics of the funniest kind. This film is what a trip to McDonald's really ought to be like. Do see it.

BEETLEJUICE (1987)

GLEEFUL GRAND GUIGNOL OF BEETLEJUICE

by Kevin Thomas

Beetlejuice, an uproarious ghost comedy, kills off its likable stars after eight minutes, but that's just the first of the chances it takes. By the time this irresistible treat is over, it has created some of the funniest moments and most inspired visual humour and design we may expect to experience at the movies all year.

The film is a dazzling display of director Tim Burton's unique pop culture sensibility. There hasn't been anything remotely like it since *Ghostbusters* or, closer still, *The Rocky Horror Picture Show*.

Talk about economy. Within those first eight minutes we're completely charmed by Adam and Barbara Maitland (Alec Baldwin and Geena Davis), an attractive homespun young couple who live in an exceptionally tall, strikingly plain old white house with a tower overlooking a Norman Rockwell New England village.

Abruptly, Burton and his writers kill off the Maitlands, a move as shocking as it is darkly amusing, since the lethal accident is also a beautifully staged sight gag, which sets the tone for the gleeful Grand Guignol to come.

But that's not the end of the Maitlands, who materialise in their home, invisible to everyone except each other and to Lydia (Winona Ryder), the teen-age daughter of their home's new owners, Charles and Delia Deetz (Jeffrey Jones and Catherine O'Hara), relentlessly upscale refugees from Manhattan.

Almost too bright and aware for her own good, Lydia, who has a penchant for dressing in elaborate mourning, possesses the necessary sensitivity to be able to see the Maitlands. They've taken refuge in their attic while Delia and her awful decorator Otho (Glenn Shadix) proceed to turn their warm, lovely, antique-filled home into a post-modern parody inside and out, complete with spray-speckled interiors, *faux* marble panelling and Delia's monstrous sculptures.

Beetlejuice reverses the usual haunted house plot. This time it's the ghosts who want to get rid of the living. (The Maitlands have been told by their 'afterlife caseworker', Sylvia Sidney, that they will be stuck in their home for the next 125 years.) But the Maitlands find it isn't as easy to scare people off as it once was. They secure the dubious services of a self-proclaimed 'bio-exorcist' (Michael Keaton), whose name just happens to be Betelgeuse but who's called Beetlejuice. Sex-crazed, wild-haired, his eyes encircled in black, Beetlejuice has a TV commercial that's like a Cal Worthington spoof and is 'dying' to be raised from the dead.

Even more than in his debut film, *Pee-wee's Big Adventure*, Burton draws upon his background as a Disney animator for the engagingly bizarre look and humour of *Beetlejuice*. (You do wonder why it didn't end up a Touchstone production.) When the Maitlands take a journey to the Other Side to seek help, they encounter a waiting room filled with other supplicants preserved in the exact state of their moment of death: a sexy show girl, doubtless an ill-fated magician's assistant, who's sawed in half; a hunter with a shrunken head; a scuba diver with a leg still down the throat of a shark, and a

Not the coolest ghoul in town, but the surprise hit of 1987 nonetheless. **Beetlejuice** *features comic actor Michael Keaton as the eponymous living-dead sleazebag.*

chain-smoker who apparently had turned himself into a cinder while smoking in bed.

Because of that darkly comic tone set at the beginning, the effect of these characters and others is hilarious rather than morbid or tasteless.

Burton and his colleagues, who include most importantly production designer Bo Welch and composer Danny Elfman, whose score is as witty and robust as Welch's designs, have no less fun with the pretensions of the Deetzes and their pals.

Exuberant scene-stealer Keaton gets some strong competition this time, especially from Ryder, Sidney (who after 60 years as a stellar dramatic actress proves to be a sharp comedian) and, above all, O'Hara, who shows us that Delia is so funny because she is absolutely humourless.

The set piece of the film is Delia's dinner party, whose guests have all graced the pages of *Vanity Fair*. Others in the film's faultless cast include Robert Goulet as a slick promoter, Dick Cavett as Delia's fed-up agent and Annie McEnroe as a comically pushy real estate agent who'd be a hit in West L.A.

There's a distinctive feel to *Beetlejuice*, a deliberate Brecht-Weill jerkiness that allows satire and just plain silliness to play off each other most successfully. Indeed, the film seems to be crying out to be a musical; one wishes it were. One thing's for sure: *Topper* was never like this.

BEETLEJUICE

review by Kim Newman

Winter River, Connecticut. Adam and Barbara Maitland, a newly dead young couple, are upset when their family home is sold to Charles Deetz, a New York businessman, whose wife Delia – aided by pretentious interior decorator Otho – sets about ruining the property with hideous sculptures and furnishings. The Maitlands contact Juno – an after-life civil servant – who says that they are bound to remain in their house for over a century and that if they want to get rid of the Deetzes they'll have to haunt the family. The Maitlands' first attempts at haunting are ignored, but the Deetzes' daughter Lydia starts seeing the ghosts and befriends them. The Maitlands finally make their presence felt by forcing the Deetzes and their dinner guests to mime to Harry Belafonte's 'Banana Boat Song' while the prawn entrees come to life. The Deetzes, however, are not terrified but enthusiastic, and through Lydia communicate to the Maitlands that they want to turn the town into a supernatural tourist attraction. In desperation, the Maitlands go against Juno's advice and call in Betelgeuse, a crazed spirit who works as a bio-exorcist, ridding ghost houses of infestations of the living. But the Maitlands can't go through with Betelgeuse's extreme measures and call him off. In an amateurish attempt at spiritualism, Otho summons the Maitlands to help the Deetzes impress investor Maxie Dean, but accidentally starts to exorcise them – which will turn them into lost souls – forcing Lydia to call on Betelgeuse. Lydia goes along with Betelgeuse's demand that she pay for his services by marrying him, but the restored Maitlands fight the spirit off and dispatch him to Juno's eternal waiting room. The Deetzes and the Maitlands find a way of comfortably living together.

With *Beetlejuice*, Tim Burton develops further the quirky, gently horrific sense of humour displayed in his first feature, *Pee-wee's Big Adventure*, and – even more distinctly – in his little-seen early shorts for Walt Disney, *Vincent* (about a boy who wants to be Vincent Price) and *Frankenweenie* (a black-and-white skit on *Frankenstein,* in which a child revives his pet dog as a monster). Although there are certain similarities between Paul Reubens' Pee-wee Herman character and Michael Keaton's Betelgeuse in terms of self-centred grotesquerie and nonstop patter, the current film is constructed less as a comic star vehicle. Keaton doesn't even take top billing for his role, allowing some of the excellent cast room to develop beyond the cameo status accorded all the supporting figures in *Pee-wee's Big Adventure*. It becomes apparent that much of what was admirable in the first film was down to the director rather than the star.

Although Burton refrains from repeating himself, *Beetlejuice* plays variations on themes from his earlier work – the use of comically exaggerated dimensional animation, make-up effects that turn characters into grotesques worthy of Don Martin or Basil Wolverton, hilariously lip-synched musical numbers, and a twisted view of what normality actually is. Given that the story is a deliberate inversion of the gentle-ghost sub-genre of screwball comedy – which takes in the knockabout *Topper*, the bittersweet *The Ghost and Mrs Muir*, and by-blows as peculiar as the TV series *Randall and Hopkirk (Deceased)* – it's interesting to note the screenplay input of novelist Michael McDowell. The latter has written some distinctive straight horror novels (the *Blackwater* sequence, *The Elementals, Cold Moon Over Babylon*) but recently turned to a series of charming entertainments very much in the screwball vein, commencing with *Jack and Susan in 1953* and *Jack and Susan in 1913*.

Burton has most fun here with the vision of an after-life run by spirits who have condemned themselves to an eternity as civil servants by committing suicide, and the film sets up a consistent and bewildering set of rules by which to play. The Maitlands must stay in their house or be transported to a matte-fringed Saturn (where *Dune*-esque sandworms lie in wait for unwary ghosts); Betelgeuse can only go into action if his name is called (and properly pronounced) three times; an unhelpful *Guidebook for the Recently Deceased* is handed out to new ghosts. Among the throwaway characters encountered in Juno's waiting room are an explorer with a shrunken head, a sawn-in-half magician's assistant, a cancerous skeleton who still can't stop smoking, a swimmer with a shark attached to his leg, and a flat-as-a-pancake road-accident victim with a tyre tread across him. These figure mainly in ingenious single gags, but somehow overwhelm the structure of the movie to such a degree that the leading characters never quite come into their own. While Keaton's Betelgeuse is a clever mix of the obnoxiously terrifying and the grossly funny, and both Catherine O'Hara and Winona Ryder make the most of their roles as the neurotic Delia Deetz and the Gothic punkette Lydia, Alec Baldwin and Geena Davis as the Maitlands and Jeffrey Jones as Charles Deetz are a little constrained by the relative non-eccentricity of their roles and McDowell and Burton's consequent lack of interest in them.

The director doesn't yet have the discipline to structure a movie as more than a series of individual skits. The down-to-earth Maitlands should be the backbone of the film, but too often they just play stooges to Betelgeuse or the Deetzes, and Burton's anything-for-an-effect approach is exemplified by the yanking in of 'guest stars' Robert Goulet, Dick Cavett and Sylvia

Winona Ryder made her first big impression in Beetlejuice, *as morbid goth-ette Lydia. In the film's anarchic climax, manic Betelgeuse tries to make her his reluctant bride.*

Sidney to no real purpose. And yet, the film keeps pulling itself together so that even the protracted business with Otho pays off in an inspired punch-line which combines the humour of the unexpected with an almost subliminal casual nastiness: the preening false sophisticate is unaffected by the most bizarre special-effects horrors but runs shrieking when Betelgeuse strips off his designer clothes to reveal a polyester leisure suit beneath. Finally, *Beetlejuice* confirms Burton's promise as a combination of Frank Tashlin and David Lynch, and establishes McDowell as a screenwriter to watch, especially in the light of the film's courageous refusal to follow the dictates of fashion in its use of Harry Belafonte rather than Harold Faltermeyer (or the like) on the soundtrack.

BEETLE MANIA

by Simon Garfield

As horror people go, Beetlejuice is not the scary creepy ghoul of your nightmares. Three-year-old American kids get their mums to open the paper to a picture of him each morning, and the kids laugh and gurgle. He's an amoral, lecherous, wildly unkempt sort of guy, but he is not evil; he is not Freddie. You can only assume that this is intentional on director Tim Burton's part. Burton *knows* scary, *knows* evil. You can bet he knows ghoulish. Why, he confronts these demons each time he peers in the mirror.

Tim Burton looks dopey and bedraggled – a bit Nicolas Cage-like – with long black tangled hair and mildly gothic garb, but this isn't what makes the Hollywood people scream. They run because here in their midst, and of their making, is a new young *enfant terrible*, a 29-year-old who's come from nowhere to make the big surprise movie of America's year, a film that contained all the seeds of comedy-horror cliche, promised no major names except Harry Belafonte, and then went on to out-gross *Rambo 3* and take $32 million in its first two weeks and over $70 million to date. It cost $14 million to make.

Tim Burton also frightens because this disgruntled Disney graduate – a pre-*Roger Rabbit* cartoon man! – has broken the classic junk Hollywood conventions with only his second feature. Small conventions, like the movie not making sense some of the time. Or making the major characters die in the first ten minutes and holding back the title character until halfway. Or making some of the special effects corny as cheese. You don't have to be George Lucas to know that this is occasionally a checklist for disaster. But not here. Why? Because select parts of *Beetlejuice* are dazzling genius.

Burton, raised in Burbank, now sits in an office in Pinewood, his makeshift home for the next year. Much of the time he fields calls from the tabloids inquiring, 'Is it true he'll be eating *dog* babies?', a reference to Burton's latest project, an update of *Batman*. Burton decides to tell them nothing, but is perversely touched at the attention the project's receiving. He remembers that for *Beetlejuice* there was no hype whatsoever. Warners were behind it in a half-hearted sort of way, but there was no big-bucks fanfare, no sense of the surefire hit.

You can appreciate the studio's dilemma. On paper they had a film that featured an unremarkable stay-at-home couple whom we meet at the top of the movie congratulating themselves on deciding not to go on holiday this year but instead, Christ, to stay at home to build models and redecorate their quaint smalltown house. Then they die. Coming back as ghosts, they try to scare away the new wanky family that buys their home – the husband to escape city pressures, the wife to do crazy sculpture, their daughter to wear black a lot and act weirdly. They fail. They seek advice from their afterlife caseworker. She warns them that however they try to get rid of this new family they must never, never, *ever* call up a strange freelance bio-exorcist called, and spelt, Betelgeuse. So they call him up

At this juncture even Warners probably realised that they had something. Beetlejuice, played by Michael Keaton with a flair he's called 'rage acting – you show up on the set and just go fucking nuts,' is a unique comic creation, a sort of horny vagrant on crack, a person gifted with destructive powers and cool one-liners of uncertain origin and awesome proportions.

You'll have gauged by now that the plot's not the thing. What Burton's achieved is a semi-surreal, oddball-sleazeball incident movie peppered with inspired ad-lib. The 'caper' is no longer a dirty word in the movies. The Harry Belafonte pop-calypso catalogue is hip again.

The afterlife to which our couple retire is a bureaucratic migraine, a stream of lunkhead clerks filling in forms. To get in you've got to loiter eternally in a waiting room. A nightmare in anyone's money. Into this appears an American football team. They join a man in a safari suit with a shrunken head. Why the team? Why the shrunken head? For big laffs, professor.

Ask Burton what gives him most pleasure about the triumph of his film and he'll probably comment on the success of its weirdness, the fact that the things that happen in *Beetlejuice* for no apparent reason seem to energise audiences most.

'I was happy to find out that the audience are a bit smarter than the studio would have you believe,' he grins. 'The current line is that if you have special effects they have to be state-of-the-art, and that you've got to have a great story that goes from A to B to C to D. You watch things like *Action Jackson*, and people are liking it, and you think, "Fuck, what am I doing here?" I've always hated that kind of story structure where every line is a new story point – you know, "Don't feed them after midnight or they'll blow up!" Fuck that shit.

'Another great thing is that I don't imagine I'll ever again work on a movie that at the beginning was more vague. Every day we never knew what would fall flat and what wouldn't, and we actually didn't know until the end. We were conceptualising the stupidest concepts. But everybody was totally into it. Talking about it we felt like college students on acid.'

American critics greeted the movie extremely. They loved it, they hated it, they were confused by it. For a while it was Burton's turn to be scared. 'I always hate it – I think I'm going to throw up for about a month. I hate those market research screenings [in the heartland sticks] to an audience of angry, troubled youths. It's valuable in a very broad-stroke way. But the way the studio look at it – every tiny reaction. If somebody in the audience twitches it's like, "Oh my God, cut that scene!" Then they conclude: "The audience for this movie is eighteen-to-nineteen-and-a-half-year-olds with moustaches."'

You can tell Burton actually quite likes Warners, which is wise; he's contracted to them for the foreseeable future. It's probable he would have liked them less had they decided to change the movie's title. Warners originally wanted something to do with 'ghosts'. 'The studio goes out to a mall and asks kids, "If you had a choice, which movie would you see: *Beetlejuice* or 'something *Ghosts*?'" I'm so grateful they let me keep *Beetlejuice*. Thank God.'

The studio also raised eyebrows over Burton's use of effects. Intentionally quick 'n' dirty – furry things on sticks, see-how-it's-done illusions, creaky Godzilla-style stop-motion techniques – Burton suggests that a much larger budget would have increased the time spent on the effects, but not the basic funky concept. He likes the Godzilla films. He sucked his rusks to them.

Burton was raised in Burbank to non-industry middle-class parents. 'I wouldn't be the one who would get in trouble at school, though I may have caused it,' he sneaks. 'My parents weren't incredibly strict, or incredibly lenient, but I thank God I wasn't sheltered from things as a kid or else I'd probably be an axe-murderer.' As a kid, Burton actually was an axe-murderer, once faking a mass slice-up of his brother so well that a neighbour called the cops.

He began his professional career animating at Disney, swiftly becoming disillusioned at what he perceived as a fundamental attitude problem – the deadbrained zombie laboriousness of the process. Also, he says, 'There was this whole yuppie shit. It's like they forgot what it's like to be kids.'

An unreleased Disney short called *Frankenweenie* came to the attention of Pee-wee Herman's people, leading to Burton's first feature, the big-money, iffy-reviewed *Pee-wee's Big Adventure*. Like *Beetlejuice* and (probably) his upcoming Batman movie, the Pee-wee film read as a kids' flick, but played as a kids-at-heart adult flick. The director prefers to see them as films for no one and everyone.

Behind Burton's grey Pinewood sofa are pinned several sketches in purple and mauve, early costume designs for the Joker. To their left you'll find photos of earlier Joker incarnations. Burton says: 'I love the idea of a man who, no matter what he does, can't help from smiling.' Burton presently suffers from a similar affliction, not least when talking about the *Batman* project. The huge Gotham City set lies grey and eerily cold on Pinewood's biggest lot, and the first day's shoot is still around a month away. But Burton can sense a sort of spiritual homecoming. He's always been a great Batman fan, he says, and was talked of as a possible new-Batman director some while before the success of *Beetlejuice*. 'Warners have had me for years, like a studio mascot. I think they ask anyone who's hot at the time.' The concrete go-ahead came only during that first megabucks week. 'Magically. Gee! I wonder if that had anything to do with it . . .'

There's been one previous shot at a Batman feature, essentially a strung-out TV episode. Burton only remembers a cool use of a shark-repellent spray. The new movie promises to keep the cape and utility belt, little more. 'It's a very difficult film. You have the TV series, which is camp, and you have *The Dark Knight* [comics by Frank Miller], which is *The Dark Knight*. What I love about *The Dark Knight* is that they've taken the Batman psychology and gone back to that, and they've blown apart the convention of comics. Hopefully the movie will do the same for movies.

'At the very start I arrived at this bottom line that you strip away all the mythology, and what you

Burton said conceptualising Beetlejuice's *ideas made the production team feel 'like college students on acid'. Barbara Maitland (Geena Davis) becomes a grotesque puppet.*

have at the root of it is a man who wears a Batsuit. Simple. And a great idea. Who just wants to copy a comic? If you're lucky you get *Superman*; if you're unlucky you get *The Legend of the Lone Ranger*.'

The central casting's a secret no more: Michael Keaton will play Batman; Jack Nicholson the Joker. Burton on Nicholson: 'He *is* that character. He's very smart. He *knows* that the Joker is the killer – you know that that's going to be great. Everything has got to be on that kind of level.' His Batman casting is less orthodox. Television original Adam West was once talked of as a keen contender, principally, it seems, by Adam West. Quizzed on his failure to land the role on a recent trip to London, West bit his lip: 'At first I was torpedoed. Shattered. *Riven*. But now it's all over, it's like a great weight off my shoulders. Somehow I really don't care anymore.' Do *you* believe him? Like fuck you do!

Michael Keaton got the role, says Burton, 'Because I can see him putting on a Batsuit. I mean truthfully. I thought about it a lot. I met a lot of what you could call square-jawed actors that I felt were good actors, but I just didn't feel it was enough. You put Arnold Schwarzenegger in a Batsuit and it's actually very absurd. You have more potential to laugh at that than anything. But with Keaton . . . there are a few actors that when you look at their eyes, you see a lot going on.'

But Keaton's career was recently in a trough, so maybe the success of *Beetlejuice* forced Burton's hand.

'Well, *Beetlejuice* is *Beetlejuice*. I had a good experience with Keaton, but that's not why he got the part. I mean I had a good experience with Pee-wee Herman, and I didn't ask *him* to play it.'

BABES IN CINEMA LAND

by David Denby

Compared to the previous decade, the eighties notoriously has not been a time in which scads of brilliant new directors have come jumping out of film school, television, theatre, and editing rooms. Looking among the newly prominent Hollywood talents, one can name, with gratitude, Oliver Stone, Barry Levinson, and Joel Coen, and also the ace Spielberg disciple Robert Zemeckis, the Australian-born Fred Schepisi, David Lynch, maybe Ron Shelton . . . Have I left anyone out? Please do not pronounce the words 'Susan Seidelman', at least not in serious company. Do not say 'Ron Howard' or 'Taylor Hackford' either, though Hackford, I admit, can be a very good entertainer. Michael Lehmann, who made the maliciously entertaining teen cult movie *Heathers*, shows a talent for gliding-camera pyrotechnics and De Palma-ish malevolence. He's certainly someone to watch. Anyone else?

Well, enough of this tease: I have left someone out – a young man who has created worlds entirely his own and who has shown the kind of wit and intelligence needed for the long run. Toy master Tim Burton, 30, director of *Pee-wee's Big Adventure*, *Beetlejuice*, and the new $30 million-plus *Batman*, starring Michael Keaton, Jack Nicholson, and Kim Basinger.

Burton broke through with a relatively inexpensive film: *Pee-wee's Big Adventure* cost $6.8 million; then he consolidated his position with a bigger-budget hit, and is now standing at that perilous place, near the edge of disaster, where a really big budget can turn a director into a quailing Hollywood sap, suddenly afraid of risk and imagination. (Compare the Ron Howard of *Cocoon* with the Ron Howard of *Splash*.) Nothing, it's said, succeeds like success, but in Hollywood, at times, nothing fails like success.

Burton's speciality is childlike reverie and an exuberant mix of ridiculous horror and social satire. He has emerged, I suppose, in the wake of the Spielberg-Lucas emphasis on fantasy; there's no reason to expect him in the near future to make domestic dramas or socially conscious melodramas or comedies about sex and ambition in the workplace. He's got his own preoccupations. In Burton's films, the childlike sensibility is thrust into an alien world and struggles to maintain its equilibrium.

Tim Burton is a movie kid. He grew up in Burbank, California, near Walt Disney Studios, and after attending California Institute of the Arts he worked in Disney's animation department making short films. One imagines him nostalgic for the magic of the great old studio days: at the end of the director's first feature film, Pee-wee Herman finally finds his lost bicycle at a movie studio, jumps on it, and rides it from soundstage to soundstage, passing through the sets of a beach-blanket-bingo movie, a cheesy Japanese monster picture, a rock video, and so on. Of course, in the past 40 years or so, no studio would have had all these movies in production on its soundstages at the same time. What comes through in Burton's nostalgia is a longing for a time when all these fantasy worlds were buzzing simultaneously, when studio-lot moviemaking was the kingdom of artifice.

Pee-wee's Big Adventure touches on the real world only to reject it. In the beginning Pee-Wee, a child-man, dreams of winning a bicycle race; he wakes from his dream to greet not the dross and drone of everyday reality but the paradise of his toy house, a place filled with one Rube Goldberg contraption after another devoted to such mundane tasks as brushing his teeth and making his breakfast. The machines – gizmos and levers and chutes of plastic and chrome – possess an exquisite complication; they are designed entirely for his delight. No turbaned and jewelled sultan, master of the most labyrinthine seraglio, with erotic fulfillment at every turn, could possess so complete a pleasure palace.

Pee-wee himself lives according to his own fierce notions of perfection. He always dresses in a silver grey suit with narrow lapels, a white shirt, and the tiny red bow-tie of a circus pitchman; his face is slightly powdered, his lips reddened, his hair a black vinyl slab. He is an unsettling, ambiguous cross between benevolent clown and decadent Weimar-era nightclub entertainer. Like the classic comics, he is always himself, as unvarying in texture as a diamond – asexual, untouchable, an infantile personality with a will of steel. By definition, his character cannot 'develop'; he cannot be altered by experience.

When Pee-wee's beautiful red bicycle is stolen, he is stricken; he doesn't need parents or a girlfriend's love, he needs his bicycle – something that *he* can love. He takes to the road to find it and meets people who have lived, people who have histories, sadness, ambitions; they are touched by him, because he's pure and doesn't want anything but his bike, but he remains essentially untouched by them. And in truth the world, as he finds it, is just as toylike as his house. There's a dinosaur park in the middle of a desert – he sits inside the mouth of a gigantic tyrannosaurus, gazing out through the teeth. The Alamo turns out merely to be a museum with life-size wax figures. Burton recreates the world as artifice; the Hollywood studio at the end is just a confirmation, a castle filled with dreamers as dedicated as Pee-wee.

Burton revels in bright primary colours, especially red and medium blue, and lots of golden sunshine; his shopping malls and streets are candied, glowing, untextured, like the streets in Disneyland. We could be looking at illustrations in a child's book were it not for the aberrant bits of humour. For instance, the movie's dip into horror – an old truck driver whose eyes bug out, revealing that she's a ghost – isn't meant to scare us as much as remind us why we love to be scared. (The yuckiness goes back to childhood pleasures in slopping the dinner soup.) The much more developed horror thrills in the great *Beetlejuice* aren't meant to scare us either. Shrunken heads, ripped-out throats, eyeballs drooping like steamed clams waving in broth, cadavers purplish

Yuppie Delia Deetz (Catherine O'Hara, right) finds – with dinner party guests Otho (Glenn Shadix) and Beryl (Adele Lutz) – that it's not so chic to have ghosts after all.

or pink – the shocks and 'Boo!'s are a comic-book idea of horror, outrageously overdone. Burton knows that we have become jaded connoisseurs of special effects, that horror can now be done only ironically, as a joke.

Beetlejuice is all jokes, with a melancholy undertone. A young couple, killed in an automobile accident, return to their lovely Connecticut house as ghosts, only to discover that dreadful new people are moving in – people so chic they find ghosts amusing. The couple hire a professional ghoul, Beetlejuice (Michael Keaton), who can really scare up a storm. For Beetlejuice, the job of scaring people is like putting on a wild show; he goes for noisy monsters and cheap, gaudy thrills. Burton and Keaton, improvising the character on the set, made him a vulgar comic – a ghost as media huckster, insistently knowing, like a guest on *Late Night with David Letterman* going over the top and then smiling at us in complicity. When Beetlejuice goes to work, it's carnival time.

Like *Pee-wee*, this movie is about a paradise ruined and then restored. The couple, Adam and Barbara, though childless, are almost as childlike as Pee-wee Herman. Both alive and dead, they want to play undisturbed in their charming, dowdy old house (it's not clear how they earned a living), a house on a hill just outside a village so peaceful that the customers in a hardware store leave their money and take change from the cash register when no one is there. In the attic, Adam has built a model of the town. Starting with the opening helicopter shot of the town itself, which dissolves into the model, Burton deliberately blurs the line between reality and toy. The town is so quaint, it seems a work of art; the model is so detailed, it has everything. Living in this toy world of charming miniatures is Burton's ideal of happiness. And yet his innocence isn't sentimental; he has the hard clarity of the lifetime melancholic who expects things to go badly.

The real ghouls in the movie are not Beetlejuice and other shrunken and empurpled denizens of the beyond, waiting so patiently in the bureaucratic outer office of Heaven (or is it Hell?), but the invaders, the fashionable idiots from New York who turn Adam and Barbara's house into a grim little art park. The new owners' sculptures and furniture and wall coverings are pure pretence, a form of real estate. The only art in *Beetlejuice*, of course, is Burton's comic horror shows. The whole movie is an aestheticised vision, a delirious potpourri of surrealism and expressionism turned to pop thrills. But unlike most directors highly conscious of visual effects, Burton is a flaky, natural-born entertainer. He gives his films a poky, stop-and-go tempo, using the quiet spots in the narrative for passing jokes, weird bits of satire. He stays in touch with the feelings of his characters, even the ones he's ridiculing.

BATMAN (1989)

BATMAN

by Taylor L. White

FADE IN:

EXT. CITYSCAPE - NIGHT

The place is Gotham City, the time 1987 - once removed.

The city of tomorrow: stark angles, creeping shadows, dense, crowded, airless, a random tangle of steel and concrete, self-generating, almost subterranean in its aspects . . . as if hell had erupted through the sidewalks and kept growing. A dangling fat moon shines overhead, ready to burst.

EXT. CATHEDRAL - NIGHT

Amid the chrome and glass sits a dark ornate Gothic anomaly: old City Cathedral, once grand, now abandoned - long since boarded up and scheduled for demolition.

On the rooftop far above us, **STONE GARGOYLES** gaze down from their shadowy, windswept perches, keeping watch over the distant street below, sightless guardians of the Gotham night.

One of them is moving.

This first half-page of Sam Hamm's screenplay for Warner Bros.' upcoming *Batman* sets a mood that is undeniably dark and ominous. The stalwart Caped Crusader of TV fame would have been laughed off the gritty streets of this Gotham City. Likewise, an inserted cartoon *Kapow!* or *Wham!* during one of its many action sequences would prove equally out of place. In this version of *Batman*, the emphasis is on *noir*, Warner Bros. having invested a reported $32 million on its filming in London.

The idea of bringing the legendary Caped Crusader – celebrating his 50th birthday this year – to the big screen has been an on-again/off-again prospect tossed around for several years. In 1984, 007 and *Superman* screenwriter Tom Mankiewicz took a stab at it with a script based loosely on the

50 years after he debuted in Detective Comics, *the title role of* Batman *was taken by Michael Keaton. Doubts about the casting were dispelled by the film's dark atmosphere.*

late seventies Steve Englehart/Marshall Rogers issues of *Detective Comics*. Directors like Joe Dante and Ivan Reitman showed interest over the years, but little came of it. It seemed *Batman* was doomed to sit on the batshelves for years to come.

Then came Hamm, whose comedy script *Pulitzer Prize* started a bidding war, landing him a two-year contract at Warner Bros., the home of *Batman*. His only prior experience came with a gruelling twelve-week stint in Alaska doing location re-writes on *Never Cry Wolf*, followed by three years of unemployment. Needless to say, the prospect of scripting a *Batman* feature was more than enticing for the 33 year-old screenwriter and comic buff.

'I was a religious reader of *Batman* when I was a kid,' he recalled. 'It was during the "time travel and pink aliens" phase when they were treating him like just another superhero in the Justice League. I think the comic writers ran out of inspiration on what kind of stories to do, so the stuff was getting pretty wild and wacky. But what really caught my fancy as a kid were the reprints from the late forties and early fifties which had the more pulpy and *noir*ish Batman with the disfigured villains.

In his script, Hamm wastes little time detailing Batman's origin, but instead has the 'winged' hero battling thugs even before the opening credits roll. Taking a different tack was Hamm's intention from the beginning. '*Superman* set the model for how to do a superhero movie by opening up with a big, spectacular origin sequence,' said Hamm. 'It stuck me that Batman was a different kind of character and couldn't be treated in quite the same way because, while being rather exaggerated, grand, and operatic, *Batman* deals with material that is within the province of possibility. You really don't have to explain why a man can fly or why bullets bounce off his chest.

'I thought the best thing was to establish Batman as a *fait accompli* and move backward by treating him as a mysterious character where you don't really know what his agenda is or what motivates him to do what he does. Therefore, the unlocking of that mystery becomes part of the plot of the story.'

In writing *Batman*, Hamm attempted to add dimension to the main character by instilling a dose of psychological depth amidst the fast-paced action. 'I tried to take the premise which had this emotionally scarred millionaire whose way of dealing with his traumas was by putting on the suit. If you look at it from this aspect that there is no world of superheroes, no DC Universe, and no real genre conventions to fall back on, you can start taking the character seriously. You can ask what if this guy actually does exist, and in turn, it'll generate a lot of plot for you.'

In writing *Batman*, Hamm also understood that his work would be under close scrutiny by comic fans everywhere, but he didn't expect bootlegged copies of early drafts of his script to reach such wide circulation. 'It's really weird that everyone in the world that I talk to seems to have read my script,' he laughed. 'At this point, I'm surprised they don't bundle them up and pass them out as a free bonus gift if you buy four issues of *Detective Comics*.'

Bootlegged scripts aside, he did feel a sense of responsibility in writing *Batman*. 'Whenever you're doing a major movie version of a beloved comic character who's been hanging around for 50 years, obviously the most rabid aficionadados are going to have strong opinions about whether you're taking the character in the right direction or not. But I had no idea that this was going to develop into the huge brouhaha that it has.'

The brouhaha in question came with the announcement that Michael Keaton would be playing Batman, a bit of casting news that rocked comic fandom from coast to coast. In response, petitions surfaced in comic stores asking fans to 'Stop the Batman Movie.'

'It's kind of disorienting to walk into a comic book store and find a petition to stop something you worked on,' said Hamm. 'It's like suddenly finding yourself on a bad episode of *The Twilight Zone*,' he joked. 'You can't do anything but laugh.'

Like most fans, Hamm does admit to being initially taken aback by the casting. 'It came as a jolt', he said. 'But I think a lot of the backlash is based on misconceptions. It's kind of a knee-jerk response from fans, because when they hear Tim Burton's name they think of *Pee-wee's Big Adventure*, and when they hear Keaton's name they think of any number of Michael Keaton comedies. It's a natural response, especially since the project has been announced again and again over the last year or two as being a serious *Batman*. In thinking about it, I can see what Burton's up to there, plus they've certainly figured out ways to cover up for the fact that he's not six foot seven and heavily muscled,' said Hamm in reference to Batman's multi-faceted Batsuit, which resembles muscled armour. 'More than anything, I think Keaton will do an interesting job as Bruce Wayne. The straighter parts I've seen him in have been really pretty good.'

Despite the left-field casting, Hamm reassured that *Batman* would be no farce. 'Keaton's casting certainly hasn't resulted in any changes in the tone of the script. The film would've been the same even if they had cast some square jawed hulk in the role.' To clarify the nature of the comedic aspects, he added, 'There's going to be plenty of nasty, dark humour all the way through the movie, but I don't think anyone's going to mistake it for a gagfest. The sense of humour is very dark and deadpan.'

Dark icon: the re-designed Batmobile creeps along the streets of a film noir-style Gotham City at night.

Although the black humour is still intact, Hamm admitted that Bruce Wayne is no longer the same psychologically mixed-up character he was in earlier drafts thanks to later rewrites by Charles McKeown and noted script doctor Warren Skaaren.

'Bruce Wayne's character has been lightened up considerably,' said Hamm with disappointment. 'My Bruce was fairly dark and tormented in addition to being charming and enigmatic, but a lot of those elements have been scaled back. Now he has a little less self-doubt about his program than he did in my version. I hate to use the term, considering the casting, but he's now a little more "square jawed" than he was when I wrote it.'

Hamm blamed the changes on what he calls the 'monolithic studio mentality'. Said Hamm, 'It's typical studio thinking that when a big, expensive picture is going into production, they start getting itchy about any of the more idiosyncratic material in the script. There's always a blind rush to change things and they start getting rid of anything that is mildly disturbing to anybody watching it. As a result, everything tends to get homogenised. They take out a lot of what I call "the organic matter", which is the material that makes it interesting to a writer.'

Although annoyed with the changes, Hamm is not entirely unsympathetic. 'I see what they're doing in that they don't want to have a larger-than-life, heroic character who is plagued with doubts about the validity of what he's doing, but it's stuff that I miss. Whether this will be a deterrent to the film, I can't really say.'

Meanwhile, Warner Bros. has left *Batman*'s Gotham City sets standing in London for a sequel to go into production in May of 1990, providing the first film turns out to be a success.

BATMAN

by Alan Jones

There's a story *Batman* director Tim Burton likes to tell. In 1978 Burton was still in school and was attending a big comic book convention in San Diego. The event was held just a few months before Richard Donner's big budget *Superman* was due to open and a Warner Bros. press officer was there to give a slide show presentation featuring scenes from the production.

'The ballroom was packed with people,' said Burton. 'All eyes were glued to the screen with the poor Warner guy trying to keep it all under control. Suddenly, one fan stood up and screamed, "Superman would never change into his costume on a ledge of a building. I'm going to boycott this movie and tell everyone you are destroying the legend!" Intense applause followed as he stormed out of the hall. Wow, I thought. And from that moment on I always knew in the back of my mind the enormous problems facing anyone taking on a film version of a comic book hero.'

The newly-married Burton faced more than his fair share of vitriol from vociferous comic book fans during the making of his multi-million dollar *Batman*, which opened to thunderous box-office for Warner Bros. Burton developed the *Batman* script with Sam Hamm at Warners after being assigned to the project when his *Pee-wee's Big Adventure* turned out to be a surprise hit for the studio. Before Hamm, Julie Hickson, who produced Burton's Disney shorts, *Hansel and Gretel* and *Frankenweenie*, had written a 30 page treatment.

'I wasn't working on it full-time,' said Burton. 'I'd just meet Sam on weekends to discuss the early writing stages. We knocked it into good shape while I directed *Beetlejuice*, but as a "go" project it was only greenlighted by Warners when the opening figures for *Beetlejuice* surprised everybody – including myself!'

The *Batman* project had been languishing at Warners for nearly ten years. Producers Mike Uslan and Benjamin Melnicker had negotiated the film rights from DC Comics in 1979. Several months later Melnicker had swung a development deal with Peter Guber's Casablanca Film Works, based at Warner Bros. Melnicker and Uslan are credited as executive producers on the film, which is produced by Guber and his partner Jon Peters.

Uslan and Melnicker hired screenwriter Tom Mankiewicz and patterned their production after *Superman* (1978), also scripted by Mankiewicz. The project was announced in late 1981 with a budget of $15 million. Set in the near future, Mankiewicz's script followed the *Superman* formula, concentrating on Batman's origins, including the murder of his parents. After a phenomenally successful run in *Detective Comics* in 1939, the character's origin had been outlined in a two-page introduction in the first issue of *Batman*, written by Bill Finger and drawn by Bob Kane, published in early 1940. That issue also introduced the Joker in its lead story, and killed him off in the issue's final strip 'The Joker Returns'. But Kane had second thoughts and redrew the strip's final panel to keep Batman's primary nemesis going in over 200 stories.

Though Burton and screenwriter Sam Hamm are credited with turning the direction of *Batman* away from the campy TV series of the sixties back to the dark, *noir*ish Kane and Finger originals, that direction was actually the stated intention of Uslan and Melnicker. 'The project has to be done right,' said Uslan in late 1983, when their version of *Batman* was being readied for a summer 1985 release on a budget of $20 million. 'The film must be about the creature of the night and capture the spirit of what *Batman* was originally about and what the comic, by and large, has reverted to in the last couple of years.'

Uslan had worked part-time for DC Comics in the early seventies on a program that taught kids how to read using comic books. He later wrote *Batman* stories for DC Comics while a law student at Indiana University in the mid-seventies. 'It was a lifelong ambition come true,' said Uslan, 'to write a couple of issues of *Batman*. I began then to think, wouldn't it be great to do a definitive *Batman* movie totally removed from the TV show, totally removed from camp; a version that went back to the original Bob Kane/Bill Finger strips.'

The Joker was the main menace in the Mankiewicz version, which also pitted Batman against 'normal' street crooks, and introduced Robin only at the very end. Directors associated with the project's development included Joe Dante and Ivan Reitman. Uslan wanted an unknown to play Batman and his cast wish-list included William Holden as Commissioner Gordon and David Niven as Alfred, Bruce Wayne's faithful butler.

But the Uslan/Melniker *Batman* would have been very different from the darkly poetic vision Burton finally realised, as Uslan's 1983 description of their idea of the Batcave illustrates. 'When you see it in the film, it'll be the Batcave that appeared in the comics: the mechanical dinosaur, the giant penny, the Joker's giant playing card.' Though Mankiewicz's script improved on the character's comic book origins – the comic's inspiration for the costume, young Bruce Wayne seeing a bat flying through his bedroom window, was dropped – the script never licked the problem of making the comic book elements believeable in screen terms.

'The very first *Batman* treatment I read was remarkably similar to *Superman*,' said Burton. 'It had the same light, jokey tone, and the story structure followed Wayne through childhood to his genesis as a crimefighter. I found it all rather disturbing because, while that route was probably fine in the case of *Superman*, there was absolutely no exploration or acknowledgement of the character's psychological structure and why he would dress up in a bat suit. In that respect, it was very much like the television series.'

Burton was wrestling with the comic's psychological aspects, trying to move the storyline in a positive direction, when he first met Hamm. 'Sam was a big comic book fan and he knew exactly what to do with the script.' Burton credited the success of Frank Miller's *The Dark Knight*, a graphic novel that explored the psychology of Batman in the style of dark, *noir*ish films, with helping sell Warners on the psychological approach and leap back to the original comics that he and Hamm wanted to take.

'The success of the graphic novels made our ideas far more acceptable,' said Burton. 'The movie doesn't wallow in darkness, but without becoming a psychological tone poem, it addresses all the issues without hammering you over the head. *The Dark Knight* works on the comic page – it seems to be a direct response to all the light-heartedness that had gone before – but it was far too dark stylistically for movie purposes. I think the movie is funny without being campy at the expense of the material. The tone is more consistent than in any other film I've made.'

When Hamm got sidelined by 1988's writer's strike, Warners brought in Warren Skaaren to help prepare the film's final shooting script. And during filming, Burton did further rewrites with an uncredited Charles McKeown. It was during those rewrites that the plot point was added making the Joker the killer of young Bruce Wayne's parents, an element not found in the comics that had earlier been part of both the rejected Mankiewicz script and Hickson treatment.

Though it didn't fit the mold of the *Batman* he wanted to make, Burton said he was a big fan of the sixties TV series starring Adam West. It was the first TV show Burton said he could recall running home to watch. 'I loved it,' said Burton, who was only seven years old when the show debuted in 1966. 'I still do, although I would never say I was ever a fanatic. But, I'm not from the hate school who thinks it's blasphemous to Bruce Wayne's memory and against everything he stood for.'

Burton said he knew that in making *Batman* he would face the ire of comic book fans, 'passionate about the minutest details,' but said he was equally aware of the pull of fans of the TV show, 'a far larger group because it was more in the public eye.' Burton saw his dilemma as a 'no win situation' and decided to follow his instincts, come what may.

'The good thing about this movie is if you liked the TV show it shares a similar flavour,' said Burton. 'I decided to take the movie in the direction I felt was right and remain unshaken by anything that would eventually happen. I was so clear about the course I was taking because what attracted me to the project in the first place were Batman and the Joker – my favourite characters. Like all great larger-than-life images, they can be explored any number of different ways. There is just as much room for the TV show and *The Dark Knight* as there is for my movie. Why shouldn't there be?'

Still, Burton and nearly everyone connected with the film was surprised by the vociferousness of the comic book brigade's up in arms protest over the casting of Michael Keaton as Batman, first suggested by producer Jon Peters. Burton has long tired of defending his controversial creative decision and merely sighs when the subject is brought up. 'There's nothing more to say apart from how comfortable I feel about Michael's contribution,' said Burton. 'The fan reaction is a surface response. The moment you mention Keaton he immediately brings to mind *Mr Mom* and *Night Shift* – the comedy/romance sit-com-type picture. Obviously I knew from the beginning that wasn't the road I would ever take. If I had been afraid of that argument, I wouldn't have asked Michael to do it in the first place. I looked at actors who were more the fan image of Batman, but I felt it was such an uninteresting way to go.'

According to the *Los Angeles Times*, other actors considered for the Batman role included Mel Gibson, Bill Murray, Charlie Sheen and Pierce Brosnan. Burton said he chose Keaton for his acting ability. 'Michael is very good,' said Burton. '*Clean and Sober* proved it. He's funny/dramatic in a way which added to what I was trying to achieve. Taking someone like Michael and making him Batman supported the whole split personality idea. The most interesting aspect I perceived in

'Wait until they get a load of me.' Jack Nicholson played the Joker as a mass murderer with a sense of fun. Financially, it was one of the most lucrative performances ever.

the story – what it was really about – has now been underscored. Michael's personality tunes into those differences, making him the perfect choice. He has a lot going on inside him, there's an explosive side; he has a temper and a great amount of anger – that was exactly the Bruce Wayne character, not some unknown, handsome, strong hunk.'

Also behind Burton's choice of Keaton as Batman was the fact that Jack Nicholson had been cast first as the Joker. Said Burton, 'I kept imagining the reviews and hearing the response in my head, "Well, Jack's great, but the unknown so-and-so is nothing special!" Michael is more straight-forward here than he's ever been in any movie. If people have problems with him then they'll have problems with the movie. But is that my problem? He's a part of the whole. He doesn't call attention to himself, and he's not doing anything but fitting seamlessly into an ensemble cast. Certain actors are so strong, they are often better than the material. Michael has the back-up strength of a great script. When you see the film, he's an actor playing a part that fits in exactly with what I envisioned. End of story. What is all the drama about?!'

The budget of *Batman* was price-tagged in the *Los Angeles Times* by producer Jon Peters at $35 million, plus $5 million in interest charges. Burton said he hadn't kept track of the film's cost and honestly didn't know the final figure. 'All I cared about was the tight, tough schedule,' he said. 'We did go over budget, but nothing that wasn't really anticipated with a project this size. I was willing to listen regarding certain cuts they wanted made. I'm not the type of person who has to rigidly stick to the script. And when I saw the rough cut, I'm happy to say every scene we shot has made it into the movie.'

At Pinewood, the production sprawled across the studio's 95-acre backlot, taking up most of its eighteen sound stages. 'Sean Young's replacement by Kim Basinger was the first problem we encountered,' said Burton. 'We were lucky not to lose more time. We had decent weather. Shooting at night didn't cause anything untoward to happen. Overall, we didn't do too badly.'

Batman was filmed at Pinewood not so much for economy, but because Burton had always wanted to work in Britain. 'To be honest, I wanted to get out of the States because of all the hype, hoopla, and controversy the film was attracting,' he said. 'It was happening in England too, but to a far lesser degree. I didn't need any extra distractions and coming here pretty much removed the stress level in that area so I could focus on the movie. There are only two places you can make a movie like this — Los Angeles or London. In many ways the craftsmen and artists are better in Britain. Even though the dollar was iffy, I'm glad I decided to base operations at Pinewood. It wouldn't have been cheaper in L.A., just more problematic.'

Pivotal to the *Batman* look is the work of production designer Anton Furst, renowned for his elaborate sets on films like *High Spirits*, *Full Metal Jacket*, and *The Company of Wolves*. Furst had been recommended to Burton by effects supervisor Derek Meddings. The designer needed no introduction to Burton, who had sought him out originally to work on *Beetlejuice*. But Burton had been told that Furst wasn't available for *Batman*, due to his commitment on Neil Jordan's *High Spirits*, so another production designer had already been assigned by Warners.

'Burton had been told I couldn't do the film, but he doggedly wouldn't believe it,' said Furst. 'Tim had wanted me to do *Beetlejuice*, but after two exhausting years working with Stanley Kubrick on *Full Metal Jacket* I didn't feel in any position to take on a new film. Tim had seen *The Company of Wolves* and had always wanted to work with me. I remember he flew from Los Angeles to San Francisco when he knew I was about to stay with friends there. He wanted to approach me before I travelled on to L.A. in case someone else got me first. Tim is really singleminded when there's something he feels strongly about. *Batman* he felt strongly about so I replaced the original choice of designer. I wish I'd done *Beetlejuice* now, rather than *High Spirits*!'

Furst budgeted *Batman* while he finished work on the filming of Neil Jordan's ghost story comedy. 'The spectacular thing about Tim is he has this extraordinary ability to get onto the pulse of a movie and define its atmosphere and general spirit,' said Furst. 'He is quite amazing in his observations. That spirit is one of the reasons why I'm sure Warners backed such a young director in the first place. They know he's got something, and even if they don't quite know what it is, they're willing to go along with it. I found his spirit contagious, and we do have a lot in common. We both wear black, for example. There was an instant affinity between us.

'I don't think I've ever felt so naturally in tune with a director,' continued Furst, 'conceptually, spiritually, visually, or artistically. There was never any problem because we never fought over anything. I often wanted his advice, but when I came up with four ideas in four different directions, he'd always choose the one I liked most. He was in America when I had to make certain decisions over the Batmobile, so I faxed over numbered designs even though the one I liked was rather radical. When I called him he said, "I've got the one in front of me." And of course it was the same one. It was always the same one.'

Furst stressed that his collaboration with Burton worked so well because they both agreed on the same philosophy of moviemaking. 'When we first met, we both independently mentioned how sick we were of the ILM school of filmmaking,' said Furst. 'You can't stun with effects anymore, you have to go back to basics. We both agreed the best special effect we could ever remember seeing was the house in *Psycho* because it registers such a strong image. Impact, that's what films are about – not effects. I felt much better after that conversation, knowing he was totally uninterested in camera tricks and the clever, clever approach.

'Texture, attitude and feelings are what [Burton] is a master at,' continued Furst. 'He's good at getting to the bottom line, or what he terms, "the broadstroke". What do we really need out of this shot? We don't want details or the icing on the cake. What do we have to put across? Tim is good at paring down to the lowest common denominator and then embellishing on that because detailing is easy. This takes a lot of intelligence and he's good at articulating this and following those ideas through. The producers always went along with him because he could always articulate why he was doing something.'

'Anton is the best in his field,' said Burton about his design collaborator. 'It's always important for me to work with people I like in these important capacities. Since my background is in illustration and design, it's the one area I'm very critical about. I have a tendency to bully departments if I'm not getting what I want. Working with someone who has real artistic talent and a strong input is a nice luxury. It excites me, and it's important for me to like them as friends. Anton's creative spark and the affinity we had went beyond a working relationship. We constantly talked back and forth; threw concepts around and discussed our thoughts openly.'

Burton and Furst came up with a look for Gotham City – actually identified as New York City in the comics from May 1939 to December 1940 – that can only be described as 'retro high-tech'. Burton abhored the term. 'I shiver at that description!' he said. 'If people say Gotham City looks like *Blade Runner*, I'll be furious!' Reading the film's reviews, Burton must be positively livid then, betcause most critics likened its architecture to Ridley Scott's effort, but also to Terry Gilliam's *Brazil*.

'So few great movie cities have been built,' said Burton. '*Metropolis* and *Blade Runner* seem to be the accepted spectrum. We tried so hard to do something different although people tend to lump things in categories. We conceptualised Gotham City as the reverse of New York in its early days. Zoning and construction was thought of in terms of letting light in. So we decided to take that in the opposite direction and darken everything by building up vertically and cramming architecture together. Gotham City is basically New York caricatured with a mix of styles squashed together – an island of big, tall cartoon buildings textured with extreme designs.'

Crucial to Burton's Gotham City concept was that nothing look new. 'Anton textured it beautifully to keep the operatic feel intact,' said Burton. 'All the sets are an extension of an opera staging and I think Anton has been very successful with my brief of timelessness. *Batman* is similar to *Beetlejuice* in that regard – it has a timeless quality with contemporary references making it believable within its own context of reality. I couldn't film any other way, although it's dangerous to describe something as timeless because the tendency is to go overboard and make it too stylised. No one feels anything but removed if you do that.'

To create the Gotham City sets on Pinewood's backlot, Furst had a $5.5 million construction budget. 'A third of that money you can't see as a lot went below the ground,' said Furst. 'On the backlot we had to piledrive into the ground to secure the set which had to withstand gale force winds. Imagine if we'd had a winter like the year before when a hurricane hit? It would have been a nightmare. That happened on *Superman* when the set was blown away. Concrete pads up to ten-feet deep with metal tubing cemented in meant the set was built to last. We weren't told to make it last for all the proposed *Batman* sequels. But we were filming through a winter, and it was cheaper in the long run to build it properly.'

Furst paced out the Pinewood lot looking through a standard medium-wide camera lens to determine the height to build the Gotham City street set, to give Burton maximum latitude. Everything was built 40-feet high, with the Cathedral 10-feet taller, so Burton could shoot freely without resorting to models or matte paintings. Only one main street was afforded by the budget, so Furst designed an alleyway in the back, and bridges over the set to provide Burton with a variety of perspectives.

'My job is to give the director as many variations on views as I can,' said Furst. 'It was important to lock in the geography early on because we had to have Gotham Square, a big parade going down the main street with the Batwing crashing into the Cathedral. These were strong parameters to lock down so the shots could be planned well in advance.'

The most remarkable element of Batman *was production designer Anton Furst's Gotham City. Tragically, Furst committed suicide in 1991, after starting work on* Batman Returns.

To combat the comic book fan backlash against their production, Warners hired artist Bob Kane, one of Batman's creators, as the project's creative consultant. 'Hiring Kane was a very intelligent move,' said Furst. 'He loved what we were doing. We sent over sketches constantly and he kept sending back these little drawings with notes attached saying, "Well done boys." He came over once to visit the set and when he was shown around, he was totally awe-inspired. Very clever, because when it comes to the American media, just to have it sanctioned by the creator makes it very difficult for [the audience] to complain. If Kane goes on record saying his concept has been brilliantly interpreted, the ardent fans buckle down. He must have a massive copyright merchan-lising deal so it's also in his interest.'

Kane had envisioned actor Jack Nicholson in the role of his Joker as far back as 1980, when he drew a likeness of the character over a still of the actor from *The Shining*. 'Kane thinks our Joker is better than the original in his strip,' said Furst. 'Very early on Bob kept saying, "Get Jack Nicholson. He is the Joker. Get the man!"'

Nicholson's hiring for the role of the Joker was credited by Anton Furst as a turning point for the production. 'Getting Jack was very important for the movie,' said Furst. 'It was so fucking obvious. I don't think there was ever a part more tailor-made for him. If he turned the part down, Tim and I both agreed we would never feel the same about the picture. As soon as he said yes, there was this great motivating force behind the movie because everyone knew that ingredient was dead right. And he fulfilled all expectations. When you have an actor with that sort of charisma, it heightens everyone else's performance and sets a standard level they all had to rise to. It was mainly because of Jack that the adrenaline ran so high.'

Called in to do Nicholson's makeup as the Joker was Nick Dudman, makeup supervisor on George Lucas' *Willow*, who trained under the tutelage of English makeup master Stuart Freeborn. Dudman was approached by Furst early in preproduction before Nicholson had been signed. 'I met Burton and Anton at a time when nobody knew whether *Batman* was a "go" project or not,' said Dudman. 'Burton told me there were two aspects to *Batman* that really scared him. One was Batman's cloak, which under no circumstances could look like an old teacloth. And the other was the look of the Joker. He didn't want him to look like an actor simply wearing white makeup.'

Batman began its twelve-week shoot in mid-October 1988 at Pinewood Studios, outside London. Though rumours were rampant during filming that Nicholson and Burton weren't getting along – and that Nicholson was trying to pressure Warner Bros. into replacing the director – Burton said Nicholson's improvisational style jibed closely with his own. 'Jack had a clear idea of the character and played around within those boundaries,' said Burton. 'I actually prefer improvi-sation, although preferably with on-page guidelines. He's a textbook actor who's very intuitive. He gets to know the character and then has quite a lot of fun with it. He'd always question how much he should laugh as the Joker and, at one point, asked me if he could go really nuts in a scene. But that comes only when both have a clear idea of the proper approach to take. He wouldn't have asked me that if he didn't feel we were in tune with each other.'

'It's not a campy perforrnance at all,' said Burton. 'Jack is absolutely brilliant at going as far as you can go, always pushing to the edge, but still making it seem real. He's less broad here than in *The Witches of Eastwick*. You can't play it too broad when you have white skin and green hair. He understood when it was time to bring his performance down.'

In the *Batman* comics, the Joker was a lab assistant who decided to stage a million-dollar robbery. When he dives in a pool of chemical waste to escape Batman, he discovers that his hair has turned green, his skin white, with his red lips spread permanently into a fiendish grin. The Joker's product-tampering victims in the film borrow imagery from the comics where his use of poison left victims with a horrified, mocking grin.

For his role as the Joker, Nicholson had what was known as an 'off-the-clock' agreement. His contract specified the number of hours he was entitled to have off each day, from the time he left the studio to the time he reported back for filming. 'Nicholson had to leave at a certain point each night – allowing time for us to clean him up – for it to be worth bringing him in the next day,' said Dudman. 'Anything over two and a half hours in the makeup chair was silly because he would only be on the floor for four hours. Although it was a crippling schedule, we got it down to two hours in all – 90 minutes to get everything on and coloured up, twenty minutes for the wig placement, and ten minutes to re-touch and finish.'

Dudman said it was a joy to work with Nicholson. 'Having Jack around was great. He's such an amusing person. He made it a pleasure to go to work.' And there were fringe benefits. 'When he didn't work, neither did we,' said Dudman. 'As Jack didn't like working weekends or too many days in a row, we always had breathing space to catch up. The prosthetics had specific foam densities and had to be absolutely flawless, so there was a lot of waste. Having extra days to review how many sets and back-ups we had was an added luxury.'

Dudman said Nicholson was a great kidder on the set. 'I'm a terrible giggler,' said Dudman, 'so I had to leave the floor several times. But he could be amusing one second and the next turn on the evil with one subtle expression. And the quality wasn't lost through overuse of makeup. My initial terror was always that the makeup would sabotage what he was trying to produce, causing him endless frustration. Jack is one of the top actors in the world. Apart from Dustin Hoffman in *Little Big Man*, I can't think of another celebrity who has consented to a total face change. He told me he wanted to play someone behind a mask, just to get an idea of what it was like. Luckily, we got him at a time he was prepared to experiment. I can see why he spent a lot of time thinking about playing the Joker. It was a brave move.'

Did Burton feel Nicholson was integral to the funding of *Batman*, as has been suggested? 'That's hard to say,' pondered the director. 'My recollection is that Warners said yes before anyone was signed. Warners definitely wanted to make the movie and an actor of Jack's calibre only helped raise the level of perception a few more notches.'

Anti-Keaton comic book protesters also took to task Bob Ringwood's superhero costume design for the film because it incorporated fake muscles, a cloak-cum-wings, and a rather large cod-piece. 'The idea was to humanise Batman,' said Burton about the design of Batman's costume. 'He dresses like this for theatrical effect. We had to find a psychological basis for his dress code. You can't just do, "Well, I'm avenging the death of my parents – Oh, a bat's flown in through the window! Yes, that's it. I'll become a Batman!" That's all stupid comic book stuff and we don't explore it at all. He dresses up as a bat because he wants to have an amazing visual impact. It all gets away from the fact he's just being a simple vigilante, something I always loathed about the character. He's creating an opera wherever he goes to provoke a strong, larger-than-life reaction. He switches identities to become something else entirely, so why wouldn't he overdo it?'

As for the costume's enlarged cod-piece, Burton sees nothing wrong with injecting a little sex into the comic imagery. 'Aren't comics always about sex anyway?' he said. 'Teens like them because they tune in to sexual fantasy at the exact time they're going through puberty. Bob's design was less an outfit, more a complete body suit. It isn't tights and underwear worn on the outside, but a complete operatic costume to overstate the image Batman has of himself. Nor is it *Robocop* inspired. We don't make as much of it as the comic fans have – it's just an image-conscious costume.'

Robin, Batman's sidekick, isn't in the finished film, though Burton and Hamm included the character in the shooting script. Burton made the decision to drop Robin shortly before filming began because he felt the character's introduction slowed the movie's pace. 'We could never get

Robin in before the last third of the movie,' said Burton of the script dynamics. 'By that time we just wanted to get on with the story rather than introduce somebody else new in tights, simply because the comic lore dictated it. Luckily, when I made the decision to cut him out entirely – something that made everyone nervous – that comic book issue was published where the fans voted to kill off Robin. The timing was very helpful in convincing Warners Robin didn't matter.'

Like *Beetlejuice*, the supporting cast of *Batman* is very 'off the wall', a penchant that is becoming one of the director's trademarks. 'I love a certain kind of casting,' said Burton. 'Jack Palance was the only person who could possibly portray Nicholson's boss. He is one of the few living actors who had the emotional weight and authority to counterpoint Nicholson's strong character. Jerry Hall [Palance's girlfriend] doesn't play herself, although you know she's a famous model. Half the time she's wearing a disfiguring mask and a lot of power is registered as a result of blurring her real life with her character role. People will read that and say, "Campy, campy, campy." But it isn't that at all. I think it's strong since she's a recognisable figure as a model, therefore it becomes much more resonant. I'm so happy with that sort of trade-off casting.'

The Palance and Hall roles, as well as Robert Wuhl as newspaper reporter Alexander Knox, were ones created especially for the script. From the comics, Burton cast Pat Hingle as Police Commissioner Gordon, a friend of Bruce Wayne's who is unaware of his associate's crime fighting alter ego. By the film's end, Gordon introduces the comic's famed Batsignal searchlight as a means of calling the crime fighter. Alfred, Wayne's faithful butler, wasn't introduced in the comics until May 1943, but, played by suberb English character actor Michael Gough, is in on Batman's film origin from the beginning.

Batman's comic book girlfriend is played by Kim Basinger, who replaced the originally cast Sean Young after she broke her leg early in the filming. 'The Vicki Vale character went from brunette to blonde – an interesting switch which didn't phase me as much as I thought it would,' said Burton. 'Incidentally, Kim isn't producer Jon Peters' girlfriend. She didn't get the part through favouritism. That was yet more salacious gossip we've had to put up with. We sued an English tabloid newspaper over that report.'

Music for *Batman* was composed by Danny Elfman, who scored Burton's *Pee-wee's Big Adventure* and *Beetlejuice*. Whereas Burton used Harry Belafonte calypsos on the soundtrack of *Beetlejuice*, *Batman* features the more contemporary songs of Prince, almost universally panned by critics and audiences alike as being out of place in the film.

'*Batman* doesn't have as blatant a soundtrack as, say, *Top Gun*,' said Burton in defence of Prince. 'The songs in the film I would call scored source pieces. They are integrated seamlessly into the soundtrack. Prince worked with Elfman to ensure the songs didn't stand out when, for example, the radio is switched on. Our eyes are not on high volume soundtrack sales.' Asked why he wasn't daring enough to include the *Batman* TV theme somewhere, Burton just shrugged.

Batman is heavy on the special visual effects, supervised by Oscar-winner Derek Meddings and his Shepperton Studios-based Meddings Magic Camera Company. The film's mechanical effects were supervised by John Evans, with whom Meddings worked on *Moonraker*. For a director whose filmic *oeuvre* is heavy on the effects work, Burton has a refreshingly nonchalant attitude about their use, which is probably why his films utilise effects so well. 'I don't like relying too heavily on effects,' said Burton. 'In *Beetlejuice* I treated this area very matter-of-factly, using them like a bridge between two shots. That's my overall attitude – integrate them into the narrative rather than make them stand out.'

Warners is said to be so confident about *Batman*'s smash box-office potential that a sequel is already in the works. Names like Robin Williams as the Riddler and Danny DeVito as the Penguin have been mentioned in conjunction with a second adventure supposedly to shoot in May 1990.

Warners bought the $2 million Gotham City set on Pinewood's backlot to use on two future productions, and are protecting their investment behind 24-hour guard dog fences. 'The set is costing $20,000 a week to keep up because of scaffolding hire charges,' said Furst. 'So when they get around to making a sequel, it probably would have cost Warners only a quarter of a million dollars to resume it, as opposed to building it from scratch. Even the cost of renovation on top probably means it was worth keeping the set up.'

Burton said there was no point talking about sequels until his movie's performance at the box-office can be analysed. 'I don't want anything to do with a sequel anyway,' said Burton. 'Sequels are only worthwhile if they give you the opportunity to do something new and interesting. It has to go beyond that, really, because you do the first for the thrill of the unknown. A sequel wipes all that out, so you must explore the next level. I don't rule out anything if the challenge is exciting.'

With a rash of cosmic book heroes about to hit the big screen, the onus is on *Batman* to prove the trend is a worthwhile investment. And Burton feels good about that. '*Batman* was the toughest job I've ever had to do,' he said. 'Actually, that isn't saying much because I had to work in a restaurant once, which was far harder!

'It was tough from the point of having no time to regroup after the script revisions,' he continued. 'I never had time to think about them. I always felt like I was catching up. I worked six days a week and exhausted myself because I feared I wasn't doing a good job. I was afraid my mental condition wasn't right for me to be making this movie, and even now I have amnesia about certain times during the shooting. But it's the movie I wanted to make and it's true to the spirit of why I wanted to do it in the first place. It's something new and original, not a copy of anything that's gone before. It has a spirit of its own that has transferred to the screen. And isn't that what you want when you go to the movies?'

BATMAN

review by Kim Newman

Gotham City. Crime czar Carl Grissom learns that his girlfriend Alicia has been seeing his associate Jack Napier, and sets Jack up to be killed during a raid on the Axis chemical works. Jack escapes Grissom's gunmen, but Batman, a masked, black-cloaked vigilante who has been terrorising petty crooks, arrives on the scene and Jack, wounded by a ricochet, falls into a vat of chemicals. Investigative reporters Vicki Vale and Alexander Knox are covering the Batman story, and happen to meet reclusive millionaire Bruce Wayne, with whom Vicki has a one-night stand. Jack emerges from the chemicals as a white-faced, green-haired, eternally grinning freak, the Joker, and murders Grissom before taking over Gotham City's underworld. Vicki is hurt because Bruce has been avoiding her, and happens to see the millionaire leaving a floral tribute in a back alley. The Joker sees Vicki's picture and decides to pay court to her, inviting her in Bruce's name to the Flugelheim Museum where he is defacing works of art. When Bruce's butler Alfred informs him that Vicki has left a message referring to their non-existent date, Batman appears at the museum and rescues her. The Joker contaminates a run of cosmetics products and terrorises the city. Knox discovers that Bruce Wayne's parents were murdered in front of him when he was a child in the alley where he laid the flowers, and Bruce realises that the hoodlum who set him on course to become the Batman was the young Jack Napier. The Joker issues a challenge to Batman to face him in a duel, and stages a parade during which he passes out millions of dollars and plans to dose the

The caped crusader protects his alter ego Bruce Wayne's lover, reporter Vicki Vale (Kim Basinger) – one of the characters taken from the comic book's long history.

crowds with lethal gas from giant balloons. Batman turns up in a Batwing aircraft and cuts the balloons free, then crashes on the steps of the Gotham City cathedral. The Joker takes Vicki, who has guessed that Bruce is Batman, to the top of the cathedral, where he is finally tackled by Batman. The Joker falls to his death and Batman presents the city with a signalling device which Commissioner Gordon can use to summon him if he is ever needed again.

Tim Burton signals his new approach to the world of Batman with his first vision of Gotham City, a tainted Metropolis of neon and steam, resembling a forties vision of a hellish future and populated by criminals and their unwary victims. A family from out of town – bumbling parents and wide-eyed son – fall prey to a pair of psychotic muggers and a black batshape detaches itself from the shadows to descend on the villains, wreaking a rough justice and telling the criminals to spread the word about the Batman. Like Alan Moore in *The Killing Joke*, Burton and screenwriters Sam Hamm and Warren Skaaren see Batman and the Joker as dramatic antitheses, and the film deals with their intertwined origins and fates to an even greater extent than any of the comic-strip stories that have played variations on their oft-told tales. Here, not only is the Joker created partially due to Batman's intervention in the Axis Chemicals raid (as in the comic story 'The Man Behind the Red Hood'), but the young Jack Napier is the mugger who attacked the Wayne family –

echoing the innocents of the first sequence – and triggered off the neuroses that led young Bruce to become the fearsome Batman (in the comics, the killer was another character entirely, Joe Chill).

The major switch in this version is that the monstrousness of Batman is emphasised to an even greater degree than in the darkest of the comic stories (Frank Miller's *The Dark Knight Returns*). The first reports of his activities suggest that he is a vampire who drains the blood of his victims, and the redesigned costume – all black rather than shades of blue and grey – is rather more reminiscent of Dracula or the Phantom of the Opera than of Batman's red-white-and-blue-hued superheroic competitors, Superman and Captain America. For most of the film, the authorities of Gotham City are as keen to track down the vigilante as the Joker, and the Laural and Hardy-style one-upmanship that characterises the relationship of hero and villain is nicely crystallised in the moment, at once funny and genuinely chilling, in which the Joker, annoyed by the headline 'WINGED FREAK TERRORISES CITY,' chortles, 'Terrorises? Wait until they get a load of me.' There is some confusion towards the end, in the moment of mutual revelation when Batman and the Joker admit that each has made a monster of the other, when the Joker seems suddenly and with no narrative explanation to be aware of Batrnan's secret identity ('I was just a kid when I knocked off your parents'). But this pays off in the powerful confrontation between the two characters in the belltower ('I have a bat in my belfry') of godless Gotham City's apparently abandoned cathedral.

During the production of the film, a great deal of hostility was generated in the fan press by the selection of a director and star known best for their comedic work, on the assumption that a Burton-Keaton *Batman* would echo the camp approach of the influential but much despised television series with Adam West. In the event, the film has found a great deal of humour in the subject but also diluted the laughter with a Gothic horror tone in keeping with Denny O'Neil's ghost-haunted approach to the character in the seventies – to such an extent, however, that it would never get past the Comics Code Authority. Jack Nicholson's Joker differs from the previous representations of the character by remaining Jack (Napier or Nicholson) under the make-up rather than, as in the original, being a nonentity (unlike the Riddler, the Penguin and the Catwoman, the Joker has, until now, had no 'real' name). Through Nicholson, Burton works cruel humour very much in the vein of *Beetlejuice* or his under-appreciated short *Vincent*, as a joy-buzzer is used to reduce a gangland figure to a smoking skeleton while the Joker snaps off a series of one-liners, or a museum full of classical pieces is desecrated ('I am the world's first fully functional homicidal artist').

In the climax, when the villain's schemes are foiled, he gratuitously shoots dead his best friend and asks his goons to kill everyone in sight: 'Because I want a minute to myself.' Beside this star turn, the figure of the hero becomes necessarily shadowy – as if areas were deliberately being left in the dark for future instalments – but Keaton holds his own remarkably well as the detached, emotionally bruised Bruce Wayne and as the Schwarzenegger-armoured dark knight. When Vicki Vale asks which of the guests at a party in Wayne Manor is Bruce Wayne, 'the most useless man in the world', Wayne honestly and disturbingly replies, 'I don't know,' a meeting-cute device that establishes how fragile the multi-millionaire's identities are. Later, Keaton manages to bridge his usual bumbling image – unable to tell Vicki the truth during a tense confrontation, he mumbles 'I'm Batman' over and over behind her back as she answers the door – and the obsessional quality necessary for the Caped Crusader.

Batman is very sparingly used in the film, always located in *noir*-ish shadows and vast rooftop sets, which means that the film isn't as overbalanced in his favour as such recent superheroic endeavours as *Superman* or *Raiders of the Lost Ark*. The little compromises necessary in any film with a budget in the $50 million region don't do any serious harm. Prince's songs, which interrupt an outstandingly old-fashioned score by Danny Elfman, could have been as disastrous as Queen's contribution to *Flash Gordon*, but only get gratuitously in the way during two scenes in which the Joker insists on a musical accompaniment to his crime sprees. And the casting of Kim Basinger – a last minute replacement for Sean Young – never quite comes off because, although she is established as an independent photojournalist and war correspondent in the mould of Margot Kidder's Lois Lane, the film mainly has her get into danger and be rescued.

Other well-remembered aspects of the Batman story – faithful Alfred the butler, irascible Commissioner Gordon, the sleek black Batmobile and Batplane, the cavernous Batcave, the crusading status of DA Harvey Dent (who, when scarred by a vindictive convict, becomes Batman's number two foe, Two-Face) – are unobtrusively but effectively worked in. The giant balloons and Flugelheim Museum even capture the wise-ass New York humour of Bob Kane's original strips, in which Gotham City was full of giant but fully functional typewriters or umbrellas, but such mainly unwelcome and 'silly' additions as Batwoman, Batgirl (two of them), Bat-mite (an extra-dimensional imp), Ace the Bat-Hound and, worst of all, Robin the Boy Wonder, have thankfully been left back in the Batcave.

Tim Burton and Vincent Price

interview by Graham Fuller

PART TWO

Where did the idea for* Edward Scissorhands *come from?
Burton: Just a very pure . . . I've always had a love of fairy tales, like 'Little Red Riding Hood' or 'Hansel and Gretel', and the idea of them was wonderful, but the psychological connection wasn't there for me. I had this conversation with somebody that made a lot of sense to me. They said, 'Imagine how "Little Red Riding Hood" was received in the world in which it was written – it probably made complete sense.' So what I love about fairy tales is something very simple and emotional in them which is shown on a much broader symbolic scale.

How do you make that felt in your film?
Burton: It's the inability to communicate, the inability to touch, being at odds with yourself. How you are perceived as opposed to what you are. What appealed to me was the idea of trying to tell a fairy tale in the classic sense but making it feel like an examination of those themes.
Price: One of the things I am dying to know if people will get – because it all happens very quickly – is when Edward is created. He comes out of a cookie cutter. My character, the inventor, picks up a heart-shaped cookie and looks at it and then looks at the machine, and he thinks, if I could put that heart into him . . .
Burton: And there's a lot of that very dreamy stuff – all very, very simple, all very, very psychological – but it doesn't hit you over the head. It's just taking things that are not literal but more of a feeling, and making a visual thing out of it and seeing if anybody can relate to it.
Price: I think it's very lucky that we have Johnny Depp. In all my scenes with him, he was so *into* it, and yet he had this smile on his face because he knew who this boy with the extraordinary hands was.
Burton: Well, he's got a purity. When you look at him, he is one of those people – and there are not many of them – who make you believe in past lives all of a sudden. It sounds kind of New Age, but you look at him and you think his soul has been around throughout the centuries. There's a lot of himself in this movie, because he is somebody who is at odds with himself and not at all how he's perceived to be in the entertainment industry. He has a very strong, tormented, passionate internal life that is very much at odds with the way he looks.

Edward Scissorhands might come across to some people as the opposite of Freddy Krueger. His hands are equally dangerous, but he couldn't be sweeter or sadder.
Burton: I never considered that at all, but when some people mentioned it to me, I thought, 'Well, that's perfect, actually, because I don't mind if anybody brings any preconceptions to the film about that look. That's fine with me.' Everybody's felt that they've wanted something in life and not been able to get it. Everybody has a couple of sides to their personality. And in a very quick, visual way, he encapsulates all that.

Sweet monster: Johnny Depp, in the title role of
Edward Scissorhands, *looks as if he has escaped*
from a German expressionist horror movie.

Vincent Price as Edward's creator. Price died on 25 October, 1993, one week after his friend Tim Burton presented him with a videotape of The Nightmare Before Christmas.

Does the film have things to say about the world that Edward comes into?

Burton: I think so. Because a lot of it is based on memories, not literal translations of growing up in a certain place. And it's a very fascinating place, suburbia. It was very important to me. It is a funny place, very strange and bizarre, but not totally negative. So in the film I hope it's presented in a way that is extreme and kind of crazy, but not judgmental and laughing at people. This is the movie that I feel closest to, and I just wanted to put images out there; hopefully people can make up their own minds about it. I mean, it's nice to do a movie again, finally, that seems to open to a little bit of interpretation.

The other image that Edward reminds me of is that famous German children's book, Der Struwwelpeter, which has all these cautionary fables for unruly children. There's this boy with a long mane of hair and long, long fingernails which he refuses to cut. Were you familiar with that?

Burton: Somebody actually gave me the book after the fact, and it's . . . My wife is German, and, you know, Germans . . . Their fairy tales are the most *horrific* . . .

Price: One hopes nobody has ever read one to a child!

Burton: Talk about nightmares.

Price: Their art is that way, too.

Burton: It was the strength and simplicity that I really loved about the expressionists' work. That and the fairy-tale element.

I wondered if that German sense of dread, the beauty in terror and the grotesque which influenced Hollywood directors such as James Whale and Tod Browning had also inspired you.

Burton: Well, there's something about it. I'm influenced by it and I think there are a lot of people who are, but I think it's important not to copy it, and I try not to do that. I can tell when people copy it, and it just doesn't have any feeling, and I hate that. Hopefully this film is more gothic or expressionistic in the feeling of it.

Price: 'Gothic' is just a word recalling a multitude of sins!

Burton: Yeah, it's kind of *Entertainment Tonight* shorthand.

Price: But I have always thought that *Frankenstein* was really one of the great, puritanical gothic novels. It's this great moral tale: 'Don't fool around with God's work.' This film, too, has that. This creature, Edward Scissorhands, has been created by the old man out of love. And love can be frustrating when it's not complete.

Burton: There's a wonderful kind of sadness to him. It's not *bad* sadness, it's just what, so far, life seems to be composed of. When people think of sadness, they usually think that it's bad, but it's not. Sadness is actually part of life, and something that keeps you going. You just don't want to fall into it too completely.

TIM CUTS UP

by Frank Rose

You expect to find bugs on a Tim Burton set, but this is ridiculous. We're in central Florida, in a freshly built tract house just off the interstate; the temperature is 98 degrees, the humidity is 110 percent, and bugs are everywhere. The house itself is so overrun that flyswatters and Raid are issued at the door. Outside there's a blizzard of lovebugs – ugly little creatures that flit about in tandem, joined at the groin (or whatever they call it in bug anatomy) and heading in different directions. The cast and crew are full of lovebug lore: how they were bred to eat other bugs but don't, how birds spit them out because they taste bad, how they do nothing but multiply. Another case of science run amok.

Denise Di Novi, Burton's co-producer, is sitting on a sofa swatting flies. 'Do you know what's the number-one reason people leave Florida?' she inquires matter-of-factly. 'Bugs.'

But there's no exit from the set of *Edward Scissorhands*, Burton's fourth feature film. Burton, who at 32 is considered Hollywood's hottest young director, is making a movie about a Frankenstein monster in the suburbs – a winsome young innocent with scissors for hands. Johnny Depp, the teen heartthrob who plays Edward, is standing uncomplainingly in the living room, barely recognisable under several layers of Salvation Army clothing, a jet black fright wig, and white makeup with scars. Plastic tubes from the cool suit he's wearing protrude from the back of his vest, dripping green coolant onto the floor. His hands, bristling with ten-inch shears, look like Swiss army knives from hell. Somewhere amid the weaponry a thoughtful designer has included a roach clip, with which he's now dragging on a cigarette.

The only person more disheveled than Depp is Burton. A tall, thin figure dressed entirely in black (except for the white skull and crossbones on his white socks), with chipmunk cheeks and a bouffant of long black hair that seems to have been created by nesting birds, Burton looks somewhat two-dimensional, like an animated caricature. Highly animated: his hands are in constant motion, gesturing, grabbing his hair, covering his face, at one point digging into his flesh as if to rip it from his skull. Huddled in this small, cluttered room, he and Depp look like brother mutants.

This is no accident. Having brought other people's fantasies to life in *Batman*, *Beetlejuice*, and *Pee-wee's Big Adventure* – his first three feature films, each cartoonish and bizarre and wildly popular – Burton has now put Depp into his own story, a Christmas fable about a misfit who's unable to touch. Edward Scissorhands was created in a typical Gothic mansion by a well-meaning inventor – played by Vincent Price – who died of a heart attack as he was about to finish the job. Tim Burton created himself in a typical suburban home by gluing himself to the TV set to watch old Vincent Price movies. Presumably, however, Edward will have a universality that transcends Burton's particulars. 'I think we're all Edward Scissorhands,' says Dianne Wiest, who plays Peg Boggs, the Avon Lady who finds him. 'Tim no more than the rest of us.'

To enhance this perception, Twentieth Century Fox spent a great deal of effort trying to interest Tom Cruise in the role. After several meetings, Cruise demurred, reportedly out of of concern over the character's lack of masculinity. 'He was never my image of the character,' Burton admits now. Other actors were considered: William Hurt, Tom Hanks, Robert Downey, Jr. Depp, best known as the teen narc on Fox's former hit TV show *21 Jump Street*, was not an obvious choice, yet now he seems perfect for the role. Not coincidentally, masculinity is all but irrelevant to his portrayal.

'He plays it like a little boy,' says Winona Ryder, Depp's fiancee and co-star, 'which is so heartbreaking. You don't feel sorry for him – he just plays it with the honesty of someone who doesn't know how to put on a face. You know how little kids can blurt out the truth? That's what he does.'

In the scene being shot today, Edward, having been taken in by the Avon Lady and her nice suburban family, has just been arrested for breaking into a neighbour's house. But Edward isn't bad, just misunderstood: the break-in was staged by the Avon Lady's daughter Kim and her jock boyfriend to get him in trouble. Now Edward and Kim, played by Ryder, are meeting for the first time after his release. The scene is muted, interior: Kim is having second thoughts, and Edward is too devoted to her to be angry. (Screenwriter Caroline Thompson based Edward partly on her dog.) Burton eyes the monitor intently, his fingers at his lips. Between takes, as a dozen hands grab for the thermostat to turn the air-conditioning back on, Depp sheds his shears so he and Ryder can touch fingertips as they gaze soulfully into each other's eyes.

Lovebugs, indeed.

With three pictures and close to $370 million in ticket sales to his credit, Tim Burton has known nothing but success. Even before *Batman*, a $50 million production that grossed five times that amount in the United States alone, he was being compared with George Lucas and Steven Spielberg. What won him that attention was *Beetlejuice*, the surprise hit of 1988: a wildly inventive, $13 million bugfest that grossed $73 million and was hailed as 'a comedy classic' by Pauline Kael. But even his first feature film, the low-budget *Pee-wee's Big Adventure*, took in more than $40 million at the box office.

Yet there's nothing conventional or predictably commercial about any of Burton's movies. He's a startlingly original director with a thrilling visual sense, outlandish humour, and a definite fondness for the bizarre. Witness *Beetlejuice*, which features a bug-munching sleazeball whose head starts spinning like a top for no apparent reason, after which he remarks, 'Don'tcha hate it when that happens?'

If people didn't line up to see this stuff by the tens of millions, Burton would be earning comparisons with such cult directors as John Waters and David Lynch instead of Lucas and Spielberg. Yet against all expectations, he's struck a nerve in the mass audience – an apparent longing for wacky unpredictability, for moody surrealism and explosive humour, for a taste of the light fantastic. The reason, says Thompson, is simple: 'David's obsessions are the obsessions of a nineteen-year-old, and Tim's are the obsessions of a twelve-year-old. And this is much more a twelve-year-old's culture.'

So you can leave the sex to Lynch; Burton is obsessed with bugs. 'I love 'em,' he admits, his voice dropping to a near-whisper as it takes on a strangely excited tone. 'I dunno – bugs, man! They're all around us. I dunno! Everyday life! Bugs! I dunno! Maybe it's growing-up with those bug movies of the seventies. Remember *Frogs*? It's the ecology – we're going to start seeing more of it, I guarantee you. A horrible new trend, just like the seventies. The nature-strikes-back movies. *Aaarrrrggghhh!* Even as we speak, they're hatching away.'

And so we find ourselves here, in a powder blue house in Land o' Lakes, Florida, that's absolutely crawling with them. Somewhat perversely, Burton says this movie won't have any. Well, maybe a couple of lovebugs for old times' sake, but that isn't the point.

Last winter, when *Scissorhands* was in pre-production, Burton showed his cast members a book called *Suburbia*, a slim volume of black-and-white photographs taken twenty years ago in California's Livermore Valley. Documented with equal parts bafflement and affection, the people in *Suburbia* are living out the American Dream as they know it. 'I enjoy giving a Tupperware party in my home,' one woman says in a caption. 'I find a sense of freedom in the suburbs,' says a man sitting with his wife in front of a painting of paper-doll clothes with tabs attached. 'You assume the mask of suburbia for outward appearances, and yet no one knows what you really do.'

'If you're culturally devoid of something – of artistry, of interesting architecture,' Burton says of his suburban upbringing, 'you manufacture those things for yourself.'

The *Scissorhands* neighbourhood – a flat, treeless area of modest stucco homes – does not look like a normal suburb. All the houses have been painted in vibrant pastel colours that accentuate their extreme plainness. Adorning the minuscule front lawns are giant wire-and-plastic 'topiaries' – a ballerina, a penguin, a dinosaur, all Edward's handiwork. At the end of the street, stone gateposts adorned with griffins and shrouded by dead branches announce the approach to the looming grey towers of Edward's mansion. Yet this location, which at first looks so bizarre that a sign at the entrance to the subdivision warns prospective home buyers that the area doesn't normally look like this, turns out to be a startlingly exact realisation of the images in *Suburbia*: generic, featureless facades masking interiors that are masterpieces of shopping-mall baroque, tricked out as they are with shag carpets, flocked wallpaper, black velvet tapestries, sunburst clocks, Italian floral wall plaques, crushed-velvet sofas, Early American TV sets, and swag lamps over the dinette set. The women wear hair curlers or bouffants; the men have beer bellies and sideburns.

A similar-looking crowd of extras has assembled across from Kim's house for a scene in which Edward is once again misunderstood by the suburban drones. Against the night sky, the intense colours of the neighborhood houses, which get washed out by the harsh Florida sun, take on a spectacularly lurid quality. It's supposed to be Christmastime, and the 'neighbours' milling about in the street are all in their holiday finery – red pantsuits with green fringe, that kind of thing. 'We wanted a feeling of timeless polyester,' explains costume designer Colleen Atwood. Wiest is radiant in a crimson dress, Alan Arkin, who plays her husband, Bill, looks a little vague in his light blue polyester slacks and burgundy sport coat, though his burgundy 'Winter Wonderland' tie adds a distinctive note. 'Oh, honey!' Wiest cries in mock delight. 'I picked that tie out special for you!'

Bill Boggs is the quintessential American dad, a man who wears an I.D. tag on his shirt but remains a mystery to those around him. 'He's into lawnmowers,' Arkin explains laconically. 'He likes thinking he's a dad. That's about it.' Bill and Peg? 'They get along beautifully. Absolutely beautifully.' But do they commnunicate? 'No. It''s like everybody's pretending to have relationships. People are remembering how people are supposed to act. They're wondering how Robert Young would do it on television.'

Edward sees the Boggses through much starrier eyes. '''They're the perfect mom and dad, the perfect family,' says Depp. 'They're what Edward has dreamed of all his life. Family. To be accepted. To be loved.' And Kim? 'I'm playing a girl who's like a prom queen,' says Ryder. 'She's a cheerleader; she has a very perfect life, except there's something in her that's sort of like Edward. In a way, she's an outsider even though she's such an insider. That's the reason they fall in love, and that's also the reason she's so frightened of him in the beginning.'

A crowd has gathered, as it has every night since filming began: local residents settling into lawn chairs with cans of beer and Pepsi to watch the show. Curiously, as the cast wanders around waiting for the crew to finish setting up, it becomes increasingly difficult to tell the neighbours in the movie from the neighbours in real life. The only giveaway is the movie neighbours' hair, which Edward, being creative with the scissors, has transformed from mere bouffants and pompadours into the supreme evocation of the beautician's art. 'Hair acting, that's what I call it,' says an actress named Caroline Aaron, unique in an asymmetrical 'do with green pipe cleaners sticking out one side. 'Everybody keeps asking if this is my real hair. I wonder what I look like during the day.'

In tonight's scene, Edward has just pushed Kim's frightened brother (played by twelve-year-old Robert Oliveri) out of the path of a speeding van and into the gutter as a crowd of neighbours is returning from a Christmas party. The neighbours, not having seen the van, assume that Edward has simply gone berserk. As Edward – played this time by Depp's stunt double – is getting his head slammed into the sidewalk by Kim's drunken boyfriend, who turns out to have been in the van, Kim looks on horrified. The triangle is complete.

After the initial takes, which are shot from above, a cushion is placed on the ground and Depp steps in for a carefully angled close-up. At this point, the script calls for the leather-jacketed boyfriend – played by Anthony Michael Hall – to be slashed as Edward tries to defend himself. But the shears are as hard for Depp to control as they're supposed to be for Edward. With the cameras rolling, one of his blades punctures Hall's jacket and sinks into his forearm. Hall, momentarily shaken, looks confused as real blood mixes with fake blood on the ground below him. But as Depp scrambles to apologise, he brushes the incident off: 'It's cool, man.'

What possessed Burton to create a hero with scissors for hands? 'It's funny, I dunno,' he says during a lull in the shooting. 'When I latch on to an idea is when it remains with me for a long time, not when I say, "Oh, it's a metaphor for this or that." But with scissors, there's something in the theme of somebody not being able to touch that I love. I just wanted a character that – visually, there he is, internally, externally. It's a visual representation of what's inside. I've always felt, just for me, for some reason, it encompassed a lot about how I feel about things. I don't know if that makes sense. But there's something about it that rings very true for me.'

Though he's eloquent with film – good at specifying what he wants, sparing and precise in the way he shoots – Burton is notoriously inarticulate with words. He usually gets his point across with his hands; Kathy Baker cites as her favorite piece of direction the time he said, 'This script, uh, uh, these words, uh, um, you know, like –' and she realised he wanted her to change her lines.

But now, three months later, relaxing in a Hudson Valley farmhouse before going into post-production in Los Angeles, Burton has regained his command of the language. Why scissors? 'I thought it was a fairly universal feeling,' he says, lounging on an old sofa in blue jeans and an

ALIEN SEX FIEND T-shirt. 'There was a long period of time when I just hadn't been able to connect with anybody or have a relationship. Everybody goes through periods like that – the feeling that you can't connect, you can't touch.'

This is no ordinary farmhouse we're in; though it belongs to a friend of Burton's, it looks like a set for one of his films. The living room is furnished in a bizarre mix of fifties modern and country cast-off, much of it painted in flame tones. Both sofas are covered with hand-stitched quilts in alarming shades of red, yellow, and orange. Out the window a dead tree sits in the middle of an overgrown apple orchard next to a tumbledown shed. In the kitchen is Burton's wife, a statuesque German painter named Lena Gieseke, whom he met while *Batman* was in production in London. Whatever his difficulty connecting in the past, that phase of his life seems to be over.

Still, it's no accident that the heavy in *Scissorhands* is a blond jock. Crispin Glover read for the part, but he and Burton had too much in common; Anthony Michael Hall was perfect. 'It's just like guys you knew in high school,' Burton says. 'I was always horrified by guys like this because – *they always had girlfriends!* I think what it is is that these guys, because they look like football captains, the image of American dream youth kind of thing, and yet they're scary and they're violent – I think girls respond to the image and then get bullied and frightened by them on a subconscious level.'

As the quintessential high school outcast, pale and withdrawn and with a well-developed taste for the macabre, Burton probably frightened them on a more conscious level. Although his dad worked for the Burbank Parks and Recreation Department (organising athletic leagues, among other things), one of Tim's favorite outdoor activities was to sit in his yard, located at the end of a Burbank Airport runway, and time the exhaust floating down as planes took off. But what he most liked to do was sit in front of the TV, lost in the electronic gloom of such Vincent Price chestnuts as *House of Wax* and *The Fly* and *The Masque of the Red Death*.

'When you go through your teenage years, which I feel like I'm still in to some degree, you have a very heavy sense of drama,' he says. 'I always had a very dramatic sense of being alone. That's why I loved Vincent Price movies and I loved the idea of Edgar Allan Poe, the theme of aloneness. And it always ended with this cathartic something or other – the house being destroyed. I always loved that because it was like, *"Yes. I understand."* And when you grow up watching certain horror films, like *King Kong*, the guys were such stiffs and the monsters had such emotion that you used to sit there as a kid going, "What the hell are they doing?"'

Burton seems to have had this reaction a lot: when he wasn't bonding with the creature some guy was trying to kill on late-night TV, he was playing amateur anthropologist in his neighborhood. Though Warner Bros., Columbia Pictures, Walt Disney, and NBC all had their studios there, Burbank was a working-class town, more like a small city in the Midwest than an outpost of Hollywood. Burton, whose mom runs a gift shop in which every item has a cat motif, might as well have dropped in from outer space.

'I used to look at my house and say, "Why is this hanging on the wall?"' he says. '"This weird blob of wood that's been shellacked and has a clock on it it?" You ask people, and it's not like other cultures, where they know why it's there. You'll ask people, and they won't remember.'

'It's funny. When you're a kid, you think everything is strange, and you think *because* you're a kid, everything is strange. Then when you get older, you realise it *is* strange. It's not just that you're a new being in the world and everything is new; there were some aspects of it that were just incredibly, you know, strange.'

Misfit Edward is the most autobiographical character in Tim Burton's films. Burton associates his scissorhands with 'the feeling that you can't connect, you can't touch'.

Edward with high school queen Kim, his unrequited love. Kim was played by Winona Ryder, Johnny Depp's fiancee at the time, poles apart from her goth look in Beetlejuice.

'A lot of this movie is how I grew up and how a lot of people grew up. I remember thinking, the houses are close together, but there's a weird feeling of "What's going on next door?" I remember there was no real communication, but if there was ever a tragedy, if there was a car accident out front, people would come out of their houses, and it would be like a block party. It's not something I can relate to, really – this blood lust. It's like a way to make yourself feel alive. It's a very strange – a funny – I just find it fascinating.'

And yet Burton is not really as alienated from ordinary existence as he might have you think. 'His work has a real affection for neighbourhood life,' Thompson points out. 'You'd never see it as condescension. And although he perpetuates this perception of himself as having been damaged, from my perspective it's just the opposite. I think he's escaped some fundamental damage that shuts most other people down.'

Despite his unusual preoccupations, Burton won a scholarship to CalArts, the interdisciplinary art school Walt Disney founded in Valencia, a mushrooming suburb on the edge of the desert. There he studied animation. Soon after, he won a job as an apprentice animator at Disney, only to discover that cartooning wasn't what he'd imagined it to be.

Disney had long since passed its peak, and Burton's ideas were a little *outre* for the caretaker regime there: birds and flowers were what they had in mind, not bugs and monsters. Still, he was able to make his own six-minute short, a wryly amusing little film about a seven-year-old boy who lives in a fantasy world of gothic horror. Titled *Vincent*, it was narrated by Vincent Price and drawn in black and white in a highly idiosyncratic style that recalled the German expressionism of *Metropolis*. Price was thrilled: 'How famous can you be that Disney does a short based on your life?' he asks. Especially one written in verse.

After *Vincent*, which was released in 1982 and won several film festival awards, Burton turned to live-action shorts. He made *Hansel and Gretel* with an all-Asian cast and then *Frankenweenie*, a 30-minute film that goes way beyond *Lassie* in the boy-loves-dog department. Unfortunately, the ratings board found such scenes as the reanimation of the dead animal in an attic laboratory too disturbing for young children, and, because it was given a PG rating, Disney refused to release it. But while it languished in the vault, word spread.

It wasn't long before Stephen King started showing *Vincent* to friends and telling them this kid was going to be big. When Bonni Lee, a production executive at Warner Bros., screened *Frankenweenie* for her boss, the wheels started to turn. Warners was looking for a director to work with Paul Reubens, a.k.a. Pee-wee Herman, and, when Reubens saw *Frankenweenie*, he knew instantly he'd found his man. Burton signed a two-year exclusive contract and went to work, crafting a movie that was at once scary, sweet, wacky, and perverse.

Then Warners sent him a script by Michael McDowell, a gothic novelist who'd decided to write 'a feel-good movie about death'. The Geffen Company, which has a distribution deal with Warners, had optioned it and wanted Burton to direct. 'My first response was, I can't believe David Geffen would want me to do this,' Burton recalls. 'It was totally opposite from everything else I'd read. It had no structure, no plot, randomly weird ideas – it just had a weird quality to it that I loved. So we made the movie.'

To say that Warner Bros. didn't realise it had a hit in the works would be an understatement. *Beetlejuice* was a marketing executive's nightmare, a movie that defied categorisation, market research, and good taste all at the same time. The title, for instance: 'It means the armpit of the giant,' says McDowell – of the constellation Orion, that is, not that Beetlejuice the character has anything to do with Betelgeuse the star anyway. But in the interest of appealing to moviegoers who might not share Burton's love of the creepy-crawly, Warner executives wanted to change the title to *House Ghosts*.

'I'll never forget this meeting,' says Burton, downshifting smoothly into marketspeak: '"See, *Beetlejuice* doesn't test, but *House Ghosts* here is going through the roof." I remember going, "*House Ghosts?*" Then I said, as a joke, "Why don't we call it *Scared Sheetless?*" And they considered it, until I threatened to jump out a window. But the thing that *Beetlejuice* did for me was it made me feel really great about audiences. I felt great that people could get into seeing something that random. Anything that fucks up the system and doesn't prove itself part of their plan, I think is positive.'

While *Beetlejuice* was being made, before *Batman* was even begun, *Edward Scissorhands* was in development at Fox. Warner Bros. had passed on it; Fox production chief Scott Rudin, a Burton fan, agreed to finance a screenplay while giving the writer-director complete creative control. Burton saw it at the time as a low-budget picture, maybe $8 million or $9 million.

When he finished *Batman*, however, Burton was a star and Fox had a new management team that was excited about his script. 'Like a lot of things – *Pinocchio, E.T.* – it's both very new and very familiar,' says Fox chairman Joe Roth. 'It takes something that's very odd and lets it show what's right about us and what's wrong about us.'

Success has left Burton curiously unspoiled – soft-spoken, businesslike, willing to listen yet quietly self-assured. He's very much in demand: Warner Bros. has *Batman 2* and reportedly *3* and *Beetlejuice 2* in development, hoping for his nod; both Warner's and Disney have animated feature films in development for him; his *Beetlejuice* cartoon is ABC's top-rated animated morning TV show; and CBS is planning to air *Family Dog*, the prime-time cartoon he's doing with Spielberg, as a mid-season replacement. However, he still hasn't been welcomed into the Hollywood establishment: *Beetlejuice* received only one Oscar nomination (for makeup, which it won), and *Batman*'s only honour was for art direction. And in an odd way, he seems to accept the snub that implies.

'I don't really consider myself a director,' he admits in a quiet moment, sitting by the window that looks out on the dead tree. 'When I read about these old directors who went from one kind of movie to another and could do – I really can't, so everything I've ever done, I have to really love it and respond to it. Which I have, but this is the first project that's a bit deeper for me. And it really shocked me, it really did a lot of strange things to me. It was a harder movie to make, and I was in a more volatile mood and more interiorised and stranger.' And in a small voice, he adds, 'I hope it turns out.'

EDWARD SCISSORHANDS

reviewed by Steve Biodrowski

Director Tim Burton survived the turbulence of teenaged adolescence by seeking solace not in rock-and-roll music but in the horror films of Vincent Price. Burton has continued to explore that fascination in his movies, all produced at Warner Bros., where he is currently preparing *Batman II*. Burton's films have been remarkably consistent for featuring weird male characters wearing makeup: Pee-wee Herman, in *Pee-wee's Big Adventure* (1985), Betelgeuse, in *Beetlejuice* (1987), and the Joker, in *Batman* (1989), which demonstrated the director's evident lack of interest in the title character. Continuing this trend is Burton's latest and most personal effort, *Edward Scissorhands*. This time, however, Burton's emphasis is not on humor, but pathos.

Produced by Burton's partner Denise Di Novi for $20 million at Fox after Warners passed on the project, *Edward Scissorhands* is the first feature which Burton has initiated himself and guided through development. The screenplay is by Caroline Thompson, based on Burton's original idea.

Special makeup and effects, including hands for the titular freak, were provided by Oscar-winner Stan Winston. The remainder of the crew includes production designer Bo Welch and many of Burton's collaborators from *Beetlejuice*, such as art director Tom Duffield, set designer Rick Heinrichs, and composer Danny Elfman.

Dianne Wiest plays Peg Boggs, an Avon lady so desperate to make a sale that she ventures to an abandoned mansion, where she finds Edward, living in isolation. Winona Ryder, the morbid young girl in *Beetlejuice*, plays a variation on that role as Peg's daughter Kim, who goes from loathing to loving Edward when her mother takes pity and brings him home.

Other cast members include Alan Arkin and Anthony Michael Hall as Kim's father and her boyfriend, and veteran genre actor Vincent Price, seen briefly in flashback as Edward's inventor, who dies of a heart attack before completing his creation, leaving him with skeletal, scissor-like hands.

Edward himself is portrayed by Ryder's real-life fiance, Johnny Depp, who, having previously abandoned the macho image of his role on *21 Jump Street* to star in John Waters' *Cry Baby*, was unfazed by the character's 'lack of virility', which (according to the *L.A. Times*) led Tom Cruise to turn down the role.

Though Fox is wont to compare their film to Steven Spielberg's *E. T.*, *Edward Scissorhands* is much closer to David Lynch's *The Elephant Man*. Set in a small section of suburbia, the story chronicles Edward's attempts as a social misfit to find some niche for himself in society. Having lived alone nearly all his life, he has no grasp of society's norms of behaviour, and his physical deformity lends an element of potential danger to even such simple actions as gesturing during a conversation.

Like Lynch's Merrick, who expressed himself by building a model of a church steeple, Edward shows considerable manual dexterity despite his deformity: using his hands as shears, he trims hedges into a menagerie of exotic animals, including a tyrannosaurus, then graduates to grooming dogs, and finally to giving elaborate haircuts.

It's hard not to see Edward as Burton's metaphor for the creative artist whose work is prized even while the man himself is despised. Burton, with his wild black hair, bears some physical resemblance to his character, and at least part of the critical admiration for his work stems from a perception of him as a strange outsider who does not quite fit into the usual Hollywood mould. Burton resists such pat autobiographical readings, hoping his film will be open to a wider interpretation.

In the time-honoured tradition of the torch-wielding villagers in the fondly remembered Universal horror films of Burton's youth, the community turns against Edward and hunts him down as if he were Frankenstein's Monster, instead of the rather benign creature Kim comes to know. Thompson's script strives for, and mostly achieves, a sense of poignant sadness by not opting for an easy happy ending. The most Edward can hope for is to escape with his life; he will never fit in, never consummate his love for Kim. For Burton, creativity is a double-edged sword, on the one hand lifting him above the commonplace, on the other, separating him from any chance of a normal life. Clearly, this time Burton, a director noted for his visual style but often faulted for his story structures, is trying to engage not only our eyes but our hearts and minds as well.

THREE GO MAD IN GOTHAM

by Jeffrey Resner

Michael Keaton is sitting in his trailer on a backlot of Warner Brothers' vast Los Angeles studio complex, cracking lame jokes as his face is systematically smeared with greasepaint and he is slowly transformed into his alter-ego, the brooding hero of this summer's – or indeed *any* summer's – biggest hit, *Batman Returns*. The greasepaint finally entirely covering his mush, the short tufts of his curly hair are carefully tucked under a nylon headband by a make-up assistant who then begins to paint large black circles around his eyes. When it's all finished, nearly an hour later, Michael Keaton looks exactly like a raccoon in a hairnet.

Suddenly, the awful screech of a car's brakes shatters the quiet of the Californian evening. Keaton leaps from the chair and bolts out of the door, doing a classic double-take when he spots a large black machine chugging loudly in front of his motor-home.

'It's the Batmobile!' shrieks Keaton, his almost childlike excitement explained by the fact that this is not, in fact, the sleek rocketcar designed at vast expense for the new movie, but the original Gotham City cruiser from the old TV series starring the paunchy Adam West as the Dark Knight. Keaton, clearly awestruck by the presence of such a legendary vehicle, races over to it, gently caressing the familiar bubbled windshield, the ominous Bat-face on the hood, the long scalloped fins jutting out from the back.

'Drive me to the set,' Keaton orders his stunt double, David Lea, who had managed to track down the Batmobile, driving it on to the studio lot as a practical joke. Now Keaton wants in on the joke too, and together they roar towards the busy soundstage where stunned crew members, extras and technicians promptly drop what they're doing to simply stand and stare. Screeching to a halt, Keaton is just about to open the car's door when he suddenly has a better idea: standing up, he hops out of the open cockpit with one fluid, graceful swoop.

'If Adam West could do it,' he giggles, giving the audience one of his his trademark cocky smirks, 'so can I.'

Suddenly, seemingly from nowhere, comes director Tim Burton, the man responsible for proving Warner Bros.' massive investment in *Batman Returns* to be a sound financial gamble, and he is making it more than clear that it is now *his* turn, bounding towards Keaton like some great gangling teenager.

'Get out of here and let me go for a ride,' he barks, jumping into the passenger seat and holding on for dear life as Lea careers around the set, giving a toothsome grin and a jolly thumbs-aloft salute to passers-by. By now, everyone is singing the old TV theme as the car barrels down the street, makes a dramatic 360-degree spin, and charges back to the cheering crowd. Finally, Tim Burton calls a halt to the fun and games, suggesting everyone thinks seriously about getting back to work. The mirthsome interlude has taken less than half-an-hour, but even such a momentary delay can do nothing but add to *Batman Returns'* estimated $80 million budget.

Burton's inspiration for Danny DeVito's Penguin seems to have come from the monsters of golden-age horror movies.

Tim Burton — A Child's Garden of Nightmares

'Just to look at that old Batmobile,' muses one crew member with a long knowing chuckle, 'must have cost them $100,000 . . .'

'Tim Burton is all over the place!' bellows Bob Kane, the comic book visionary who created the neurotic superhero Batman back in 1939. Today, walking around his bright, airy condominium just below Sunset Boulevard filled with colourful oil renderings of the Caped Crusader, the Joker, the Penguin and Catwoman, the gaunt and softly spoken Kane is discussing his role as spiritual adviser on *Batman Returns*. Already more than happy with the movie depiction of his creation in the original *Batman*, Kane appears genuinely puzzled when asked about Tim Burton's manic yet highly stylised approach to moviemaking.

'Tim doesn't relate to you as a very seriously *concentrated* director,' he muses. 'He's running around doing things, he's got rips in his pants and his wallet is ready to fall out of his pocket. You wouldn't think he's on top of things. But he's right there, and he's got his finger on it.'

What Burton has his finger on at the present moment is, of course, the sequel to one of the most profitable and hyped movies of all time. When we last left the Caped Crusader three short years ago, he had just got the better of the Joker after a battle in the belfry, presented Gotham City with a cool new bat signal, and had Kim Basinger climb into the back seat of his limousine. Meanwhile, in the real world, *Batman* earned more than $406 million in worldwide ticket sales, $150 million on video and $750 million in merchandise, including bat-pyjamas and bat-vitamins. It was more than just a movie, it was an *industry*.

Although a sequel was an obvious move, neither Michael Keaton nor Tim Burton had been signed up in advance – indeed, after the release of the original, Burton publicly described a sequel as 'a most dumbfounded idea'. Both eventually caved in to Warner's wishes, however, after the studio bent over backwards to satisfy their requests, with Keaton declining to get involved until his salary was *seriously* increased, and Burton refusing to come aboard until he was happy with a script – not an easy task considering his mixed emotions about the original film.

'There's *parts* I liked, but it was a little boring at times,' says the 33-year-old Burton with typical candour. 'Oftentimes with sequels, they're like the same movie except everything gets jacked up a little. I didn't feel I could *do* that; I wanted to treat this like it was another *Batman* movie altogether.'

After a disappointing first draft by *Batman*'s screenwriter Sam Hamm that had the Penguin and Catwoman going after hidden treasure, the next scribbler brought in to attempt to please the tousle-haired *auteur* was Daniel Waters, screenwriter of 1990's cult black comedy *Heathers* and the similarly insane *Meet the Applegates*. Clearly more on the Burton wavelength than his predecessor, Waters came up with a social satire that had an evil mogul (Christopher Walken) backing a bid for the Mayor's office by the Penguin.

'I wanted to show that the true villains of our world don't necessarily wear costumes,' says Waters, although fans of the sixties TV show will perhaps also recall the episode called 'Hizzoner the Penguin, Dizzoner the Penguin' which similarly had the bird-brained criminal running for Gotham's highest office. Besides the political slant, Waters also contributed a more profound understanding of Catwoman, giving her character deep psycho-sexual overtones and turning the feline foe into a decidedly nineties feminist.

'My idea was to ground her supervillainy in feminine psychology,' considers Waters, 'which is a volatile thing to begin with. It was Tim's inspired idea to give her this ripped costume that shredded worse whenever she got into trouble.'

Although writer Wesley Strick would later refine and doctor the script, it was Waters' draft that finally encouraged Burton to sign on the dotted line and start gearing up for production. His enthusiasm was clearly contagious, with Keaton joining up almost immediately afterwards, and Danny De Vito coming on board to play the Penguin after a single meeting with Burton. All that was left was the casting of Catwoman, a decision Burton made as soon as he left the cinema having seen Annette Bening in *The Grifters*.

Bening, of course, dropped out of the production when she became pregnant with the small human being that was to become Kathlyn Bening-Beatty, leading to the legendary visit to the set by the 'slightly' eccentric Sean Young, who stormed on to the lot in full Catwoman costume, demanding an audition.

'I didn't even get to *talk* to anyone,' sulked Young afterwards – hardly surprising since Tim Burton has admitted that he actually hid behind his desk when he heard Young was at large on the Warner lot. 'Hollywood is just a bunch of *weenies* . . .'

Subsequently, of course, Michelle Pfeiffer was offered the role, nabbing a percentage of the gross and a flat fee of $3 million – about $2 million more than Bening was offered. Indeed, Pfeiffer may well have been the best choice after all, since back in 1988, after separating from her husband, she spent a few months dallying with her fellow thespians; as well as walking out with her *Married to the Mob* co-star Alec Baldwin and her *Dangerous Liaisons* partner John Malkovich, there was another actor in her black book: one Michael Keaton.

'They have a *lot* of sparks flying between them,' admits *Batman Returns* co-producer Denise Di Novi, garnering a disapproving look from her director.

'Let's not get into that,' sighs Burton wearily. 'We've got enough problems on this movie already.'

Finally, with the team in place and all small requests dealt with, and with what amounted to a blank cheque from those nice people at Warner Brothers for the special effects and sets sticking out of his back pocket, Tim Burton and his merry band were at last ready to start shooting . . .

Beginning in early 1991, two of Hollywood's largest sound stages – Stage 16 at Warner and

Burton's control over **Batman Returns** *let him develop the story's most interesting element: the villains. Here he directs Michelle Pfeiffer as a fetishised Catwoman.*

Stage 12 at Universal – were prepared for the production of the monumentally complex sets for *Batman Returns*, as were eight other buildings on the Warner lot, at least 50 per cent of which was occupied by Gotham City. Stage 16 became home to the mammoth Gotham Plaza, based on New York's Rockefeller Centre and covered with white foam and polyester fabric stuffing to stimulate snowdrifts. Universal's Stage 12, meanwhile, housed the Penguin's underground lair, an enormous tank filled with half-a-million gallons of water and a simulated ice floe island. Before Burton even began considering the structure of the movie, the studio had made clear that – within reason – money was not an object.

Which is all very well, of course, when the rewards for such a monumental endeavour are so potentially enormous. The problem, though, is that sitting at Pinewood Studios, just west of London town, there are the late Anton Furst's vast sets built for the original *Batman*, untouched since 1989 and awaiting the inevitable return of the filmmakers for a sequel.

'I wanted to use American actors in supporting parts,' says Tim Burton of the fantastically expensive decision to make the second movie in Southern California, 'and I felt *Batman* suffered from a British subtext. I *loved* being over there, but it's such a different culture that things got filtered. They could have brought somebody else in for the sequel, and had the same sets, and shot in London, but I couldn't do that because I'd have lost interest. I wanted to treat it like it was another movie altogether – there's no point in doing the exact same thing again.'

And did the sheer scale of the whole affair ever affect the redoubtable Burton, leading him to wonder if really anyone can possibly keep a movie like *Batman Returns* in their head?

'There were moments,' begins Burton, clicking into typically existential mode. 'There were moments sometimes when I'd just sit there, looking at the set and the way the light hit a certain thing – like a boom guy sitting up in the rafters reading the paper, and he's got this incredibly beautiful shadow he's projecting. It's something no one else will ever see, but the juxtaposition of images makes you feel very private and very special, in a way.'

Of course, the sets (kept frozen to simulate a snowy winter and keep the penguins happy), the make-up (including two hours a day for De Vito), and the special effects (a collapsing Batmobile, helicopter umbrellas, computer-generated bats) were only *part* of the logistical nightmare confronting Burton. Because of the inherently bizarre nature of the story – a birdman and a catlady fighting with a batman – every technical and dramatic problem apparently took on almost surreal proportions.

'No one can fully understand the emotion, and the psychological aspects of this,' insists Tim Burton. 'The stress and the *pain* – you can't put it in normal perspective because it's completely *absurd*. You have people almost having a heart attack over how long somebody's nose should be. Also, it's very hard for the actors because *everything* is in the way of their acting. They're not allowed to just walk on to the set and act, because of the technical nature of things.'

'We've been in this movie for three months,' adds Michael Keaton of the difficulty of acting around the effects, 'and I've only completed one scene – and it's not even a very *long* scene. I go a month between ending one part of a scene and going back and picking it up.'

Indeed, to keep a lid on the movie's extraordinary visuals and technical wizardry, a number of ultra-paranoid security tactics were devised by Warner Bros. Picture ID cards were issued to everyone on set, with an ominous code name, 'Dictel' (short, insists Burton, for 'Dictatorial') being stamped on sensitive documents. Art department personnel were advised keep their office curtains closed at all times; no visitors were allowed near the sets, with even Kevin Costner being refused a peek; and everyone involved was required to sign a document garanteeing tight lips all round. With some cast members suggesting that the obsessively tight measures were enforced to increase sales of an exclusive behind-the-scenes book written by the unit publicist, and others insisting it was all about the studio desperately trying to keep images away from the T-shirt bootleggers, the Gestapo-type secrecy *almost* worked.

About midway through the shoot, however, a few test shots of Danny De Vito in costume found their way into the US tabloids, prompting Warner executives to employ a firm of private investigators to track down the culprit – a ploy that ultimately failed.

'It was a *big* deal to them,' remembers production designer Bo Welch of the panic among Warner's control freaks. 'Every day we'd come into work expecting a big bust.'

'The first time, people got hyped up and then burnt out,' admits Tim Burton, sitting in his office during a break in editing *Batman Returns*, and looking a little hollow-eyed himself. 'I know how I feel about that, and that was what was so odd for me about going through the process. I'm a regular person in that way – if things get too hyped up I have a tendency to resist it. It's like, "*Enough* already." I felt what happened on the first one is that it got hyped up, and the movie can't support that. So I thought it was best to forget all of that and try to make another movie completely . . .'

Sitting on a comfy black leather sofa in his office at the Writer's Building in the Warner studio complex, Tim Burton is feeling secure surrounded by his treasured toys. There are robots, dinosaur models, Mexican folk art skeletons, and enough other loopy artefacts to fill the next Pop Art show at the Royal Academy. Next to the Vincent Price autobiography and other books on a shelf are items like a Beetlejuice sweet display and a small metal box festooned with photos of masked wrestlers. There is also a dead baby bat ghoulishly embalmed in a jar of formaldehyde – a gift, he's quick to point out, not a personal purchase.

Burton leaves the office to head for a screening of the first rough cut of *Batman Returns*, hacked into vague shape just 48 hours after the director shut down the production and waved the cast and crew goodbye. Throughout the screening, Burton is remarkably quiet, grunting occasionally, but otherwise passing no comment whatsoever on the $80 million-worth of celluloid that is flickering before his eyes. As the lights go up, those few insiders attending the screening stretch themselves and look over to the director for some kind of comment. Smiling broadly at the assembled company, Tim Burton runs his hands through the Medusa-like shock of madness that passes for his hair, and gives his verdict on his latest baby.

'It's six months of agony,' he chuckles mirthlessly, 'compressed into two hours . . .'

BATTIER AND BATTIER

by Richard Corliss

Batman Returns is a funny, gorgeous improvement on the original and a lesson on how pop entertainment can soar into the realm of poetry.

Scared, scarred Selina Kyle is trudging homeward after another wretched day as secretary to the mighty Power & Light lord Max Shreck when she bumps into a fellow in a black cape. 'Wow! The Batman!' she apostrophises. 'Or is it just – Batman?'

The 1989 movie *Batman*, director Tim Burton's first go at the Bob Kane comic-book character, earned well over $1 billion in its theatrical and video release and in a boffo merchandise blitz. Yet, however imposing its grosses, however many kids in developing countries wore T-shirts with the logo that is supposed to look like a bat in a halo but inevitably suggests a gaping mouth with five rotten teeth, the film was wan, jangled, lost in meandering murk.

Tim Burton – A Child's Garden of Nightmares

That one was 'just – Batman'. Now Burton has made *Batman Returns*, and it looks as though Warner Bros., which produced the film, got its $55 million worth. It is a funny, gorgeous, midsummer night's Christmas story about . . . well, dating, actually. But hang on. This is the goods: 'The Batman'. Accept no prequels.

Like a superhero for cinema, *Batman Returns* arrives in the nick of time. Movies are in big trouble. The magic is gone; the danger is missing. Genres that vitalised the box office a decade ago – the sci-fi epic, the horror movie, the adult comedy – look sapped. Top directors like Steven Spielberg and Martin Scorsese remake their own or other people's movies. So does everybody else. *Lethal Weapon 3* and *Patriot Games* and *Sister Act* may bring millions into a cool theatre on a hot evening, but are audiences getting the fresh kick that good films are supposed to deliver? Movies today are like the Bush Administration in its fourth year: aimless, exhausted, myopic. They lack the vision thing.

The first *Batman* seemed a symptom of that malaise. *Batman Returns* is an antidote. For a start, it's alive, not an effects showcase in a shroud. Daniel Waters' script delights in elaborate wordplay and complex characters. 'The characters are all screwed up,' Burton notes. 'I find that much more interesting.' *Returns* tops the first movie's shrill wrestling match between Batman (Michael Keaton) and the Joker (Jack Nicholson) with a funnier, more lithe and daring villain: the Penguin (Danny De Vito). He is a vicious troll with a righteous grudge: his rich parents dumped him in the sewer when they saw he had flippers for hands. Now he wants to be loved and, even more, elected – Mayor of Gotham City. In DeVito's ripe performance, Penguin is a creature of Dickensian rhetoric, proportions and comic depth.

The Cat and the Penguin. While Pfeiffer's Catwoman is an ambiguous heroine, Danny DeVito's Penguin is a sympathetic grotesque.

But this brisk, buoyant movie gets its emotional weight from an entirely other conflict: the tangle of opposites between – and within – two credible people. Wealthy orphan Bruce Wayne (Keaton again) – the 'trust-fund goody-goody', as Max Shreck (Christopher Walken) calls him – is also Batman, a trussed-up do-gooder who cannot reveal his identity. Selina Kyle, the single woman with a lousy love life, is also the vengeful kitten with a whip: 'I am Catwoman! Hear me roar!' Bruce and Selina are drawn to each other's worldly wise grace and the hint of hidden wounds. They are attracted by the fear of what they might find. And when they don their business good – Batman, of course – and white or bright is bad. Max, the rapacious industrialist, has a Stokowskian white mane that helps Gothamites think of him as Santa Claus, though Selina derisively calls him 'Anti Claus'. The Penguin's sewer-level lair, Arctic World, is a garishly colorful place; it has ice-white walls, chartreuse toxic bile and a giant yellow ducky that serves as the Penguin's Stygian barge.

Burton knows that moviegoers, just like the Penguin, need their oversize playthings. So he and production designer Bo Welch provided toys for the kids. The new-model Batmobile can get ultraslim (fast!) and slip through the narrowest crevice. The Penguin's parasol becomes an Umbrella-Copter, spiriting him out of the trouble he loves to make. At the end he sends his commando squadron of penguins to destroy the city: tuxedoed birds wearing embossed shields, tiny helmets and missiles with candy-cane stripes (it is Christmas) on their backs. Some of the penguins were real, some were robot puppets, some were little people in costume and others were computer generated.

There are lovely toys for adults too. From the eight-ft. logs and six-ft. andirons in Bruce Wayne's fireplace to the neon lettering (HELLO THERE) on Selina's bedroom wall (which Catwoman alters to read HELL HERE), the picture gives you the chance to luxuriate in a cartoon world made flesh and concrete. Massive Deco-style buildings – a Rockefeller Centre gone bats – stretch skyward to put heroes and villains in ironic perspective. 'The movie is very vertical,' says Welch, who also designed *Beetlejuice* and *Edward Scissorhands*. 'It goes from the penguin in the sewers to a flying rodent. So these are aggressive sets, not passive backdrops incidental to the action.' The visual contrasts – big on little, bright on brooding, snow on soot – give the film a distinct, witty style: Dark Lite.

There's wit aplenty in Danny Elfman's discordantly lush score, with its sugarplum fairy exploding over meowing violins. And imposing performances from Walken, as a master builder who out-Trumps himself and Keaton, sturdily imploding from *Batman*'s unresolved, not quite explicable nobility. But the flashy turns are from DeVito and Pfeiffer.

In the sixties *Batman* TV series, Burgess Meredith played Penguin as a kind of deranged F.D.R. This was not for DeVito. 'I didn't see myself playing a weird Nick Charles with a martini glass and a tuxedo,' he says. 'It just didn't tickle my fancy.' Then Burton showed him a painting he had done of 'a toddler with a big round head and big eyes and a protrusion in the nose and mouth and a bulbous body with little appendages. And there was a caption that said, "My name is Jimmy, but they call me the hideous penguin boy." And I got this weird chill.' As Penguin, DeVito gamely spewed black bile (food colouring and mouthwash) and ate raw fish (seasoned with lemon). DeVito, *auteur* of his own dark comedies *Throw Momma from the Train* and *War of the Roses*, says the only thing he would have done differently if he had directed *Batman Returns* is 'make love to the leading lady'.

In the movie, Penguin and Catwoman make hilarious hate. Pfeiffer had cats crawling over her supine body and, in one scene, a live bird in her mouth. 'Fortunately,' she says, 'I have a pretty big mouth.' She also had a longtime crush on her character. 'Catwoman was a childhood heroine of mine,' she says. 'She's good, bad, evil, dangerous, vulnerable and sexual. She is allowed to be all of those things, and we are still allowed to care about her.'

In *Batman Returns* she is a lot more, thanks to Waters, who wrote *Heathers*, the brilliant 1989 tale of feminine competitiveness and desperation (and on *Batman Returns* got story help from Sam Hamm and dialogue 'normalising' from Wesley Strick). 'We didn't want to make her a macho woman,' he says, 'or a sultry, coquettish *uber*-vixen curling on a penthouse couch. We wanted her tied deep into female psychology. Female rage is interesting: we made her a mythic woman you can sympathise with. Catwoman isn't a villain, and she isn't Wonder Woman fighting for the greater good of society. That has no meaning for a lonely, lowly, harassed secretary toiling away in the depths of Gotham City. But she does have her own agenda. She's nobody's toy. She's a wild card – the movie's independent variable.'

Waters sees the story of Bruce and Selina, Batman and Catwoman, as a parable of the strangers men and women are to each other. 'In the daylight they have a sweet, tentative romance,' he says, 'but at night their ids are out, beating the heck out of each other. In costume the ids are active. No kissing there, only one good lick.' It is the reverse of a fantasy like *Pretty Woman*. Pretty Woman goes into the store and shops; Catwoman goes in and whips off the heads of the mannequins. Julia Roberts tells Richard Gere she wants the fairy tale. Cat tells Bat, 'I would love to live with you forever in your castle, just like in a fairy tale. I just couldn't live with myself. So don't pretend this is a happy ending.'

Batman Returns could mark a happy beginning for Hollywood – not because it might make a mint but because it dispenses with realism and aspires to animation, to the freedom of idea and image found in the best feature-length cartoons. Most directors think pictures have to be anchored in the narrowest form of reality: the one that Hollywood has presented since the dawn of sound 65 years ago. Burton, once an animator at Disney, understands that to go deeper, you must fly higher, to liberation from plot into poetry. Here he's done it. This Batman soars.

TROUBLE IN GOTHAM

from 'Front Desk', *Empire*, September 1992

While matching its record-shattering US box office opening with a similarly impressive initial performance in the UK – trouncing *Terminator 2: Judgment Day*'s year-old £2.6 million first weekend record with a £2.8 million opening shot – the question of the Bat-sequel's staying power continues to trouble Hollywood studio executives, with a shocking 45 per cent drop in the US now lowering the estimated final box office tally to a comparitively disappointing $170 million. Indeed, Tim Burton's dark vision now looks set to earn the ignominious distinction of having earned 40 per cent of its final tally in its first *week* on release.

Equally troubling for the Burbank community is the first display of a parental backlash against the Warner Brothers blockbuster. Charging that the various outbursts of violence in the film and the specifically sexual references scattered throughout are wholly unsuitable for their young offspring to view, concerned citizens are directing their disapproval at the marketing campaign which targets the PG-13 rated sequel as just another fun-filled family night out at the pictures. The McDonald's empire – with its *Batman Returns* Happy Meal promotional tie-in – is first in the firing line of this parental ire, with unsuspecting moms and pops and their pleading kiddies allegedly lured into the den of violence and sexual adventures inhabited by the Bat, the Cat and the Penguin.

McDonald's have now already begun to downplay this promotional link, claiming they did not actually mean to *encourage* people to see the movie and quietly closing down the Happy Meal campaign. In the UK, where *Batman Returns* goes out with a 12 certificate, the marketing campaign seems set to adopt a different tone.

'Who *said* it was being marketed as a children's movie?' asks Paul Lewis, head of marketing at Warner's UK office. 'It has a 12 certificate so children under the age of twelve are precluded from going to it. There has been *no* negative reaction that I'm aware of.'

Putting a further dampener on the general Bat-excitement is the embarrassing $30 million legal suit launched by *Batman* executive producers Ben Melnicker and Michael Uslan against original producers Peter Guber and Jon Peters, with Melnicker and Uslan alleging they were coerced into striking a 'net profit agreement' rather than the gross profit arrangement manoeuvred by, among others, Joker Jack Nicholson. Highlighting yet again the highly dubious accounting methods studios use when determining whether or not a film has actually gone into profit, Warners are claiming that *Batman* is still $20 million in the red despite being the fifth biggest box office hit of all time and there is therefore nothing in the coffers to offer the disgruntled pair. Instead, Warners has now offered a $1 million out-of-court pay-off for each of the duo, a sum described by the pair's attorney as 'two popcorns and two Cokes'.

TIM BURTON

by Ken Hanke

Now that it seems more than a little likely that Tim Burton is about to become Warner Bros.' – and by extension, Hollywood's – favourite whipping boy thanks not just to the relative box-office 'failure' of *Batman Returns*, but also because of the extremely vocal parental outrage levelled against the film by people who apparently cannot read words like PG-13 and Parents Are Strongly Cautioned, it is perhaps more than high time that we pause to take a serious look at the director's career thus far.

Despite a certain thematic slightness to most of his work (at least on a surface reading), Burton is quite possibly the most visually gifted American filmmaker of our time with only Woody Allen, Gus Van Sant, the Coen Brothers and, marginally, Barry Sonnenfeld offering any serious competition. (Cases will undoubtedly be made here for Martin Scorsese and Barry Levinson, but I maintain that the mere juggling trick of keeping the camera in a state of a perpetual flux of generally arbitrary motion is little more than window dressing.) More to the point, there is a thematic import – and certainly a consistency – to his work if we bother to go beyond the surface of some admittedly slender and often absurd storylines.

Thanks to Disney's long overdue release of Burton's short, *Frankenweenie*, it is possible to take the filmmaker's career back a step from *Pee-wee's Big Adventure* on something other than hearsay. *Frankenweenie* answers a number of question about Burton, helps to dispel at least on popular misconception, and makes it very clear why he could not function within the confines of the Disney factory far better than his own statement that he 'couldn't draw cute foxes'.

Frankenweenie is, first and foremost, a kind of homage to James Whale's horror films. Shot in beautiful black and white against often stylised backgrounds, the little film perfectly captures the stark studio quality of Whale's original *Frankenstein* right down to the painted sky backdrops. While Burton has made it clear that he dislikes and distrusts the concept of 'being in touch with the child within', this is nothing more than a fantasticated piece of autobiographical work.

Nearly all modern filmmakers (that is movie generation filmmakers) start out (some never get over this!) by imitating films they admired in childhood, but Burton truly takes this a very important step further in *Frankenweenie*. He rethinks the model film in terms that recall both the early experiences of any kid let loose with a movie camera for the first time, and, more importantly, the essence of transforming your own surroundings into the glamorously mysterious world of the source film. As a result, a pet cemetery becomes a Gothic Whale set, an attic and array of seemingly useless junk is converted into Henry Frankenstein's tower, and a disused putt-putt golf course provides the climactic windmill setting. All this is very charming, but the point is something other than that, as anyone who ever 'played out' last night's late show in the backyard of their own childhood can easily attest. We are here very much inside childhood in a way that less ingenuous filmmakers – from Disney to Spielberg – have never quite grasped. Rather than thrusting a child hero into an impossible adventure (though the re-animation of a dead dog is certainly fantastic), Burton transforms the everyday into an adventure in the same way a child does within the confines of his own mind. The results are the product of childhood imagination brought startlingly to life, and are almost certainly of greater interest and appeal to the adult who has forgotten than to the child for whom this personal fantastication is commonplace.

It isn't hard to understand why the Disney people were more than a little taken aback by this striking and unique film. Its simple story about a young boy filmmaker who brings his dead dog back to life is too savvy and lacks the proper ending for the mindset that brought us *Old Yeller*. The mere fact that the neighbours (or villagers, if you will) recognise the error of their ways when the dog saves the boy from the burning golf course windmill and help bring the second-time dead animal back to life (with jumper cables on their cars!) is at odds with the Disney outlook. It is as if the film was actually made *by* children, rather than *for* them. The theory that a film like *Old Yeller* teaches a child how to come to terms with the reality of death may hold water, or may simply be a measure of a kind of adult 'I know what's best for you' sadistic mentality, but it is clearly an *adult* view. No child would make such a film. On the other hand, a child would make *Frankenweenie* if he or she had the technical grasp to do so. Indeed, children make this film every day of the week, but only in their own minds. Interestingly, Burton himself recognises this, since the film-within-a-film childhood home movie, *Monsters from Long Ago*, is both an on-target recreation of the sort of over-ambitious, charmingly inept film children do make, and a deft comment on the innate loneliness suffered by the creative child in that it features no actors, only the child's dog.

Also out of keeping with the Disneyised approach is the film's portrayal of the well-meaning parents. Not only do they not know best (the parents in any teenage-meat-on-the-hoof horror film are about as bright), but they are singularly distracted and remarkably uninvolved. It isn't that they are evil. They're merely uninterested until it becomes impossible not to take notice of the situation. In this regard, too, the film is at odds with the studio policy – almost to the point of being subversive.

As the cornerstone of Burton's work, *Frankenweenie* is both stylistically and thematically important. It establishes him as the logical successor to James Whale in a way that his subsequent films have done somewhat less overtly. The typical Burton hero (the only Burton hero) is somehow outside the realm of society. He is mentally and often physically different than those who make up the 'normal' world. This is exactly the case with every James Whale hero (and villain, for that matter), and despite the fact that Whale's attraction to those who are different was almost certainly an extension of his homosexuality, the distance between Whale and Burton is almost unnoticeable. The major difference between the two filmmakers (apart from the fact that Burton is not as yet quite the showman that Whale was) is that Whale could be termed Studio Gothic, while Burton, in spite of often astronomical budgets, would be more properly pegged as Backyard Gothic.

As a filmmaker, Burton is more than slightly at odds with his cinematic brethren. There really is

Two freaks meet in the darkness. The neon sign signifies the corrupt character Max Shreck – after the actor who played Dracula in the shadowy silent classic Nosferatu.

no one like him (just as there was no one like Whale) working in film today, and, indeed, his unique mixture of childhood and adulthood, combined with his empathy for the alienated characters that people the world of his films, probably bring him far more in alignment with the more serious side of the pop music world. It is hardly surprising therefore that all of his feature films have been scored in collaboration with Danny Elfman, the founder and driving force of the rock band Oingo Boingo, who, under Burton's auspices, is currently on his way to becoming a filmmaker in his own right.

The connection to Elfman goes far deeper than might be imagined on the basis of filmmaker and film scorer. In interviews, Elfman always speaks of their working relationship in terms of collaboration, indicating that Burton very clearly does not simply hand him an answer print of the final cut and ask him to put music to it. The release of *Frankenweenie* with its sweeping score by Michael Convertino and David Newman makes it obvious that this is so, since it is but a small step from this to the Elfman scores. It is, however, a very important step. The similarity in approach between the Convertino-Newman soundtrack and those of Danny Elfman is simply in the *type* of music. Elfman's scores are far more creative, far more in line with Burton's combined sense of charm, irony, and absurdity, and generally just better music.

Elfman himself tends to minimise the connection between his movie scores and his work for Oingo Boingo, but this is at least partly a bit of self-deception. Orchestration differences are not composition differences, and while Elfman's scores are richer and more varied than his rock music, the core of Oingo Boingo is always just around the corner. This is not a bad thing, though,

From masked vigilante to saviour. Gotham City authorities and press await the return of Batman almost as keenly as the marketing department of Warner Bros.

since it is part of what keeps Elfman's work from crossing over into the realm of John Williams' sub-Wagnerian big-for-big's-sake scoring. The blending of such diverse influences as 1930s jazz/pop music with high energy rock and a taste for ornate film scoring produces an effect as unique as Burton's visual sense.

For Burton the connection to Oingo Boingo may well be more pronounced than either he or Elfman would care to admit, especially if one carefully examines Burton's first feature, *Pee-wee's Big Adventure*. A passing familiarity with the distinctive album cover art that adorns the Oingo Boingo work immediately attests to a striking influence on the design of the film, while an even more obvious design and approach can be found in Danny Elfman's brother's (Richard) 1981 avant-gardist film, *Forbidden Zone*, for which Danny composed the music (including Oingo Boingo songs this time) and even played the part of Satan (or Satan rethought as Cab Calloway in a Max Fleischer cartoon). Richard Elfman's low-budget cult classic, a homage to the world of Max Fleischer prior to the Production Code, is very much at one with Burton's work, even though it is far more overtly sexual than Burton has thus far allowed in his own films. Where Burton was bizarrely out of step with Disney, he would have been quite at home with Max and Dave Fleischer in the early 1930s, and his own 'cartoonish' qualities, like those of Richard Elfman, are distinctly more Betty Boop than Mickey Mouse.

It would be unfair to say that *Pee-wee's Big Adventure* is a sanitised knock-off of *Forbidden Zone*.

It would also be incorrect, but the connection is undeniably present – not so much cleaned up as made more overtly mainstream. The curious thing about this is that ultimately *Pee-wee's Big Adventure* is the more subversive of the two films, simply because it can and does pass muster as a mainstream personality work for the singular talents of Paul Reubens (Pee-wee Herman). And those talents are so central to the film that Burton's exact creative position on the project is not as easily defined as on his other works. In fact, it is more than a little possible that Reubens had a good deal to do with the hiring of Danny Elfman and the overall Oingo Boingo influence, thereby bringing the composer and the filmmaker together. Whatever the case, the result is quite a remarkable film, and the subsequent artistic and commercial failure of the follow-up film, *Big Top Pee-wee*, attests to the fact that Burton was a key factor in *Pee-wee's Big Adventure*'s success.

The basic concept of the Pee-wee Herman character is bizarre in the extreme. Presented as a cross between an overgrown child and a seriously demented kiddie show host, Pee-wee is a nightmarish role model of contradictions. It is impossible for any rational parent to object to his basic decency and the obvious object lessons of accepting one's self, enjoying life, and relying on a generous nature and a good heart.

However, his appearance and demeanour are another matter. Despite a basically sexless pose (to the degree that a pose incorporating the idea of a grown man stuck in a latency period can be construed as sexless), the character insists on wearing indelicately tailored trousers that are quite at odds with his 'safe' image. Worse, he wears lipstick and make-up that makes him look like a female impersonator in training, and his relationship with the young boys in his neighbourhood is clearly tinged with pederastic overtones. 'There are a lot of things about me you don't know anything about,' he tells his borderline girlfriend, adding, 'things you wouldn't understand; things you couldn't understand; things you *shouldn't* understand.' Long before Reubens' personal legal troubles made this line of thought take on a new resonance, the words carried a curious sense of saying more than was apparent on the surface. Here lies the tantalising appeal of Pee-wee Herman. He could not be objected to, yet it was always obvious that he was neither quite 'normal', nor quite 'safe'. (Parents objecting to his irritating voice, laugh, and mannerisms, which may well have been an intentionally distracting smokescreen, were in reality alarmed by something else they either could not or would not see.) Here then was the perfect Burton hero.

Owing to his borderline status as a weirdly androgynous man masquerading as a boy, Pee-wee provided Burton with a character who successfully straddled the boundary between childhood and adulthood, allowing the director to cross over from the child heroes of *Frankenweenie* and his stop-frame animated Disney short, *Vincent*. Moreover, the character's status as someone outside the realm of normal human existence brought him fully into line with the director's innate empathy with the 'different'. It would be a mistake, though, to take the resultant film too seriously. It is very much a 'fun' project and an enjoyably obvious – and quite successful – attempt by the filmmaker to dazzle the viewer and Hollywood with his technical panache. The subversive nature of the Pee-wee character, the sharp (and again very anti-Disney) insights into the adult world's often imbecilic attitude on how to deal with children (the satirical tour of the Alamo alone is worth the price of admission), etc., are really icing on a cake that exists primarily to make the viewer go, 'Wow!'

Burton's stated attraction to the project – that he immediately identified with Pee-wee's obsessive behaviour toward something (a stolen bicycle) no one else cared about or understood – is what gives the film the little weight it has. What remains with the viewer, however, is the insane pop art sensibility of its design, the over-the-top poster-like colours of the photography (which bears no relation to the usual work of cinematographer Victor J. Kemper and must be attributed to Burton), and Burton's boundless creativity in presenting both very original scenes and pastiches of the work of his cinematic ancestors and indeed his own work. The amazing sequence that follows the theft of Pee-wee's bike is, in three minutes, a better evocation of Hitchcock (blithely dismissed as 'that fat guy on television' in *Frankenweenie*) than the entire running time of Mel Brooks' *High Anxiety*. The climactic drive-in premiere of Warner Bros.' film of Pee-wee's story is an assured bit of Felliniesque filmmaking. (In both cases, Elfman's score comes through, offering ersatz Bernard Herrmann and Nino Rota respectively.) At the same time, there's the purely Burtonesque bonus of Pee-wee running riot on the Warner lot and destroying the production of a Godzilla movie (complete with Japanese director and crew) that is nothing more nor less than young Victor Frankenstein's *Monsters from Long Ago* out of *Frankenweenie*! For that matter, the sequence where Pee-wee ends up preferring to jump from a moving train rather than be subjected to the further cacophonous singing of a hobo seems more than a little like a satirical jab at Frank Capra's most forced homespun sensibilities. A more assured feature film debut is hard to imagine.

The success of *Pee-wee's Big Adventure* led to Burton's more controlled and direct involvement in *Beetlejuice*, which might be viewed as a greater success than *Pee-wee's Big Adventure*, if only because it doesn't hinge solely on one's taste for – or toleration of – the pre-packaged Pee-wee Herman character. Unfortunately, this undeniable plus is slightly offset by Burton's obvious inability to give a damn about the painfully dull and normal Alec Baldwin and Geena Davis characters. When the film is good, it is very good indeed, but that is mostly when Michael Keaton, Sylvia Sidney, Winona Ryder, and, to lesser degrees, Glenn Shaddix, Catherine O'Hara and Jeffrey Jones are in the forefront. He responds well to Keaton's outrageousness, Sidney's sharpness, Ryder's morbidity, Shaddix's prissy snobbery ('Deliver me from L. L. Bean!' sneers Shaddix upon discovering a too, too folksy den, and this could well be Burton's own attitude toward the film's normalcy factor), O'Hara's pretentious bitchery, and Jones' hopelessly wrong-headed pursuit of a 'normal' existence. There is something of Burton in all these characters, but not a trace of him in the romantic leads, and when they take the reins the film lies there and dies there.

The leads all too often threaten to be reduced to buffoons, though some of this is done with engagingly on-target satire. That these almost willfully dull characters meet their demise while driving their safety-minded Volvo and wearing their seatbelts is certainly no accident. The problem is that they never seem to grow as a result of any of their experiences, and we leave them pretty much as we found them – a couple of stiffs in flannel and calico.

A mixed experience, *Beetlejuice* is nonetheless notably more personal than its predecessor. Danny Elfman is, of course, back on hand with an even better score than before. Replacing veteran cinematographer Victor J. Kemper is Burton's own Thomas Ackerman, who had shot *Frankenweenie*, and the production design is now in the hands of Bo Welch in the first (so far) of three brilliant collaborations with Burton. On this level, *Beetlejuice* is an unqualified success, if only because it registers as something approaching the mature Burton of his two most recent films.

Beetlejuice is notable for establishing certain Burtonian trademarks on both a stylistic and thematic level. The film's opening, for example, has become a Burton staple – a sweeping travelling shot across a skilfully constructed model that serves to literally waft the viewer right into the film. Burton's approach here is what might be called radical-reactionary, utilising model work in much the same manner one finds in early talkies like Roland West's *The Bat Whispers* (1931) and Archie Mayo's *Svengali* (1931). Perhaps this is merely a small step from the Whalean pet cemetery and golf course of *Frankenweenie*, but it is nonetheless startling and refreshing in modern cinema where this almost forgotten, visually stunning approach has long been limited to science fiction films and

Burton and his designers took Catwoman's kinky comic-book costume and turned it into PVC fetish-wear. Though the instrument is unseen here, she is truly a kitten with a whip.

oversized adventure epics where its use is dictated by necessity, not aesthetics. It's interesting to see Burton's careful evolution of the effect. Apparently not quite certain whether modern audiences will accept that which their filmgoing ancestors took for granted (check out the slick, offhand use of models in Rouben Mamoulian's *Love Me Tonight* [1932] and Frank Tuttle's *The Big Broadcast* [1932]), he stages the effect here as a gag with the payoff being that we are supposed to be looking at a model all along. Lightweight cameras, helicopter shots, high speed film, and generally greater flexibility had replaced the use of models for elaborate travelling shots, despite the fact that this more realistic approach still didn't allow for the full effect of the earlier method, which was often only detectable as model work because we knew the shot was otherwise impossible.

Beyond this most obvious trademark, there is a sneaky thematic undercurrent here that will crop up again and again in Burton's work – and which his earlier work had already suggested. It is significant in retrospect to consider the fact that there is no sermonising attached to young Victor Frankenstein's re-animation of his dog, no trace of 'things men should leave alone', no moral about 'tampering in God's domain'. In *Beetlejuice* Burton offers us an afterlife that has no relation to anything religious. 'Are we halfway to heaven? Are we halfway to hell?' asks Geena Davis, only to have Baldwin tell her that their copy of the *Handbook for the Recently Deceased* 'doesn't mention heaven or hell'. The afterlife offered by the film is a fantasticated fun-house bureaucracy presided over by suicides (the punishment for which is eternity as a civil servant) where a false step out of your assigned space lands you on the Dali-esque surface of Saturn. It's an engaging enough notion, but the point of it all is distinctly that of a secular humanist sensibility. Its inclusion in a comic-fantasy framework tends to allow it to be overlooked, yet it is very much present and quirkily somewhat out of step with our conservative era. Not surprisingly, when Burton makes his first wholly personal feature, *Edward Scissorhands*, the humanistic subtext emerges with much more force, since the artificially created hero's possession of basic goodness or a soul is never in doubt, and the film's marginal villain is the neighbourhood religious fanatic, who is presented as destructive, foolish, and none too bright.

Moral questions of quite a different sort arise in *Batman*, namely the filmmaker's own apparent discomfort with the fascistic overtones inherent in any superhero. The Burton-Michael Keaton Batman is a far cry from Adam West's campy TV hero. In his stead we find a deeply-troubled individual who is easily as dark-tinged as the film's nominal villain. Burton constantly presents him in a questionably heroic light, even going so far as to stage one of the most strikingly mythic images of the character so that he is directly in front of the equally powerful neon sign for Axis Chemicals.

Batman is a rich film filled with powerful images and Burton's own sense of fun and cinematic invention. It is also an uneven film as its creator is himself all too willing to point out. The title sequence is a marvel, with Burton's camera prowling around, through, and finally out of a sculpted Batman symbol (the Burton travelling shot-model work opening turned into an abstraction), and Elfman's score is his best work for the director up to this time. The opening is similarly assured, but also hints at one of the film's most troubling aspects – the gap between Anton Furst's production design and Burton's own visual style.

Putting aside the pop art day-glo colours of *Pee-wee's Big Adventure* (Burton's only collaboration with designer David L. Snyder), the director's signature colour is clearly blue (even *Pee-wee* hints at this in Burton's now-typical bright blue skyscape backgrounds, and his cool blue night scenes). Anton Furst's was not. Furst's designs are predominantly brown and grey, while the sets themselves are often so smoky as to come across as refugees from a Ridley Scott picture. The upshot is that *Batman*, handsome as it is, looks like a Tim Burton picture once removed. (Indeed, a case could be made that Barry Sonnenfeld's heavily Burton-influenced *The Addams Family* looks more like a Burton film than does *Batman*.) Occasionally, the purest of Burton shines through –

the travelling shot up Jack Palance's office building, the scenes in the Batcave, the Axis Chemicals sequences, a wonderful trip through a stylised forest at night – but the film's look verges on the schizophrenic if we judge it as a Burton film.

Equally disturbing is *Batman*'s basic inability to suggest that Gotham City itself extends much beyond its single big street set. For a production this big, the film often seems cramped, and the casual use of matte paintings to increase its sense of *size* don't much help. It is ironic, but not inapt, that two of the film's most striking visuals, the shot up the office building and the trip through the forest, are Burton's re-workings of shots from Roland West's *The Bat Whispers*. It's almost as though Burton's ability to communicate with Furst and cinematographer Roger Pratt worked best when he could direct their attention to something 'outside' his own style, even if that something had already been absorbed and filtered into his personal vision.

Moreover, Burton was clearly uncomfortable with the move to a project of this size with this much pressure attached to it. In this, it's amazing that he left his fingerprints on the film as much as he did, and that so much of the work is good and vital. Unfortunately, one of his most accomplished bits of filmmaking was subverted by the film's high-pressure advertising campaign. The build-up to our first look at Jack Nicholson's Joker is a fine throwback to James Whale's slow build-up introduction to the Frankenstein Monster (with perhaps a passing nod to the fire-scarred Peter Lorre in Robert Florey's *The Face Behind the Mask* [1941]). Alas, the image of the Joker was just too tempting for the advertising department, so that the careful avoidance of letting us see him is technically impressive, but minus the pay-off.

Regardless of any reservations one may have about the film, it was undeniably a popular success of almost unheard of proportions – something that is not easy to grasp in light of the fact that it's long, rather slow paced, thoughtful, and as concerned with elegance as action. And, in fact, it does not play all that well with an audience. Having seen the film in its theatrical release a number of times, I was invariably struck by the fact that the audiences grew quite restless (occasionally to the point of milling around the back of the theatre!) during the climactic encounter between Batman and the Joker – the pace of which is perhaps best judged by the title of Elfman's music for the scene, 'Waltz to the Death'.

What then appears to hold the film together for an audience is Nicholson's Joker, and while this is undeniably a *tour de force*, it is also perhaps detrimental to the film as a film. All too often there is a sense of the film turning into little more than Nicholson spouting one-liners. Worse, his bravura theatrics threaten to swamp the rest of the cast (does anyone really think that Jack Palance *wasn't* making up for this with his hysterically hammy villainy in *Tango and Cash*?).

The best of the script lies in its exploration of the duality of Batman and the Joker, and the implication that the hero is just as crazy – and potentially just as dangerous – as the villain. Whatever else it is, Burton's *Batman* is a universe or so away from Richard Donner's *Superman* and its progeny.

One of the most interesting aspects of the film lies neither in the script, nor the performances, but in Burton's sense of time frame. The proceedings seem to take place in the present day, but not *exactly*. Rather, the film exists in a time of its own that roughly seems to encompass the period from Burton's childhood to the present. Curiously, this skewed presentation of time first clearly surfaced in David Lynch's *Blue Velvet*, where it was used to make a more overt point about Reaganism's manufactured (and one might say Disneyised) hallucination of an idealised 1950s. Just prior to *Batman* it had surfaced again in Ken Russell's *The Lair of the White Worm* – a film with a distinctively Edwardian flavour that is filtered through a clearly 1960s sensibility, yet featuring a villainess with a taste for heavy metal head-banging music and a very modern state-of-the-art CD player. Russell's film, too, seems to be taking a snipe at 1980s materialism, since it is only the villainess who is up to date. Burton's approach differs in that it seems more pathological. Burton's 'everytime' is less utilitarian, more personal, and mostly used to create a separate world. The everytime concept did not reach full flower for Burton until his next film, *Edward Scissorhands*, the director's most personal feature to date and his best.

Edward Scissorhands is one of the most original, striking, romantic, and charming works to come out of American film in decades. Unfortunately, its unique qualities tended to be overlooked on the critical front owing to its fantasticated subject matter and the commercially shrewd casting of Johnny Depp in the title role. (This so nettled some reviewers that the claim was made that it was impossible to determine whether or not Depp could act since he had so little dialogue – a judgement call that very neatly disposes of Boris Karloff's Frankenstein Monster as non-acting, too.)

Interestingly, the film came not from Warner Bros. (for whom Burton had created three money makers in a row), but from Twentieth Century Fox, who seemed more receptive to Burton's personal vision – even to allowing the film to boast its own version of the studio logo (with snow falling on it and without the traditional fanfare). This is even more striking when one stops to consider that Fox, on the whole, has tended to contribute more to popular culture than the art of film over the years. And, despite a quotient of studio sets and the usual Burton model work, the film is largely not a studio-oriented project. Shot in a tract housing development (slightly rethought by painting the houses in solid, bright, kitschy colours) in Lutz, Florida (a small town a few miles north of Tampa) with side trips to Lakeland for a very 1960s shopping-centre location (presented exactly as it exists!), Burton and designer Welch create a kind of generic suburbia that more or less dovetails with the time frame of Burton's own adolescence.

Once again, the apparent time frame is far from exact, and thrown off even more by the film's framing story where an old woman tells the story of the film to her grand-daughter. The interior of the grandmother's house is cosily old-fashioned with oversized furniture and an even more oversized fireplace, yet it turns out supposedly to be a home in the housing development of the central story – or perhaps a child's eye view of one. Moreover, this Grimm's fairy story setting is ultimately shown to be taking place 60-odd years after the events of the film, despite the central film's late sixties-early seventies ambience, which in itself is combined with the more modern accoutrements of CD players and VCRs (and as in Russell's film these items seem to exist solely in the realm of the film's villainous characters). Rounding it all out is the incongruous (especially in geographically-flat Florida) Inventor's Castle perched high atop a mountain at the end of the street (thanks to an old-fashioned glass shot). This is the Backyard Gothic of childhood imagining from *Frankenweenie* with a vengeance. What, after all, is the castle at the end of the street but a literalised version of the one creepy house that seems to exist in every neighbourhood, and about which children imagine the most mysterious, fantastic and horrific things? The result is Burton's most successfully realised 'everytime'.

Apart from the more romantic and fantastic elements of this deceptively simple work, *Edward Scissorhands* is a gem of suburban observance. Making sport of suburbia is easy, though Hollywood has always tended to aim for a more upscale version of it than Burton does here. Despite its fantastication, this is much nearer reality both as a setting and as a state of mind. Apart from the imaginary castle, there is nothing in Burton's neighbourhood that couldn't be purchased in any discount store in America – from the tacky knick knacks that festoon the sets to the bunny Christmas wrapping paper Conchata Ferrell uses in one scene. The minor characters are of necessity rather broad caricatures, but none of them (with the exception of O-Lan Jones' religious looney tune) are fools.

Burton's characters are generally both believable and likeable. There is a sense of autobiographical remembrance in Alan Arkin's wonderfully distracted father (a character that seems at least partly modelled on Burton's mother, judging by remarks he's made in interviews). Dianne Wiest's role as the mother in the film is even better. The character in Wiest's hands manages to be absurdly optimistic and nice without ever once becoming irritating. In Burton's view, you have to admire anyone who can go on being the neighbourhood Avon lady year in and year out despite the fact that no one ever buys anything from her, while her innate goodness (no sooner does she meet Edward than she decides to simply take him home with her) is leavened with a degree of perception and a ditsy quality that prevents her from slipping into the stick-figure boredom of Geena Davis in *Beetlejuice*. The rest of the adults in the film are pretty much types, but they're realistic types with the vestiges of actual lives outside the plot of the film. Strict urbanites may not recognise them, but anyone who has ever lived in a neighbourhood like the one in the film certainly will. The over-sexed, stretch-pants clad single lady, the hefty, nosey-but-nice woman down the street, the back-slapping husbands, the upscale family (heard about but never seen), the war veteran who never tires of discussing his shrapnel-ridden leg – all have the stamp of truth on them.

The children are perhaps a bit sketchier, especially on the villainous side. Anthony Michael Hall's character is thoroughly unlikeable, for example, and there is some (perhaps justifiable) criticism that he becomes unbelievable. However, the validity of that complaint exists only if we insist on applying objective terms to a subjective fantasy. The popular jock character with the

Beetlejuice presents a Disneyland version of Hell/Limbo and detailed miniature sets. Sets and star become one as Betelgeuse (Michael Keaton) conjures a demonic carousel.

Burton directs Jack Nicholson in Batman, *as Jack Napier, the thug who becomes the Joker. Once in make-up, the film is a showcase for his comic-book histrionics.*

cheerleader girlfriend would seem every bit this ghastly (possibly more so) to an outsider like Burton, whose artistic introversion and gawky demeanour would have made him a natural target for such a person. In subjective terms, Burton knows whereof he speaks. It might be more to the point to criticise the fantasy projection of Winona Ryder's character. Burton's assertion here that the popular cheerleader type would, if exposed to him rather than her boyfriend, have a spiritual awakening at the hands of a sensitive young man like Edward (by implication, Burton himself) is actually more suspect. But this is *his* fantasy, and there's no denying that he presents a moving, if not objectively convincing, picture.

The title character is, of course, Burton's onscreen alter ego (though to some degree this may be said of the little brother character). Part Frankenstein Monster, part Cesare from *The Cabinet of Dr Caligari*, Edward is the eternal outsider. Created from a combination of mechanical chopping devices and a heart-shaped cookie by Vincent Price's inventor (a character who exists solely in relation to Edward – or perhaps Edward's imagination), Edward is almost classically too good to live. Yet, thankfully, this wondrously creative and imaginative soulful being has a darker side. There is a threat of (ultimately real, if justifiable) violence in his very being – a danger that lurks beneath the surface. Where Burton himself played out his frustrations in drawing, Edward creates fantasy topiary sculptures with his scissor hands – a clear indication that artistic ability is as much a curse (because it makes you different) as a blessing. Burton merely externalises that difference. That

Edward is potentially dangerous when put into society is in itself a comment on the inherent dangers of art and the artist. The best art and the best artists are *not* safe. They turn things upside down, leave us different from the way they found us, make us see the world in their own skewed fashion. Perhaps Warner Bros. should have studied *Edward Scissorhands* before entrusting Burton with *Batman Returns*.

Technically, *Edward Scissorhands* is Burton's purest, most seamless creation. Nearly everything about it is inspired – from Welch's designs to Elfman's score to newcomer Stefan Czapsky's photography. Czapsky proves here (and again on *Batman Returns*) that he is exactly who Burton needed to best realise his vision. The skyscapes of Burton's earlier work – aided by the flat Florida landscape which lends itself to angles accentuating the sky as the only interesting 'geographical' feature – here become the magical backdrop against which the exteriors are played. The Burtonian blues of the first films are here deeper, richer, purer in the film's studio-created sections. There is an effortlessness about the film's imagery that makes its seemingly offhand creation of resonant images that smack of the truly mythic all the more astonishing.

By all rights, *Batman Returns* should have been a triumph – and artistically it is. The absurd things that have been said about it will fade into insignificance with time. The film will not. Even so, Burton here seems doomed to play out the worst aspects of Edward's dilemma. It's as if Burton's previous work equates to Edward's topiary sculptures and avant-gardist hairstyles, while *Batman Returns* is Burton as Edward after he comes to be viewed as dangerous. In essence, Burton warned us of this potentiality in his previous film, but no one took the hint. The resulting film is dangerous and disturbing – and brilliant.

Gone is the muddy production design of the first film. In its place is a totally convincing stylised centre set that manages to convey a sense of being part of a great city, rather than a single huge set that reduces the city to one street. Everything is sharply defined and crisp. As in other Burton works, the accent is on blue, and, like *Edward*, the film makes canny use of a snowy setting, the better to reflect Burton's blue lighting scheme – and a telling bit of the magically unfamiliar for a Southern California born and bred filmmaker. The cinematography flows in the sequel in a way it never did in the first film. The Burtonesque opening – detailing the birth of the Penguin and his descent into the sewers – carries the sweeping pull-the-viewer-into-the-film opening to even greater extremes. The characters are considerably more complex, appealing, and *real* than in the first film, which, along with the dark and consistent tone of the film, is the source of the film's box office and public relations troubles.

Undoubtedly, *Batman Returns* is not a film for four-year-olds – and a damn good thing, too, since any film aimed at a four-year-old isn't going to be of much use to anyone else. Its PG-13 rating should have been sufficient to warn parents of this fact, but it did not, and the upshot of protest frankly says more about the parents than it does about the film. That young children are going to find the film disturbing (especially in its first violent scene) is to be expected, but this is a hard area to judge in any case. As a four-year-old child, I sat through *Journey to the Centre of the Earth* without a twinge, but was found cowering under my seat due to a Donald Duck cartoon with a depiction of hell in it (so much for the safety of Uncle Walt on a subjective level!). Moreover, Burton didn't make his film for four-year-olds. Warner Bros. marketing is to blame for that.

One of the more obscure complaints about the film on a parental level are those directed at the script's innuendo-ridden dialogue. And again, Burton is taking the heat, which seems curious since, although he was certainly involved in the development process, he did not write the script. Beyond that, am I to seriously believe that no one at Warner Bros. read this script, viewed any rushes, or saw a rough print? This strains my credulity more than a little. Regardless of this, the film's innuendoes are unlikely to be understood by even the most worldly pre-teen (and if they are, it seems equally unlikely that there's much potential corrupting influence on so savvy a child). But perhaps the most curious aspect of all this comes from a comparison of the basic set-up of the first film with the second.

In *Batman*, the Batman character and the Vicki Vale character meet, have dinner at his mansion, and promptly jump into bed together. No eyebrows were raised over this. In *Batman Returns*, Batman in his normal state meets Catwoman in her normal guise, they have dinner at his mansion, and do *not* jump into bed. Indeed, their love is never consummated. Yet this film has been attacked for its sexual content. The reason, I suspect, is more psychological than actual. *Batman* gave us a pretty traditional (read: acceptable) lady in distress in Vicki Vale. *Batman Returns* offers a much less palatable, much more feminist point of view in Catwoman, who transforms herself from victim into self-styled avenger. This is no lady in distress, and, indeed, she ultimately rejects Batman's advances to be Mrs Bruce Wayne. 'I'd love to live with you in your mansion, but I couldn't live with myself,' she tells him. It is this attitude, I suggest, that is unacceptable to the reactionary mindset, not any actual physical content. We may have come a goodly distance in our accepting a 'liberated' heroine – after all, Vicki Vale was supposedly a talented career-woman photographer – but, by and large, this acceptance only exists so long as the heroine takes a subservient role to that of the hero in the final reel. Note carefully, *Batman* concludes with Vicki Vale playing maid in waiting to our hero, who seems to prefer striking a dramatic pose to riding off with Miss Vale. *Batman Returns* concludes with Batman rescuing a stray cat, riding into the night with his butler, Alfred, talking about the season of 'good will toward men – and women', while Catwoman is the lone mythic figure on which the film ends.

Controversy to one side, *Batman Returns* is almost pure Burton where its parent film was maybe 70 per cent Burton, and the film is all the stronger because of this, if only because it boasts a single, strong point of view. This isn't surprising. What is surprising is that the second film's narrative is far less muddled – an oddity in that dramatic construction has never been Burton's strong suit, a fact Burton seems only too willing to recognise. To date, none of his films have been actually scripted by him, though *Frankenweenie* and *Edward Scissorhands* are from Burton stories, yet they all bear his stamp and are clearly written to his ideas and specifications. In the case of his least personal film, *Batman,* this is mostly evident in bits and pieces – not all of them good. Burton's work has always shown an engaging willingness to veer off on a digression, combined with a somewhat less desirable cavalier attitude toward narrative. The most glaring example of this is in *Batman* where – without thought or build-up – Alfred happily waltzes into the 'secret' Batcave with an unannounced Vicki Vale in tow (a narrative gaffe that invariably sends a buzz of whispering through the audience, and which serves as the source for a withering in-joke in the second film). There is also every reason to believe that Burton is responsible for the slow pace of the first film. In *Batman Returns*, where he was in charge of the development, we end up with a film nearly fifteen minutes longer than its predecessor that seems much shorter, moves in a reasonably straightforward fashion, and is constructed for maximum dramatic impact. Indeed, *Batman Returns* suggests that it is perhaps time for Burton to write his own material.

The effortless mythic quality of *Edward Scissorhands* crosses over into *Batman Returns*. The occasionally startling images of *Batman* are here almost constantly bombarding the viewer, and, in fact, it would be safe to say that *Batman Returns* is far more closely related to *Edward Scissorhands* than to its source film. Elfman's score combines some of the original *Batman* themes with the wordless choir of *Edward*, while the snow-covered setting clearly links the two. Most interesting, though, is Burton's concept of Michelle Pfeiffer's Catwoman. If we take Edward Scissorhands as Burton's onscreen alter ego in that film, then we must also accept Catwoman as the most clearly defined personification of Burton in this film. Even her costume – sewn together out of an old raincoat – is designed to resemble that of Edward. Again, Burton provides the clue the studio might have grasped – Catwoman is the embodiment of the dangerous side of Edward Scissorhands, and by implication of Burton himself. But where Catwoman goes on a campaign of revenge, Burton merely creates a troubling and, for the studio, troublesome film.

Burton, however, does not limit himself to Catwoman, since he obviously identifies with the Batman and the Penguin as well. The first Batman character was frankly something of a stiff. Apart from his aberrant behaviour and mental instability, his personality was about as interesting as Alec Baldwin in *Beetlejuice*. This time round he is more savvy, more aware of his own quirks, and a lot more fun. Burton could better identify with the Joker, except that the Joker never really became a character. He was stubbornly Jack Nicholson in a purple suit. The script's reference to his aptitude for art seemed more in line with Burton than the character on the screen, while the Joker's claim that he is 'the world's first fully functioning homicidal artist' seems equally Burtonesque. In *Batman Returns* Danny DeVito gives Burton a performance, where Nicholson gave him a stand-up routine, and the result is a more clearly defined relationship between filmmaker and character.

Regardless, the script is at pains to make another point. In their climactic fight, the Penguin sneers, 'You're just jealous because I'm a real freak and you have to wear a mask!' 'Maybe you're right,' responds Batman. This is the crux of both the film and perhaps of Burton's career. His strong identification with characters who are both mentally and physically different suggests that this is a moment of personal catharsis. Burton as a lonely, imaginative child enmeshed in a world of old horror movies on television could identify with those films' monsters and misfits. He knew he was more like them inside, but, of course, the perception of his parents and the rest of the world was something else again. They saw and expected a normal young boy, since the things that made him different were not physically apparent. It is hardly a wonder that this desire for externalised 'freakishness' would find its way into Burton's art. And this by itself is a large measure of what is disturbing about Burton's work in general and *Batman Returns* in particular.

That this rich, dense, dark film should be the subject of a controversy is as regrettable as it was inevitable. *Batman Returns* isn't quite as secure as *Edward Scissorhands*, but it only just misses that mark, and perhaps makes up for it in its disquieting ambience. The worst of it is that its lack of acceptance may well damage Burton's career. There is talk of a third Batman film (which, truth to tell, we need about as much as a *Friday the 13th Part IX*), either without Burton, or with a properly subdued and contrite Burton subjugating his own vision to the mentality of corporate filmmaking. Hopefully, this will not happen. It would be a great pity to see one of our most original – and, so far, constantly evolving – filmmakers reduced to this level at a time when his work is looking ever more promising. With any degree of luck or justice, Burton will instead get the chance to deliver on that promise.

TIM BURTON'S THE NIGHTMARE BEFORE CHRISTMAS (1993)

GHOUL WORLD

by Mimi Avins

The naked woman stood immobile under the fluorescent lights until, in a brief stolen moment, she stretched, a flicker of relief stretching across her previously expressionless face. Most of the group gathered for the life drawing class at the Burbank Adult School that evening were indigenous blue-haired ladies satisfying a long-dormant lust for creativity. A few guys, barely into their twenties, stood near the back of the room, including a rangy, towheaded artist intent on his sketch pad. These nude models, Henry Selick thought. They're always more what you'd call interesting than beautiful. The things you gotta do to keep your drawing skills up.

Unlike the model, the figure Selick's pencil described was a fully clothed male, wearing loose khaki pants, a rumpled short-sleeved shirt, and the kind of big Converse gym shoes that had been part of the unofficial uniform at Burbank High in the late seventies. With his anarchic black hair and long, slender fingers, Tim Burton seemed a far more compelling subject than the fleshy mannequin struggling to hold her pose. Selick finished his portrait of Burton and scrawled a caption: 'Typical Disney geek.'

Actually, of the young artists who flocked to Disney in the early eighties, eager to draw adorable little animals, few were less typical than Burton and Selick. Burton conjured up stories of ghoul-obsessed boys, and Selick found experimental German animation as inspirational as Mickey Mouse. Although they were both too weirdly gifted to stay at the studio for long, the fact that they have now, respectively, produced and directed a Disney feature is in itself a tale of the Revenge of the Art Nerds.

The movie is *Tim Burton's The Nightmare Before Christmas*, a twisted holiday fable that takes place on a night when the sky is so dark and the moon shines so bright and a million small children pretending to slumber nearly don't have a Christmas at all to remember. Although it is an animated musical, it is as different from recent Disney toons as Dr Seuss is from Dr Ruth. Sure, *Aladdin* was hip, but it still has a conventional hero, a hissable villain, and tunes that wouldn't be out of place in an old fashioned Broadway musical. *Nightmare* features less melodic, narrative songs by Danny Elfman, the rock star-film score composer who put calypso in *Beetlejuice* and added musical menace to *Batman* and its sequel. A manic-depressive skeleton serves as the movie's confused antihero, and what he's up against is more a bad situation than a clearly identifiable bad guy.

And *Nightmare* isn't a cartoon. It uses an animation technique called stop-motion that dates back to the silent era but has rarely been employed for a full-length feature. In the same way that drawn (or cel) animation projects 24 static, two-dimensional images per second to give the illusion of movement, in stop-motion, three-dimensional puppets or objects appear animate because their positions are slightly altered in each frame of film.

The idea for *Nightmare* came to Burton a long time ago, longer now than it seems, in a place he had seen in his most favourite dreams. 'I was born in Burbank, right down the street from the

Loveably grotesque sweethearts, Jack Skellington and ragdoll Sally, meet under the full moon. They star in the most bizarre animated musical comedy yet produced by Disney.

Disney studio,' Burton says, 'and like a lot of people who grew up liking to draw, I thought Disney would be a great place to do it. But the turnaround period from dream to nightmare was about as quick as it could get.'

The early eighties were the Dark Ages at Disney animation, when charmless movies were worked on endlessly with scant enthusiasm. Burton was hopelessly miscast, set to drawing a fox named Vixey in *The Fox and the Hound* that matched Sandy Duncan's voice. 'I felt they were saying, "Okay, this is Disney – this is supposed to be the most incredible gathering of artists in the world." At the same time they were saying, "Just do it this way; shut up and become like a zombie factory worker." After a while I was thinking, Is my restaurant job still available? I realised I'd rather be dead than work for five years on this movie.'

While he was suffering from massive Disney disillusionment, Burton found allies – other misfits – such as Rick Heinrichs, a sculptor, and Selick, a former art prodigy from New Jersey who had already scored a grant to make a short animated film combining cel and stop-motion animation. They appreciated Burton's brilliant doodles – skeletons with pumpkins for heads, an odd Burbankite observed on the street, a canine Frankenstein – all rendered in his spidery drawing style. 'I thought that people, especially kids, would love his work in the way they loved Charles Addams,' says Selick. 'But nobody recognised that at Disney. They thought, Oh, this is just too weird.'

Times change. Studio heads' heads roll, and new management teams take power, bringing with them fresh philosophies. Fast-forward to 1989. After the critical and financial success of his first three features – *Pee-wee's Big Adventure*, *Beetlejuice*, and *Batman* – Burton was now Hollywood's great white hope (although he had taken to dressing only in black) and was savvy enough to know he had the clout to make a movie based on his dental records. Jeffrey Katzenberg was chairman of the Walt Disney Studios and a passionate supporter of its animation division, recognising it as the studio's valuable birthright. Burton, flexing his new muscles, tried to rescue the children's story he conceived seven years before from the black hole it had fallen into at Disney.

The story, *Nightmare Before Christmas*, was written as a poem and described the parallel worlds of Halloweentown and Christmastown, where the holidays are made ready for presentation in the Real World (think Burbank). Jack, the Pumpkin King and chief architect of Halloween, is a misguided, albeit benevolent, Grinch who wreaks havoc when he kidnaps Santa and tries to take over Christmas. Burton initially drew three characters: Jack Skellington, a skeleton as delicate as a dragonfly; Zero, his ghost dog, complete with Rudolph-like light-bulb nose; and a big hill of a Santa Claus, with a paramecium-shaped, fringed beard and a circle for a face. The seminal colour sketches appeared to be either clever, visionary, or the work of someone who is seriously disturbed.

Burton had a personal affection for the holidays that encompassed an appreciation of their distinctive palettes and iconography. To even his childish artist's eye, Burbank looked bland. But dress it in Christmas lights or decorate it with Halloween symbols and it became a place touched by magic. No stranger to alienation, he felt a kinship to Jack Skellington, tortured by his own soulsickness. Since the visual imagery, story and characters of *Nightmare Before Christmas* were close to his heart, Burton had felt particularly frustrated when Disney and all the TV networks to whom he and Heinrichs originally brought the project rejected the idea of making it as a half-hour television special. Burton thought of *Nightmare* often as the years passed and it slumbered, like Sleeping Beauty, in Disney's development dormitory. And though he wasn't sure what form the prince's quickening kiss would take, he always believed his beloved story would somehow be awakened.

Since Burton had been a Disney employee when the notion of a stop-motion movie based on the holidays came to him, the studio had sole rights to pucker up to *Nightmare*. 'You signed your soul away in blood when you worked there. They owned your firstborn,' Burton explains. 'I kind of gently said, "Could I just have it back?"'

Could the Indians just have Manhattan back? 'When it comes to animation, we believe in and enjoy the notion of a monopoly,' Katzenberg has proclaimed. But Disney wanted its prodigal son to return. David Hoberman, president of Walt Disney Pictures and Touchstone, was smarting from criticism that the company's formulaic comedies were mind candy full of empty calories. It became his personal mission to persuade Burton to make *Nightmare* for Disney. 'We were looking to do something completely unique,' Hoberman says. 'This was an opportunity for us to be in business with Tim Burton and to say, "We can think outside the envelope. We can do different and unusual things."'

'Disney understood from the beginning that it was a really personal project for Tim,' says Denise Di Novi, Burton's co-producer. With the contractual promise of creative autonomy, a deal was struck to make *Nightmare Before Christmas* as Disney's first stop-motion animated feature.

Skellington Productions moved into a warehouse in San Francisco's South of Market district in July 1991, and production on *Nightmare Before Christmas* began the following October. Since then, in this place north of L.A., just a bit far away, all the goblins and ghosts go to work every day.

It is winter's end, 1993, and *Nightmare* won't be finished till late in the summer. Most of the crew of 110 men and women have been toiling in virtual isolation here for so long that members of the group have experienced everything that occurs on an extended submarine voyage: feuds, love affairs, marriages, births, illness. The process of stop-motion animation is agonisingly slow. If observing a typical movie being shot is usually as exciting as watching paint dry, then stop-motion filming would compare to the thrill-a-minute spectacle of a mountain eroding.

Headway is measured in seconds of film completed per week; the weekly goal is 70. Animators work on twenty stages at once, manipulating puppets on any one of 230 exquisitely detailed sets built for the movie. Black curtains function as dividers in the ground floor area where the makeshift stages are, creating an atmosphere like that of a fun house rigged by children in an abandoned building.

The puppet shop fills two rooms on the second floor. Puppets in various stages of undress litter wooden worktables, boxes of their snap-on facial features looking like so many Mr Potato Head parts. No one thought puppet maintenance would become such a constant chore. (No one had worked on a stop-motion movie for more than a year at a time.) Stop-motion has traditionally been used as a special effect in short experimental films, commercials, and in children's television. Gumby is a stop-motion character, as were the 1933 King Kong and, in some scenes, Robocop. The dancing California Raisins are Claymation, a stop-motion technique in which clay is sculpted and resculpted between shots.

A number of special effects and commercial production houses with stop-motion expertise, including Industrial Light and Magic, are located near San Francisco. The Bay Area offered psychic and real distance from the studio, but the veteran talent pool available was the paramount factor in locating the production there. It also happened to be where Henry Selick lived. If Selick wasn't born for the job of directing this movie, he does seem to have spent the last twenty years in training for it. After he left Disney, he worked in special effects, designing, storyboarding, and executing elaborate stop-motion sequences before landing his dream job, creating a series of station IDs for MTV. Selick became sought after as a director of stop-motion commercials and did 30 featuring the Pillsbury Doughboy.

Tacked on walls throughout the warehouse is Selick's schedule for the day; he inevitably misplaces any copy handed to him. But it would be a mistake to label him the absentminded artist. 'Henry thinks in animation frames,' Heinrichs says. He has been known to take note of a distinctively lit scene in dailies, identify another scene 25 minutes earlier in the film in which the identical

Burton's creations (Jack seen here with the Mayor of Halloweentown and a monstrous baby) were influenced by macabre illustrators Charles Addams and Edward Gorey.

effect was created, and suggest an alternative lighting scheme to avoid repetition. As much as Selick has insisted on elevating the movie's production values – lighting the scenes as beautifully as if he were working with vain movie stars, attempting sophisticated camera movements like those used in big-budget live-action films – he is admired for his restraint and sense of pace. Technological bells and whistles can dazzle an audience, he knows, or exhaust them.

Burton journeys to the warehouse every few months, but the daily crafting of the movie is overseen by Selick. Shuttling between two editing machines, he suggests a puppet be repositioned within a frame, decides a different camera angle would intensify the emotional content of a shot, then rises from his chair to act out the body moves he'd like to see a singing Wolfman mimic. He reassures, praises, challenges, never forgetting the common, Gepetto-like goal of willing puppets to life. 'What the animators do is as hard as neurosurgery,' Selick says. 'They have to almost bleed their energy into the puppet.'

It was always understood that *Nightmare* would, in every way, be a Tim Burton movie. But what is that? It is a film, his critics would say, in which details of the extraordinary production design are given more attention than the story. (The script is the work of Caroline Thompson, who also wrote Burton's *Edward Scissorhands*.)

In *Nightmare Before Christmas* design always ruled, even if serving Burton's vision meant discarding long-held conventions. 'The first rule of animation is to give your characters expressive eyes,' Burton says. 'We designed these characters that are pretty weird. The lead character doesn't have any eyeballs.' Even the film's palette proved problematic. A puppet needs to stand out against the background, but in Halloweentown almost everything and everyone is black and grey.

Burton's carefully cross-hatched illustration style, reminiscent of Ronald Searle and Edward Gorey, has been faithfully maintained. Selick describes the movie as having the look of a pop-up book, and at times it appears as if the characters are moving around in a fantastic drawing that's spookily bathed in light and shadow.

Background characters created for the movie had to be appropriately Burtonesque. A particular favorite is the corpse kid, who, with his little eyes sewn shut, is, as Heinrich puts it, 'just the right combination of cute and ghastly.' The corpse kid, like the other denizens of Halloweentown, is blissfully un-self-conscious, and such transparent vulnerability illustrates several themes that recur in Burton's films: It's okay to be different, it's okay to screw up, and it's okay to be miserable. Jack, the tortured artist, is bored with his life and plagued by an inner emptiness even success has not mollified.

Whether children will relate to such mid-life angst remains to be seen. But frequent Burton collaborator Danny Elfman does. Elfman, who temporarily walked away from his rock band, Oingo Boingo, to find fulfillment as a film composer, found writing *Nightmare*'s ten songs one of the easiest jobs he's ever had. 'I have a lot in common with Jack,' he says. 'I made demos of all the songs, but I felt with Jack's character I had nailed it, and no one else would be able to do a better job than I had.' Elfman convinced Burton to let him be Jack's singing voice. (Chris Sarandon provided Jack's speaking voice, and Catherine O'Hara is Sally, Jack's rag doll love interest.)

Questions remain at the end of the day. Will children go for the ghouls, or will they be scared away? Will Evil Scientist dolls with heads that open to reveal their gooky brains be a hot Christmas item for children with a finely tuned taste for the macabre? 'I hope it goes out and makes a fortune,' says Hoberman. 'If it does – great. If it doesn't, that doesn't negate the validity of the process.' The budget of *Nightmare* was considerably less than that of a Disney animated blockbuster, so it won't have to earn *Aladdin*-size grosses to satisfy the studio.

Burton is already satisfied: 'People will look at the movie and go, "Oh, this is really great," and a lot of stop-motion will be done, and some of it will be really great. Some will be really bad. Too much will be done, and then we'll put a pillow over it and smother it for another 30 years, and then it will come up again. Cycle of life, you know?'

ANIMATED DREAMS

by Leslie Felperin

As far as the general public is concerned, animation directors barely exist, while producers get all the glory – for instance, everyone assumed for years that Walt Disney was solely responsible for the studio's string of hits. Today, independent animation directors may be recognised as *auteurs*, but, within the Hollywood mainstream, directors are still seen as only a few steps up the food chain from inkers and painters.

In keeping with the tradition, Disney is marketing its latest feature as *Tim Burton's The Nightmare Before Christmas*. But though the film is based on a poem and treatment Burton wrote while employed at Disney in the early eighties (and therefore is still under the studio's copyright control), it was shaped as much by the interpretation of its director, Henry Selick, as *Apocalypse Now* was by Coppola's reading of *Heart of Darkness*. It was Selick who put flesh on Burton's original, literally, skeletal concept.

Skinnier than Kate Moss, the hero of *The Nightmare Before Christmas*, Jack Skellington, is the king of Halloweentown, populated by a freakish cast that could have made Tod Browning shudder. Stumbling across Christmastown by accident, Jack decides to try his hand at a different kind of holiday. Halloweentown swings into action, making teddy bears with teeth and other ghoulish Christmas presents, and arranges for Kris Kringle to be Santa-napped. All goes predictably wrong as the presents produce tears instead of joy and Santa falls into the hands of malevolent gambling-man Oogie Boogie. Assisted by his fetching rag-doll girlfriend Sally and his ghost dog Zero (a gem-nosed scene-stealer), Jack tries to set things right.

Strongly evocative, in the familiar dark nightshades of Burton's visual signature, the film marks a departure for Disney. Apart from the disastrous experiment in the macabre of *The Black Cauldron* (1985), the studio hasn't made anything as creepily sinister as this since Pinocchio visited Pleasure Island and turned into a donkey. Moreover, the use of stop-motion or three-dimensional animation has traditionally been the province of cheap children's television or of avant-gardists like Jan Svankmajer and the Brothers Quay.

After establishing a studio in San Francisco, Selick was given the difficult brief of trying to remain true to Burton's original murky concept while keeping the film anodyne enough for the 'suits' at co-financers Disney. The result is a film often visually spectacular but not as crisply structured as it could be. For instance, the climax, when the children in the beautifully skewed 'real world' open their presents, is generally hilarious, but over far too quickly. Nor do regular Burton collaborator Danny Elfman's lugubrious songs help, often reminiscent of Kurt Weill on a bad cocktail of Mogadon and Prozac. Nonetheless, after a slow start the film eventually took a respectable $60 million in the US.

Modest and professionally circumspect, Selick is pragmatic about being eclipsed by his star producer. After all, they have been friends since they served their apprenticeship together at Disney in the early eighties. Like Burton, Selick started his animation career at CalArts in Jules Engel's experimental animation programme. His early films – for instance, *Phases* (1978) and *Seepage* (1981) – with their mix of techniques and tendency towards abstraction, bear witness to this training.

After leaving Disney in disgust at having had to draw one too many 'cute foxes', Selick moonlighted doing short animated films for MTV and *Sesame Street* together with some second-unit directing and storyboarding for live-action films. In 1989 he made *Slow Bob in the Lower*

Dimensions, a powerful mixture of pixilation and animation for MTV, as technically flawless as it is narratively obscure, which returned him to a full-time career in animation. Selick has a remarkable eye for imagery, and is gifted with an impressive command of the medium coupled with a perfectionist streak. If his next project, *James and the Giant Peach*, is successful, he may finally break out of the anonymity ghetto.

How much of your training with Jules Engel in experimental animation filters into your current work as a mainstream director?

I'm on the fence here. I'm definitely working in commercial films – the budgets are high enough to mean that I have to respect the fact that we want the films to pay for themselves so we can make more – but the audience is more open than Hollywood imagines. So I'm always trying to put in more than an audience can handle: new imagery, new techniques, even pushing novel storylines. The commercial rule for me is, the stranger the imagery, the straighter the story. You can't bend it

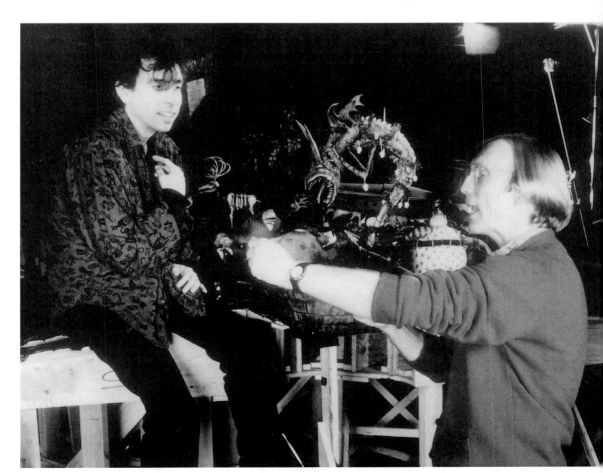

Burton with Henry Selick, friend and former Disney animator. While Burton worked on **Batman Returns** *and* **Ed Wood,** *Selick brought* **The Nightmare Before Christmas** *to life.*

Adapted from an illustrated poem by Burton, The Nightmare Before Christmas *recalled* Vincent, *while its imagery foreshadowed his book,* The Melancholy Death of Oyster Boy.

too much. In my own films, I've often used very realistic images and very disjointed storylines because I'm more interested in tone poems than in tight little stories. But in the films I'm doing now I like to have understandable stories so I can go further on the visual side.

Are you pleased with The Nightmare Before Christmas?

The flaws are still painful but what's good about it is excellent. I had an amazing group of people to work with including some fine British animators – Paul Berry, whose *The Sandman* was nominated for an Academy Award, and Loyd Price, among others. It was very gratifying not to have the typical Disney structure. Instead, there was Tim Burton – an 800-pound gorilla with creative control – who basically passed that creative control to me for most of the project while he was off making *Batman Returns* and *Ed Wood*. Tim is that lone filmmaker who does very unusual films, every one of which has been successful. Even with their story flaws and rhythm flaws, what's good in his films is so brilliant that the audience always responds.

The film has been marketed as **Tim Burton's The Nightmare Before Christmas,** *but you're the director. What do you think is distinctively yours about the film?*
It's as though he laid the egg, but I sat on it and hatched it, so it came out looking a bit like both of us. He wasn't involved in a hands-on way, but his hand is in it. It was my job in a way to make it look like a 'Tim Burton film', which is not so different from my own films. We can collaborate because we often think of the same solution to a problem. It's why we hit it off at Disney – we were not having fun drawing cute foxes and little animals. But I would wager that in *The Nightmare Before Christmas* most of the lines you laugh at are mine. I did most sequences like the battle, or any action sequences – Tim always gives live action to a second-unit director. Every shot of the movie is something I looked at through a camera and composed.

I don't want to take away from Tim, but he was not here in San Francisco when we made it. He came up five times over two years, and spent no more than eight or ten days here in total. It's more like he wrote a children's book and gave it to us and we went from there. But the bottom line was that Tim Burton's name before the title was going to bring in more people than mine would.

Nightmare *centres on three different worlds: those of Halloweentown, Christmastown and the 'real world'. You have the same contrast of worlds in one of your earlier films,* **Slow Bob in the Lower Dimensions.** *Is this a concern of yours?*
It's pure coincidence – in fact, the idea of different holiday worlds came from Tim. But most of my other personal work, including several short films, is about the collision of worlds. For example, a nine-minute film I made in 1981, *Seepage*, depicts stop-motion animated life-size figures by a pool who experience a collision between their world and an imaginary world they speak of.

What kind of visual influences went into the design of **Nightmare Before Christmas** *apart from Tim Burton's original drawings? Did you draw on the gothic tradition for ways of expressing nightmarishness?*
I drew on some of my favourite films, including *The Night of the Hunter*, the only Hollywood feature Charles Laughton directed. It was a low-budget film but it had a lot of high-contrast imagery, a fairy-tale quality. Then there were illustrators who were Tim's inspirations, including Edward Gorey and Charles Addams. We tried to put a lot of Gorey-type textures on our sets.

That sort of knobbly quality . . .
Yes, though the set for Christmastown was more Dr Seuss inspired, much softer, rounder, a fluffy look.

Were you inspired by any other artists?
Rick Heinrichs was the visual consultant on the film – he has worked with Tim on every film Tim has made, he's Tim's hidden partner. He exposed us to a Russian animator, one of the earliest . . . Starevich. We looked at Starevich's films not so much for style but because he would use real material, real cloth, hair, insects, things that shudder and shake and pixilate and catch your attention needlessly that most animators would avoid. It loosened us up a little.

Anyone else?
A lot of painters have affected me – for instance Francis Bacon, and some of Kandinsky's work before he went abstract. He would do these Russian fables, quite beautiful, fairy-tale paintings, very simple with colour on what he wants, light on what he wants, then the rest just disappears into a medium ground. Also the Polish animator and poster designer Jan Lenica crept in.

Tim Burton — A Child's Garden of Nightmares

I know that Caroline Thompson wrote the script, but you must have had a big influence on it.

There are very few final lines of dialogue in the movie that are Caroline's. We worked with her, but she's off on other films and we were constantly rewriting, reconfiguring, developing the film visually. I'd like to do a silent movie, quite honestly, because especially in stop-motion I think the characters could tell the story quite well without any dialogue.

To return to nightmares and the gothic, do you think animation is especially good at expressing these?

I think animation lends itself to illustrating dreams of any sort. As a kid I was deeply impressed by the 'Night on the Bare Mountain' sequence from *Fantasia*. That felt like nightmare and dreams to me, and was very powerful. Another important influence was Lotte Reiniger. I saw a lot of her films as a kid on a local television station. All her films are primarily silhouettes. They are very dreamlike, you have to use a lot of imagination to make them work. These two influences plugged into a kind of dream imagery where you don't fill in all the blanks, just as you'll get isolated figures in limbo in dreams, moving at unnatural speeds, usually in slow motion but sometimes faster, falling, exaggeration.

How did that feed into the design of the nightmare landscape in the film?

One of our criteria was to make the Halloween characters look really scary, though they weren't bad people except for Oogie Boogie, and even with him it was just his nature to be voracious. When Tim was a kid he watched a lot of films like the original *Frankenstein* or *The Creature from the Black Lagoon*. Those creatures weren't inherently bad, they were just misunderstood and people were terrified of them and tried to destroy them. Tim had sympathy for them and it's something he wanted to carry through to the denizens of Halloweentown .

One thing that has caused controversy is that Oogie Bogie, the only malevolent character, has an 'obviously' black voice attached to him. How do you respond to this criticism?

We did consider this. In some parts of the world, like in Alabama where my mother is from, a 'boogie man' is a monstrous black person, so it had racial connotations. It really came from Betty Boop cartoons though, which would have Cab Calloway, the jazz band leader and a great singer, serve as the basis of what they would call 'specialty numbers'. He would dance his inimitable jazz dance and sing 'Minnie the Moocher' or 'Old Man of the Mountain', and they would rotoscope him, trace him, turn him into a cartoon character, often transforming him into an animal, like a walrus. I think those are some of the most inventive moments in cartoon history, in no way racist, even though he was sometimes a villain.

It's not completely resolved in myself – it's controversial and I've got a slight twinge of guilt. But in the end we went with Ken Page, who is a black singer, because he was the best guy to sing the song. He had no problem with it.

There has been a lot of publicity about animation experiencing a renaissance, with Disney leading the way. Do you think that's the case?

It really is happening. *This* is the golden age of animation – it wasn't 1939-41. There's far more production going on, there are more independent animators, though it's not easy for everyone. Disney wants to do everything in-house and to gobble up the rest of the world. They want to own anyone who is doing great animation. I think they have a deal with the Aardman Studio. I hope they leave them alone and let them do what they do so well, though I wouldn't trust them to do so. They are also doing a film with Pixar [*Toy Story*], which is a company that does computer films with John Lasseter. They've been very hard on them, insisting on making things very obvious and working them over and over. They're doing incredibly well with this semi-formulaic approach to film-making, trying to reach the largest audience.

For independents it's still very tough. There's no equivalent in the US of Channel 4 or the BBC for funding and showing short films. There's MTV, which will pay a little bit of money for short pieces – that's what got my own career back on track. All kinds of techniques are being used - ancient ones like the ones we use combined with computer, pure computer, independents using wire, sand and so on. It's a good time but it's not easy, and it never will be unless you want to do Disney animation and that's who you work for.

Did you break new ground technically with Nightmare?
We took an old technique and did the highest-quality stop-motion that has ever been done for that many minutes. I think we moved stop-motion up to a high level of performance in timing, lighting and computer-aided camera moves. We made it a serious contender rather than things that look like toys on a table top with two glaring lights.

What are you working on now?
A Roald Dahl children's book called *James and the Giant Peach*, for Skellington Productions [with Tim Burton as executive producer], a company I set up for the last one. We're casting the part of James at the moment. The Disney people didn't get it at first, it's not their type of film, but then neither was *The Nightmare Before Christmas*. It's going to start live and then everything turns into stop-motion. Then the boy emerges, live again in New York, a drearier New York, flatter than he expected. Then there will be a combination of animation of the giant bugs who live in the peach emerging and interacting with the live world.

It sounds a little like Jan Svankmajer's features Alice *and* Faust. *There's a European surrealist sensibility in both Svankmajer and Dahl that seems related to the visual tone of* Nightmare.
When I went to work at Disney you had to do tests to get a job, and everyone would say, 'That's kind of European.' They didn't mean it as a compliment. There is that strong puppet tradition in eastern Europe, which was an influence on me. And I love Svankmajer's *Alice* – I'd like to see everything the guy has done.

The live world James starts to live in should be very stilted and lifeless. It will look like sets, like theatre work, and when James enters the peach, he transforms into a puppet. It's almost as though the live world is flatter. There was a book written around the turn of the century called *Flatlanders* that I read as a kid and it has stuck with me. I've always loved moving from dimension to dimension – when we go into the animated world things will just fall away into a more rich dimensional world, more alive than the live world.

Svankmajer's Faust *has just opened in London and there have already been articles comparing it to* Nightmare.
Sure, sure. Of course, he's the pure artist and we're the Hollywood schlockmeisters, right?

TIM BURTON'S THE NIGHTMARE BEFORE CHRISTMAS

review by Kim Newman

Under the direction of Jack Skellington the Pumpkin King, the people of Halloweentown spend the whole year planning the tricks and frights they unleash on the world each October 31st. After yet another successful Halloween, Jack feels trapped in a rut. Wandering into a forest and through a door in a tree, Jack comes upon Christmastown, which is ruled by Santa Claus, and is struck by the notion of taking over this other holiday. Sally, a rag doll abused by her Frankensteinian creator, loves Jack and worries that his ambitions will lead to disaster. Jack despatches Lock, Shock and Barrel, Halloween's prominent trick or treaters, to kidnap Santa Claus, and orders Sally's creator to make a team of reindeer to pull a coffin-shaped sleigh. The rest of the townsfolk try to make Christmas presents, but are unable to make anything that isn't scary. Lock, Shock and Barrel, after mistakenly kidnapping the Easter Bunny, snatch Santa and, against Jack's orders, turn him over to Oogie Boogie, a malevolent creature who is too extreme even for Halloweentown.

Sally whips up a fog on Christmas Eve to prevent Jack's sleigh taking off, but Jack's ghost dog Zero guides the team with his glowing nose. Jack distributes presents to children, who are terrified by various unleashed creatures, prompting the army to try to blast the Santa impersonator out of the sky. Realising his error, Jack returns to Halloweentown, defeats Oogie Boogie and releases Santa, who sets things right on Earth. Jack, having learned his lesson, admits that he reciprocates Sally's love.

This animated feature is billed as *Tim Burton's The Nightmare Before Christmas*, although co-producer Burton neither directed nor wrote it. He did, however, originate the characters and story, which date back to the period when he was an animator in the Disney galleys, toiling on *The Fox and the Hound* and discomforting the management with the shorts *Vincent* and *Frankenweenie*. It is to these underrated (and underseen) films that the current feature is closest in animation style and a gentle macabre feel, far more benevolent than that of such obvious influences as Charles Addams and Edward Gorey. Through the work of Henry Selick and writers Michael McDowell (of *Beetlejuice*) and Caroline Thompson (of *Edward Scissorhands*), this feels like another of Burton's veiled experiments in autobiography (cf *Edward Scissorhands*, *Ed Wood*), as it deals with the frustrations of a one-note creator who wants to break out and do something else, only to learn that he should stick with what he does best.

Considered 'risky' because of its 'darkness', *Nightmare* is actually far less unsettling in its implications than such 'unproblematic' Disneys as *The Little Mermaid* (message: it's all right to be a bitch if you're cute and privileged) or *The Lion King* (alpha males have a divine right to rule the jungle). Halloweentown does have its genuine nasties, like the infantile Frankenstein who created Sally, and the bag-of-worms Boogie Oogie (seemingly related to the cartoon incarnation of Cab Calloway who once co-starred with Betty Boop). But most of its residents – from the two-faced mayor through sundry werewolves and vampires to uncategorisable Burton creations with all-round mouths or too many eyes – are as mushy-hearted and eager to please as the wistful skull-on-a-stick Jack. Santa Claus, understandably cross for most of the film, seems far more a tyrant than the Pumpkin King and, regardless of the makers' stated or unconscious intentions, most audiences will derive far more pleasure from the hilarious gag sequences of Jack's gruesome Christmas presents terrorising a cross-section of multi-racial children than they will get from the perfunctory follow-up scenes showing Santa putting things right.

While the riotous Nightmare Before Christmas *influenced hits like* Toy Story, *Hollywood would reject painstaking stop-motion techniques in favour of CGI effects.*

The grotesques in Burton's films are harmless and usually pathetically lovelorn, save for those bloated freaks (Penguin, Joker, Oogie Boogie) whose malevolence keeps the plot boiling. If his slight distance means that *Nightmare* seems like a film *about* rather than *by* Tim Burton, there are also signs that the collaborators, gaining the upper hand, have flattened out his tendency to all-over-the-show plotting and simplified his sometimes over-fussy designs. The streak of psychotic knowingness that will presumably overflow in the forthcoming *Ed Wood* is represented not only in an evocation of Ray Bradbury and *Mad Monster Party*, but in adapting the plot of the well-remembered cult disaster *Santa Claus Conquers the Martians*. Although a fragile conceit, *The Nightmare Before Christmas* is certainly more worthy of your attention than any Disney 2-D cartoon since *Basil – The Great Mouse Detective*, and has a rich, inventive score by Danny Elfman (who also provides Jack's singing voice), which shows just how inadequate the trite pseudo-Broadway muzak of Menken, Ashman and Rice has become.

THE WOOD, THE BAD, AND THE UGLY

by John Clark

The curtains part and out walks Johnny Depp. He's wearing high heels, black nylons, a blue dress, a beige corset, a pink blouse, and red lipstick. His biceps are tattooed, the left reading PATTY SUE, the right WINONA FOREVER. He looks pretty hot. 'Ruff!' he barks at onlookers. 'Ruff! Ruff!' It's not an attack dog's bark. Rather, it's a poodle's. Depp continues on to what can only be described as the smoking circle, where cast members of *Ed Wood*, filming in a warehouse in West Los Angeles, can stretch out and have a cigarette. The place looks like a firetrap. Pigeons roost in the rafters, sometimes screwing up takes. The air would probably drop one of those singing canaries they send down mine shafts. It can get very hot. But at least it's home. The crew has spent much of this 72-day shoot bouncing from one location to the next, most of them in the scummiest parts of Hollywood, and that's saying a lot. It is in these places that Ed Wood, arguably the worst director in the history of the medium, lived and worked during the forties and fifties.

Today they are shooting reenactments from his best-known film, *Plan 9 from Outer Space*, which is about aliens who bring earthly corpses back to life. The corpses are Wood regulars Tor Johnson (played by Jim Myers, aka George 'the Animal' Steele), a former wrestler so huge he was famed for breaking hotel toilet seats; and Vampira (model Lisa Marie), a local late-night horror-show hostess who had a seventeen-inch waist, fifties-style 'headlights', and skin that can only be described as dead. They recite – or rather Steele recites, since Vampira was too proud to utter this stilted dialogue – the original movie's language word for word in a deliberately bogus-looking graveyard. Behind an ancient camera supposedly filming this scene is Depp. He's giving direction through a megaphone. His manner is spectacularly earnest – a game-show host's, as one cast member puts it.

And behind this scene is none other than Tim Burton, director of *Pee-wee's Big Adventure, Beetlejuice, Edward Scissorhands,* and, of course, the hugely successful *Batman* movies. He's wearing a baggy brown suit and black Dr Martens and sporting his trademark rat's-nest hair. As Burton stares animatedly into the monitor, laughing in that private way exhibited by obsessives, it becomes clear that there's a family resemblance between one of the most successful moviemakers in Hollywood and one of the least. It's like Ed Wood said about the resemblance between Bela Lugosi and the chiropractor who doubled for him in *Plan 9* after the star's death, 'It's uncanny. The whole thing is uncanny.'

'It's uncanny' has become one of the crew's favourite lines. While it may in some weird way be applicable to Wood and Burton, it's ludicrous when applied to Lugosi and his double, 'Dr Tom' Mason. Dr. Tom was taller and younger than Lugosi. This is plainly evident even though Dr Tom stalks through *Plan 9* with a cape drawn across the lower part of his face. Only someone as blind as Wood wouldn't have noticed or would have chosen to ignore it. His movies are full of such howlers. According to a colleague, one of his favourite expressions was 'dramatic licence'.

In Angora sweater and otherwise all-male attire, Ed Wood's transvestism was as half-assed as his movies. Note the vintage horror movie posters behind Johnny Depp.

Tim Burton — A Child's Garden of Nightmares

The irony of *Ed Wood* is that it takes considerable licence with Wood's life, in search of a larger truth, or truths – although certainly the facts of his life are large enough. Consider: Wood was a decorated World War II veteran who stormed enemy beaches while wearing women's panties under his uniform. During one such skirmish, his mouth was caved in by a rifle butt, necessitating false teeth. After the war and a stint as a geek and half man-half woman in a travelling circus, he went to Hollywood. There he wrote, acted in, or directed various Grade Z plays, revues, and films until his 'break-out' movie, *Glen or Glenda*, which is based on the real-life experiences of transsexual Christine Jorgensen. In Wood's hands, however, it became a bizarre plea for understanding of his own transvestism (he particularly favoured angora sweaters). It stars Wood himself, in and out of drag, and his then girlfriend, Dolores Fuller, acting (if that's the right word) in scenes that no doubt were uncomfortably close to home.

Glen or Glenda also features Lugosi, an actor who came to figure prominently in Wood's life and had been an idol of his since Wood was a child. But Lugosi was no longer the star of Wood's youth. By the fifties his career essentially was over and he was a morphine addict. Typically, Wood chose to overlook these facts, and the two of them formed a kind of symbiotic relationship. Lugosi's 'star power' secured shoestring financing for Wood's pictures, and Wood's pictures supplied Lugosi with work. In addition to *Glen or Glenda*, he appeared in Wood's most conventionally coherent movie, *Bride of the Monster*, and unrelated footage taken of him smelling a flower and bursting into tears was used in *Plan 9*. Wood promoted *Plan 9* as Lugosi's last appearance and sold the idea to his landlord, who thought he could use the profits to finance a cycle of religious films. So, in a sense, Wood was dancing with Lugosi even after his death.

Lugosi (played by Martin Landau in *Ed Wood*), Fuller (Sarah Jessica Parker), Tor, and Vampira weren't the only members of Wood's troupe. There was Criswell (Jeffrey Jones), the charlatan psychic who in *Plan 9* utters the immortal lines, 'We are all interested in the future – for that is where you and I are going to spend the rest of our lives'; John 'Bunny' Breckinridge (Bill Murray), fey alien ruler in *Plan 9* and reputed transsexual wannabe; Wood's wife, Kathy (Patricia Arquette), seemingly the straightest person in all of this; Loretta King (Juliet Landau, Martin's daughter), the *Bride of the Monster* starlet who allegedly would not take fluids, not even water; and a whole slew of down-on-their-luck contract players and hangers-on.

Most of these people inhabit the periphery of *Ed Wood*. If the movie is 'about' anything, it's about the relationship between Wood and Lugosi. It ends with Lugosi's posthumous appearance in *Plan 9* and does not follow Wood's long decline into alcoholism and pornographic writing. He died, broke and broken, in 1978 at the age of 54. Though the movie takes liberties with the events it does cover, what really happened is open to debate. The only 'history', aside from several documentaries, is Rudolph Grey's *Nightmare of Ecstasy: The Life and Art of Edward D. Wood, Jr.*, published in 1992. In it the surviving members of Wood's troupe talk without any authorial interference (although there is a splendid filmography in the back), resulting in contradiction and confusion. Was Wood a hustler or a dreamer? Were *Plan 9*'s flying saucers made out of pie tins, paper plates, hubcaps, or flying saucer models?

Reaching into this mess, and doing a lot of research of their own, particularly about Lugosi, were two young screenwriters, Scott Alexander and Larry Karaszewski, whose previous credits are the *Problem Child* movies. They took the idea of an Ed Wood movie to Michael Lehmann, director of *Hudson Hawk* and *Heathers*.

'Part of the joke with Scott and Larry was: Wouldn't it be funny for the guys who wrote *Problem Child* and the guy who made *Hudson Hawk* to make a movie about Ed Wood, because our movies had also been called the worst movies of all time,' says Lehmann. 'We looked at his work

Phoney psychic Criswell (Jeffrey Jones), bizarre Ed Wood regular, acts as the film's narrator in a pastiche of Wood's **Night of the Ghouls.**

and said, "Here is a committed artist. He's terrible, his movies are terrible, but all the other aspects of his endeavour were carried out the way a committed artist would carry them out. What if someone had the drive and ego of Orson Welles and none of the talent?'"

Figuring he had to find people with clout and taste, Lehmann brought the idea to Denise Di Novi, who had produced *Heathers* and was partnered with Tim Burton. She passed it along to Burton. His reaction was almost visceral: Rather than produce it or see someone else make it, he wanted to direct it himself. Stories then began to circulate that he muscled Lehmann off the project. Not so, say Di Novi and Lehmann, who was given an executive producer credit.

'Somewhere during the treatment process, I found the script for *Airheads*,' says Lehmann. 'So when we presented *Ed Wood* to Denise and Tim, we really didn't have a game plan. Tim read the treatment and flipped. He said he really wanted to do the movie, and I was committed to *Airheads*.'

Burton responded to the same things Lehmann had in the material, and a few others beside. 'When I was a child and saw *Plan 9*,' Burton says, 'it . . . stood out. I lived near a cemetery near the Burbank airport and there was a reference in the movie to the Burbank airport and cemetery. It was very real to me because it was taking place in houses that were like the houses I lived in.'

He never thought Wood's movies were bad. 'I've always felt that if anybody shows a style and their own belief, then it's not a bad movie.' And he didn't have a problem with the contradictory source material either. In fact he embraced it. 'It says more about the nature of memory and how we all perceive things,' he says. 'It reminds me of my own memory, which is somewhat revisionist and foggy. I can definitely relate to that kind of denial and reinvention. I get the impression – and I don't mean this disrespectfully, because I feel this way myself – that everybody [in *Nightmare of Ecstasy*] is a little out of it.'

In putting together the final script, the screenwriters decided to focus on the relationship between Wood and Lugosi, because, says Alexander, 'we knew Tim could relate to that. He felt the same way about Vincent Price.' Burton had idolised Price for years, using him as a mad scientist in

Dolores Fuller offers cross-dresser Ed Wood her pink Angora sweater in his film Glen or Glenda, *replicated by Johnny Depp and Sarah Jessica Parker in Tim Burton's* Ed Wood.

Edward Scissorhands and directing an animated short about him. As for whether he saw himself and Price in Wood and Lugosi, Burton says, 'I'd say 50 to 75 per cent of it had to do with that.' Sadly, Price died during the production.

Before production could begin, however, Burton had a major obstacle to overcome, one he had in fact created himself. He had decided to shoot *Ed Wood* in black and white.

'I actually resisted it for a long time,' he says. 'But any period movie I see, especially movies that take place in Hollywood, I just don't like the way they look in colour.'

This line of reasoning didn't wash with Columbia, which had green-lit the project. The studio claimed it couldn't sell a black and white picture in ancillary markets (foreign, video, etc.). As a compromise, it was suggested that Burton shoot in black and white on colour stock.

'I went through that ten years ago on *Frankenweenie*,' Burton says. 'It looks like shit. If you're going to make a decision, make a decision. You don't hedge it. There's enough of that.'

Columbia put the project into turnaround. Burton responded by dropping out of *Mary Reilly*, a production he had in development there. Although he won't say it in so many words, he was irritated by Columbia's lack of respect and enthusiasm for *Ed Wood* and, by implication, for his instincts as a filmmaker.

Remember, this is the guy who has never made a bomb. 'It's amazing to me,' says Lehmann, 'that Tim, with his sensibility, has been so successful in Hollywood, because he could just as easily have ended up like Ed Wood.'

Apparently the folks at Disney didn't have such doubts. They snapped up the project, although some observers felt they were more interested in securing Burton's long-term services than in *Ed Wood*. Negotiations did go on during production, with not only Burton's future movies on the table but theme park-related issues as well. After reportedly nearly signing on several occasions, Burton ended up returning to Warner Bros., which had produced his *Batman* movies. Whether this dampens Disney's enthusiasm for *Ed Wood* remains to be seen. It's going to have trouble enough trying to market the movie as it is. For one thing, the film doesn't have a strong narrative – a characteristic of all of Burton's movies and a continual source of criticism.

'It's like a given now,' he says. 'Why even mention it anymore? Things either work or they don't. This movie is like the book [*Nightmare of Ecstasy*]. It's like someone's memory of a life. It just kind of happens and you try to give it shape. I find that much more realistic in terms of the way I perceive, the way I remember things, the way life is for me.'

It was Johnny Depp's job to flesh out – and dress up – 'someone's memory of a life'. And since accounts of Wood's behaviour are so contradictory, Depp pretty much had a free hand. His 'game-show host' interpretation of Wood – easily the broadest, most theatrical thing Depp has ever done – was inspired not by the memories of Kathy Wood or Dolores Fuller but by . . . Andy Hardy.

'Tim would say things like, "Andy Hardy, Andy Hardy," says Depp. 'So I saw some Andy Hardy stuff. I had a couple of other things that spiced it up a bit. I came to him and I said, "Listen, Andy Hardy, but look: Ronald Reagan." And Tim went, "Wizard of Oz or Casey Kasem." "Yeah, yeah, yeah." We just boiled up this stew and shot it.'

'It was important to find someone good-looking to play Ed,' says Alexander. 'We didn't want him to be laughable in drag. Johnny walks like a truck driver. There's nothing swishy about it.'

'He looked so good in drag, it upset me,' says Sarah Jessica Parker. 'He's beautiful to begin with as a man, and then you put him in drag and he looks way better than I did. Beautiful legs.'

Asked about it, Depp says, 'It doesn't feel weird at all. In fact it's spookily comfortable. The only time it felt weird was when I had to do a striptease.' That's when attention was focused below the belt. 'They had to mash things up. But I'm getting better at walking in heels.'

Depp passed the acid test one day when they were shooting exteriors in Hollywood. Kathy Wood, who was aware of the production but had no real involvement in it, was on her way home from shopping when she stumbled across the set. After identifying herself and staying in the background, she was finally ushered onto the set to meet some of the principals.

'It was a bad drag day,' says Patricia Arquette. 'It was one of those days when it was raining and your lipstick is smudged and your mascara is smeared, so I think Johnny was nervous. But she loved Johnny. She gave him Eddie's wallet with his phone book and everything.'

'I don't know what prompted me to do it,' says Kathy, who has very few things of Ed's left. 'But I just felt Eddie would have wanted that.'

As the script would have it, and as Kathy verifies, Ed's dressing up didn't bother her. Although she was initially taken aback, she says, 'I knew the real Eddie, and that's why I loved him.' But it's also true, contrary to what the script says, that Wood didn't do much parading around in public. 'He didn't flaunt it,' she says. 'Once in a while on a set he put on a sweater or something like that, but he didn't make a point of it. It wasn't offensive like some of the things you see nowadays.'

Actually, Wood might be considered one of the patron saints of some of the things you see nowadays. His outrageousness certainly accounts for some of his following. At a recent screening of his films in Hollywood, one 'woman' was heard to remark to a male friend, apropos of the undergarments Wood wore as a Marine, 'I was in the Army eleven years. Special Forces. It hasn't changed.'

For Burton, Wood's cross-dressing plays into the preoccupation with masks and disguises so evident in his *Batman* movies. 'Everybody has many aspects to their personality, and I think we live in a culture where it remains hidden a lot of the time,' he says. 'I always felt that this society's pressures are to keep you in the closet. Masks can be liberating. By covering up, it allows people to be freer. That's why I always loved Halloween, because you look at people and you don't know anything about them, but if you look at them in their costumes, they're actually very telling.'

Aside from Wood, the most prominent masked figure is Vampira, with her pancake makeup, cinched waist, artificial fingernails, and black wig. The get-up was torture for Lisa Marie, whose first film this is and who also happens to be Burton's girlfriend. Nevertheless she got into the role. She lunched and shopped with the real Vampira, Maila Nurmi, and she walked around the house dressed like a ghoul – among other activities.

'As a vampire, you get to do a lot of things,' she says. 'Have you ever sucked blood from one of your lovers? You should try it. Just a little taste. You'll never go back.' She says her boyfriend loved it.

Nurmi, apparently, didn't go quite as far with the character. She well understood its darker underpinnings without trafficking in them. Although forever linked in fans' minds with Wood, she was around only during the *Plan 9* period. However, like Wood, she has a following.

'Vampira fans were young men who were very effete, if not effeminate,' Nurmi says. 'And they were tall and anorexic and would dye their hair black and would wear white makeup and black clothing. I think they were Vampira in their fantasy. I don't think they were men, really. They were males who were a little androgynous, and if they were women, that's who they would be.'

Burton rehearses a scene with Johnny Depp and Sarah Jessica Parker. Though shot in the low-rent sector of Hollywood that Ed Wood inhabited, the film omits his final decline.

She has no idea how well Lisa Marie will do with the role, but she does have definite ideas about the script's dialogue: 'They talk like Beavis and Butt-head. They have Bela, who never used a four-letter word, talking like Howard Stern. They have me talking like a nineties bimbo.'

And they have Kathy Wood knitting! 'I don't know where they dreamed that up,' Kathy says, laughing. Although she was anything but a Doris Day character, she does say, 'I was naive and gauche. I didn't know anything about Hollywood. I was a secretary and kept on being a secretary all the time Eddie and I were married. I was out of my element, I guess. Once you met Eddie, you couldn't resist him. All his actresses fell in love with him. He was that kind of guy.'

She's thrilled to have someone as 'pretty and glamorous' as Arquette playing her. She even gave her a zirconia ring Eddie had given her. Arquette, for her part, internalised what the script told her to be. She became the little housewife, knitting and doing spring-cleaning. She definitely connects with Kathy's acceptance of her husband's transvestism.

'When you find somebody you really love and that's the person for you, they're bound to have flaws,' Arquette says. 'But if their worst fault is that they like to wear a skirt now and then, that's okay.'

While Nurmi and Kathy are more or less accepting of their characters, Bela Lugosi's son, Bela, Jr., who practices law in Los Angeles, is unhappy with how his father is depicted. 'I read enough of the script to decide he wasn't portrayed either accurately or respectfully, and so I stopped reading,' he says. He doesn't want to discuss the matter further, although he is interested in how one gets in touch with Disney.

Lugosi is no doubt upset by the four-letter tirades that arise whenever someone mentions the name of his father's rival, Boris Karloff, and by scenes of drug taking and lecherousness. Martin Landau did a lot of homework to portray Lugosi and defends this interpretation. He is not unsympathetic to Lugosi – he even gives points to him for being a good, if theatrical, actor. Landau, in turn, gives a theatrical performance, though he insists it's not strictly an imitative one. More important than the approach, at least to Burton, is the weight Landau gives the role.

'Martin, I think, has had the kind of career that he understands this stuff completely,' Burton says. 'You just look at everything he's done – working with Hitchcock and doing a guest spot on *Gilligan's Island*.'

Dolores Fuller is also upset about the movie, although it's hard to see why: She comes off as relatively normal. Fuller left Wood after *Bride of the Monster* premiered, fed up with being associated with a bunch of 'freaks'. Though the movie doesn't cover this, she went on to become a successful songwriter (for Elvis Presley, among others) and manager (for Tanya Tucker). When reached in Las Vegas, she and her husband, Philip Chamberlin, said their lawyer was 'interfacing' with Disney's legal department, but that she would comment on the distortions in the script when the dust settled. When the dust settled, they said she would comment only on condition that any interfacing with Disney not be mentioned. When contacted a third time, Chamberlin said, in reference to questions of a settlement, 'Contract? What contract?' Disney had no comment.

The worst that can be said about the depiction of Fuller in the movie is that she's a bit of a stiff, particularly as an actress. 'Dolores Fuller is probably – and I don't think arguably – the worst actress I've ever seen,' says Landau.

This presented a problem for Sarah Jessica Parker. Being deliberately bad is not easy. 'I watched *Glen or Glenda* a lot,' says Parker. 'I watched how bad she was over and over again and then in doing it I just didn't comment on it. She was totally self-conscious. Totally uncomfortable in front of the camera, totally tight and not creative at all. Nothing instinctual about her. It was great fun, I have to say.'

Burton has a lot of affection for these characters, and if an early test screening is any indication, it shows. The movie was described by one insider as funny and sweet, perhaps closest in feeling and tone to *Edward Scissorhands*. 'There was just something that struck me about those people,' Burton says. 'A weird naivete. And there's something I respond to in people who have gone through lots of things and still have a certain belief.'

No one has gone through more than Kathy Wood. She endured her husband's long descent, and, in the fifteen years since his death, she's basically been destitute, living on welfare, social security, etc. (Ed was a lousy money manager, and the rights to his movies are nearly impossible to determine.) She's had a couple of heart attacks. She's had open-heart surgery. She didn't even know that a movie about Ed was being made until a neighbour apprised her of it. She secured a lawyer, Robert Jay Weinberg, who negotiated a deal with Disney that gives Disney merchandising rights to the movie (which Kathy gets a small piece of) while Kathy retains rights to Ed's image (which Disney does not own). Disney is backing a campaign to get Ed a star on the Hollywood Walk of Fame. Burton, Depp, Landau, Arquette, and others have written letters in support. It's nice, but it's a little late.

'It was like I was in a big, grey, bottomless pit,' says Kathy of those years after he died. 'It's foggy and there's no beginning and no end, and it was just like the world had stopped.' Her voice catches. 'The whole thing wasn't fair, the way he died. All this publicity and fanfare – why didn't it happen before? He would've loved it.'

ED WOOD . . . NOT

by J. Hoberman

Only in America: Tim Burton, one of the most bankable filmmakers who ever lived, expends the credit of his success in sincere, black-and-white tribute to the obscure, tawdry vision of Edward D. Wood, Jnr. (1924-78), the alcoholic, heterosexual transvestite and sometime pornographer known affectionately as 'the world's worst director'. As nothing in America can be said to exist outside the media's glare, there is no such thing as negative publicity. (The value of celebrity is absolute, as Wood well knew.) To be the World's Worst Filmmaker is to personify a particular high concept.

Playing both ends against the middlebrow, Burton's feature opened in the US, bearing the imprimaturs of both Walt Disney and the New York Film Festival. There's no mistaking it for anything but an art film, yet it's sweeter than *Cinderella* (and nearly as sexless). The dank aroma of Salvation Army thrift stores that clings to the Wood *oeuvre* evaporates in the simulated sunlight of a Disney production with a hot young cast: Ed Wood as Johnny Depp, loved by the luscious Sarah Jessica Parker and Patricia Arquette – and admired, if only platonically, by Bill Murray. Ed Wood, recovered failure, subject of a feel-good movie for creeps!

Wood flourished, if that is the word, during the mid-fifties heyday of skid-row supernaturalism, the period of exploitation horror flicks and cold war science fiction, produced for downtown grind theatres and the presumably uncritical teenage audience of the drive-in trade. Wood's peers include schlockmeisters William Castle and Roger Corman, although he had neither the former's knack for exploitation nor the latter's gift for low-budget filmmaking. A casual *mise-en-scene* of half-dressed sets and visible Klieg lights is Wood's hallmark, and an unbridled pragmatism (three consecutive scenes shot in the same location) is his *modus operandi*.

What characterises the laughably inept *Plan 9 from Outer Space* (1959) – a movie constructed around a few shots of Bela Lugosi taken shortly before Lugosi's death – and Wood's other features is their non-existent pacing; their long, pointless exchanges between untalented performers; and their near-documentary atmosphere of genuine befuddlement. Wood's action montages are so perfunctory as to be a slap in the face of public taste. His major innovation is a checkerboard effect of mismatched day and night scenes. *Bride of the Monster* (1954), also with Bela Lugosi, is less of an actual horror film than the idea of one.

Wood established himself in a fringe Hollywood beyond the imagining of Nathanael West. (It's not surprising to learn that he ended up directing hardcore porn, and that his last opus was an 8mm 'home study' segment of *The Encyclopedia of Sex*.) In addition to the burnt-out, pitifully emaciated Lugosi, B-movie workhorse Lye Talbot, the talentless progeny of the money-men who bankrolled him and sundry veterans of thirties Westerns, Wood's impoverished productions feature such showbiz oddities as Criswell the television psychic, Tor Johnson the 400-pound Swedish wrestler, Vampira the beatnik ghoul girl, and a defective prop octopus that had been stolen from Republic Studios.

No more oddball that his side-show entourage, Wood was a cross-dresser with a particular fetish for Angora sweaters – the unconvincing magic, crackpot logic, and decomposing glamour of his films mirror his own. *Glen or Glenda* (1953), his first and most substantial feature, is a passionate defence of transvestism – and thus free expression – cast in the mode of a half-heartedly 'scientific' exploitation flick. Wood's convoluted narrative is based on two case histories, which are recounted (with Foucaultian aptness) by a psychiatrist to a police officer. In the first, the tormented Glen, forever ogling the lingerie displays on Hollywood Boulevard and played by Wood himself, gets married and lives happily ever after with his wife's wardrobe. In the second, inspired

'It's uncanny.' Left: Lisa Marie, then Burton's girlfriend, as Vampira in Ed Wood; *Right: 1950s horror-show hostess Vampira herself in Ed Wood's* **Plan 9 from Outer Space.**

by the then-recent example of Christine Jorgensen, a disgruntled G.I. goes all the way and gets an operation.

With *Glen or Glenda*, the Wood style is already full-blown. Every significant moment – and there are many – is underscored by the same flash of stock-footage lightning. Everyone from a bearded lady to the cop on the beat sits around glomming the same dog-eared copy of a tabloid, headlined 'World Shocked By Sex Change.' (The end of the film is announced when this well-thumbed paper lands in the garbage.) Formally, the entire movie is structured to suggest an anterior parody of Alain Resnais' *Mon oncle d'Amerique*, with Lugosi instead of Professor Henri Laborit. Like Laborit, the star never interacts with other characters. Cloistered in his laboratory (littered with test tubes, human skulls, a crystal ball), he kibbitzes the action in cutaway: 'Bevare! Bevare! The story must be told!'

As bad filmmakers go, Wood is less provocative and mindboggling than the Black Pioneer, Oscar Micheaux, or than the Great Negation, Andy Warhol. Still, at his best (which is to say, at his worst), Wood's mysterious illogic deforms the simplest narrative cliches so absolutely that you're forced to consider them anew. As the big lie of chronology is confounded by Wood's imperfect continuity, so the nature of screen acting is foregrounded by cloddish bits of business, the notion of

Bela Lugosi (right) and Ed Wood on the set of Glen or Glenda. *Lugosi's weird narrator intones the surreal order 'Pull the string!' over stock footage of stampeding buffalos.*

originality undermined by the interpolation of library footage.

The rich realism induced by Wood's failure to convince is of incomparably greater aesthetic interest than the seamless naturalism of conventional narrative films – but this particular form of radical demystification is not the source of his current appeal. Opening to overwhelmingly positive reviews (a 'very good film about a very bad film-maker', said *The New York Times*), Burton's *Ed Wood* is only the most visible instance of the Ed Wood revival that began with Harry and Michael Medved's 1980 wise-guy paean to bad movies, *The Golden Turkey Awards*.

The excavation of the Wood *oeuvre* continued throughout the 1980s. (Michael Medved, meanwhile, opportunistically parlayed the adolescent facetiousness of *The Golden Turkeys* into a career as a television movie-reviewer and, in his 1992 tract *Hollywood vs. America*, a right-wing proponent of so-called family values.) There was even money to be made. The distributor who obtained posthumous rights to Wood's official *chef d'oeuvre*, *Plan 9 from Outer Space*, proved his business acumen by making a small fortune with a decade of Bad Movie festivals.

Variety, which ignored Wood's movies when they first appeared, now has advertisements for 'The Ed Wood collection' and, according to *Premiere*, there's a campaign underway to get Wood a star on the pavement of Hollywood Boulevard. Rudolph Grey's 1992 oral history *Nightmare of Ecstasy: The Life and Art of Edward D. Wood Jr.*, has been followed by two made-for-video documentaries, *Look Back in Angora* and *The Haunted World of Ed Wood*, and two as-yet unproduced biographical musical plays, *The Worst!* by Josh Alan Friedman, and *Plan 9 from Yucca Street* by the New York film reviewer known as the Phantom of the Movies.

Despite (or perhaps, because of) the fact that its score is entirely uncredited library music, the original *Plan 9 from Outer Space* soundtrack has been released on CD. *Plan 9* has also inspired a 111-minute video documentary, *Flying Saucers Over Hollywood: The Plan 9 Companion*, John Wooley's meticulous recreation of the movie as a graphic novel, and a touring musical. (The most daring of recent Wood homages is Trent Harris' *Plan 10 from Outer Space*, an independent feature made in Salt Lake City which treats Mormon cosmology as the stuff of fifties sci-fi.)

Thanks to Burton, however, the Ed Wood story makes the leap from cult to religion. By celebrating the career of so sodden a loser, *Ed Wood* may seem to be a travesty of the classic Hollywood biopic – a form which, disproportionately concerned with showbusiness personalities, peaked (numerically, if not aesthetically) during the same fifties that brought *Plan 9 from Outer Space* and now functions, in American popular culture, as an eternal theme park of national innocence. In fact, *Ed Wood* is as blatantly inspirational as any paean to Alexander Graham Bell or Al Jolson – a success story preaching the importance of self-belief and the power of positive thinking, demonstrating by its very existence the pay-off for doing one's thing.

There's a moment in the film where an incredulous Hollywood producer, amazed by a private screening of *Glen or Glenda*, anachronistically proclaims that this grotesque melodrama has got to be a 'put-on'. That's exactly what they said of Van Gogh, schmuck. We always knew he was great – didn't we?

Burton is a Wood fan. (Like Joe Dante, who celebrated William Castle in his 1993 *Matinee*, he belongs to the *Famous Monsters of Filmland* school of adolescent fetishes.) Written by Scott Alexander and Larry Karaszewski from *Nightmare of Ecstasy*, *Ed Wood* is nothing if not knowing. The movie opens with an extravagant pastiche of *Plan 9 from Outer Space* – tombstone credits illuminated by lightning, a crescendo of thunder yielding to mad bongo drums – and thereafter, there's scarcely an Ed Wood joke that isn't made. 'Gosh, where's my pink sweater?' is his girlfriend's first line. 'Why, if I had the chance, I could make half a movie out of this stock footage,' the aspiring filmmaker tells a friend.

Just as *Mystery Theater 3000*, a regular feature on American cable television's Comedy Central,

Bela Lugosi (Martin Landau) teaches Ed Wood a vampire's hand movements. His evocation of the Wood/Lugosi relationship won Landau the Best Supporting Actor Oscar.

inscribes an animated pair of wise-cracking humanoid spectators over the old drive-in movies presented, so Wood's contemporary incarnation is rigorously overdetermined. Depp plays the director as a wide-eyed, wired enthusiast, suave but disjointed, lips accentuated by pencil-line moustache, teeth bared in a ventriloquist dummy's idiot grin, every word illuminated by faith in his own dream.

Depp aside, the movie's *typage* is remarkable: Jeffrey Jones' Criswell, Lisa Marie's Vampira, George 'the Animal' Steele's Tor Johnson, Vincent D'Onofrio's Orson Welles are all impressively hyperreal, and Martin Landau's Lugosi is a good deal more. ('No one gives two fucks for Bela,' Lugosi says sadly upon meeting avid fan Eddie Wood.) Thanks to Landau's performance, a mixture of wounded pride and agonised gratitude, *Ed Wood* is as much footnote to the Lugosi canon as it is celebration of Wood's. Condemned to self-parody, resurrected by the camera, Lugosi functions as the pure essence of negative stardom – he's a successful failure, Ed Wood's Ed Wood. Landau's Oscar proves it.

While skirting the sleaze and pathos of its subject's life, *Ed Wood* is heavily dependent on Wood's films. Burton in a sense naturalises the video doc *Look Back in Angora*, which used clips from the Wood *oeuvre* as the basis for a biography, while puzzling over the miracle of how these sacred texts came to be created. The most thematically apposite sequence has Ed and his cast submitting to mass baptism (true story!) to secure the Baptist Church of Beverly Hills' backing for *Plan 9 from Outer Space.*

In the gospel according to Burton, Wood is so solicitous of his actors that he shoots every scene in one take; like Warhol, his mantra is 'That was perfect.' *Ed Wood*, of course, is absolutely flawless – as fastidiously crafted as any previous Burton production. (Columbia reportedly put it in turnaround because Burton refused to trade 'first look' for the right to shoot in black and white.) The painstaking replication of Wood's haphazard compositions suggests another Hollywood landmark, the Buena Park Palace of Living Art where the Mona Lisa or Whistler's Mother are reproduced as garish wax dioramas and the Venus De Milo is improved upon: not only is she colourised, but her lost limbs are restored. *Ed Wood* is the Palace of Living Art in reverse. Art is not reproduced as kitsch; living kitsch is embalmed as art.

No less than its subject, albeit in a different way, *Ed Wood* is deeply solipsistic. For however ostensibly mediated by film or television, the entire world is subsumed to the director's vision: everything is stippled with *noir* lighting and awash in studio rain, a lavish version of a cheap horror movie. The most elaborate gag involves the mechanism of an amusement-park spook house; the most powerful moment has Lugosi reprise his tormented speech from *Bride of the Monster* ('Home? I have no home!') on a Hollywood street corner; the most inspirational sequence allows Ed to meet his idol Orson Welles in a cheap bar and thus draw strength to finish his 'masterpiece', *Plan 9 from Outer Space*.

Opening as it does in a movie movie-graveyard, Ed Wood evokes Hollywood as a mansion populated by unquiet ghosts, but it's a Hollywood haunted house just the same. Unlike *Look Back in Angora*, which includes footage documenting Wood's bloated descent into porn, Burton ends the story on a positive note. According to *Nightmare of Ecstasy*, *Plan 9* never enjoyed a Los Angeles theatrical release; in *Ed Wood*, it is accorded a gala premiere at the packed Pantages Theatre. Recognised in the movies as he never was in life, the genius of *Plan 9* is feted by an ecstatically appreciative audience: us!

The circuit of self-congratulation is complete. 'This is the one they'll remember me for!' Burton's prescient hero gushes at *Plan 9*'s imaginary premiere. If it seems inconceivable that Hollywood directors D. W. Griffith, Josef von Sternberg or even Orson Welles (to name only three) would ever be so canonised, it may be that their very presence would reproach the audience. But then *Ed Wood* is really a form of alternative film history. It's the aesthetic equivalent of those contemporary releases – *Forrest Gump*, *Nell*, *IQ*, *Dumb and Dumber*, *The Brady Bunch*, the upcoming *The Stupids* – in which simple minds are synonymous with appealing innocence and virtue is a factor of low intelligence.

Deliberately or not, Ed Wood served to deconstruct all manner of Hollywood pretence. *Ed Wood* builds it all back up, shiny and new. In the great American tradition, Ed Wood is born again, born to win. (The panic over *The Bell Curve* notwithstanding, dumbing down is democratic.) Let the lowest common denominator rule. Although the closing credits note that Tor Johnson achieved his 'greatest fame as a bestselling Halloween mask', the movie's greatest irony is the liquidation of irony itself.

ED WOOD

review by Kim Newman

Hollywood, 1951. Edward D. Wood Jnr, a studio flunkey with ambitions to be a writer-director-star, stages an unsuccessful play starring his girlfriend Dolores Fuller. Learning that producer George Weiss plans a film about Christine Jorgensen, Ed pitches to direct *I Changed My Sex*, claiming to be qualified because, like Jorgensen, he is a transvestite and can persuade the washed-up Bela Lugosi to appear in the film. Ed uses his script to reveal his fetish for angora sweaters to Dolores, who is shocked but agrees to appear in the film in a role based on herself.

When the retitled *Glen or Glenda* fails to land him a studio contract, Ed tries to run up finance for a horror film, *Bride of the Atom*, to star Bela, Dolores and wrestler Tor Johnson. Ed casts Loretta King, an actress he meets in a bar, in Dolores' role because she appears to offer to invest $60,000. It turns out that Loretta only has $300, forcing Ed to raise the money from a meat packer who insists his son is cast as the hero. When the retitled *Bride of the Monster* opens, Dolores walks out. Ed persuades Bela to admit himself to hospital to be treated for morphine addiction. There he meets Kathy O'Hara, who falls in love with him though he admits to his transvestism. Bela leaves hospital and Ed shoots footage with him for a future movie, but the actor dies.

Ed's landlord mentions that his Baptist Church wants to finance religious films. Ed persuades them to invest in his science fiction script *Grave Robbers from Outer Space*, which is built around the Bela footage. Ed has his whole cast (including flamboyant homosexual Bunny Breckinridge, bogus prophet Criswell and unemployed horror hostess Vampira) baptised, and casts Kathy's chiropodist Tom Mason as Bela's double. During filming, the Baptists insist the title be changed to *Plan 9 from Outer Space*. Pressure forces Ed to flee the set to a bar where he runs into his idol Orson Welles, similarly despondent at career reversals, and is inspired to finish the film he is confident he will be remembered for.

The bravura credits sequence of *Ed Wood* perfectly evokes the look and sound of *Plan 9 from Outer Space*, complete with cast names on tombstones and a cheesy black and white mock-up model of a rainswept Hollywood. It follows a mock intro by Jeffrey Jones cum Criswell in the first of the film's many uncanny impersonations/interpretations of bizarre real-life characters. But a secondary layer of reference is touched on as the camera swoops over the model, evoking memories not only of the real Ed Wood's fondly-remembered but mainly boring pictures but also of the similar opening of Tim Burton's *Beetlejuice*. Though nurtured as a project by executive producer Michael Lehmann, and based on a strange, anecdotal biography (*Nightmare of Ecstasy: The Life and Art of Edward D. Wood Jr.* by Rudolph Grey), *Ed Wood* has been thoroughly infiltrated by the Life and Art of its own director.

Tor Johnson – portrayed here by fellow wrestler George 'the Animal' Steele – was a faithful member of Ed Wood's ham-actor ensemble, playing monsters without make-up.

Continual evocation of Burton's previous films intermingles with the recreation of *Glen or Glenda* and *Bride of the Monster*: the central thread of Ed's relationship with Bela Lugosi is a clear echo of Burton's own well-documented (in *Vincent*) relationship with Vincent Price. The presence of Johnny Depp, like the tract house exterior and gothic cluttered interior of Lugosi's last home, evokes *Edward Scissorhands*, while Ed's hyperactive monomania and peculiar high voice echo the first of Burton's feature-length alter egos, Pee-wee Herman. Burton shares with Wood a lack of interest in conventional Hollywood notions of construction and character, compensating for the waywardness of his films with a bizarre, unreplicable flavour. It is ironic that for all its anecdotal and elliptical approach, *Ed Wood* is Burton's most successful piece of proper storytelling, its visuals never overwhelming its emotions, its consistent strangeness never interrupted by the second unit action stuff that flaws the *Batman* movies.

Given the Grey book as source material, the technical veracity of *Ed Wood* is often in doubt: Loretta King and Dolores Fuller give diametrically opposed accounts of how one came to replace the other in the lead role of *Bride of the Monster*, prompting screenwriters Scott Alexander and Larry Karaszewski to pick the interpretation that offers the most humour and the strangest side detail (Loretta's no liquids diet). Much is omitted that would contradict the film's takes on Wood and Lugosi, including unmentioned marriages for each of them and important professional contacts (Wood's with producer Alex Gordon and Lugosi's late role in *The Black Sleep*). Wood's meeting with Welles is an inspired fiction given life by an uncanny Vincent D'Onofrio performance. His self-involved Welles is just as much a movie-struck outsider as Ed, fitting in perfectly with the film's other eccentrics by holding a casual conversation without once questioning why Ed is dressed in women's clothing.

Although the film does not resist the temptation to score easy laughs from Ed's eccentricities and the shortcomings of his films ('Perfect,' he snaps after every botched take, 'print it'), Burton and his collaborators invest them with a skewed dignity that is ultimately very moving. There is a touch of contemporary irony in Lugosi's proud claim, 'I'm the first celebrity that ever checked into rehab,' but the film is as smitten as Ed with the old ham.

Marvellously incarnated by a crusty Martin Landau (himself a talented veteran of too many dreadful horror programmers), Lugosi sadly admits in his first scene that 'Nobody gives two focs for Bela' and goes from wistfully explaining his hypnotic finger waving with 'You have to be double-jointed and you have to be Hungarian' to fulminating against an old rival by claiming 'Karloff doesn't deserve to smell my shit.' The cast is perfect down to the walk-ons: from Bill Murray's Bunny Breckinridge, who returns from a failed sex change in Mexico with a whole mariachi band in tow, alleging, 'Without these men, I would be dead,' to Lisa Marie's Vampira, resisting induction into Wood's circle but finally swamped by her own invented Morticia Addams character.

Tim Burton remains a reticent director, unwilling to show his hand even as he continues obsessively to experiment with autobiography. This is reflected in a strange void at the centre of the film, as he refuses to examine the sources of Wood's insane, naive, ruthless drive or his off-centre integrity (in its own cracked way, *Glen or Glenda* is an art movie) or even his transvestism. All the emotional highs of the film come from Ed's devotion to his associates (when told he's 'the only guy in town who doesn't pass judgement', he says, 'If I could, I wouldn't have any friends') or from their unexplained devotion to him (Bela envies Ed the love of Kathy, saying none of his wives would ever have jumped onto a moving car for him).

When Kathy, played with sweetly subtle seriousness by Patricia Arquette, presses Ed about his past, he talks not about himself but his love for pulp magazines and radio serials. Like Kathy, we are charmed, entertained and introduced to unforgettable people, but left no wiser about the Lives and Art of either Ed Wood or Tim Burton.

MARTIAN INSPIRATION
THE BUBBLEGUM CARDS

by Chuck Wagner

The 1950s had seen the first of the large wave of flying saucer sightings. Soon, the movies were filled with those twin pillars of menace of the Eisenhower Age: UFOs and war. It was during this period that a young man named Len Brown began his career. Working for Topps, he and a dedicated team in 1962 created perhaps the ultimate evocation of leftover late fifties paranoia: the infamous *Mars Attacks!* card series. Topps – which owns sole right to the concept of packing cards with gum – added macabre menace from the Red Planet to go along with their pink squares of gum.

Brown, who wrote the cards and still works for Topps, was just 21 at the time. He had gone to work for Topps at the age of eighteen, mentored by Woody Gelman, a friend and former magazine publisher hired by Topps to dream up new ideas for bubblegum trading cards. Under Gelman, Brown worked on Topps' 1962 Civil War Centennial Cards, an unlikely forerunner to *Mars Attacks!*. 'It was during that series that a veteran pulp artist named Norm Saunders was hired by Woody Gelman to paint some wonderfully detailed pictures that were no bigger than five" x seven",' said Brown. 'The series, gore and all, was pretty successful.'

The success of the Civil War cards led Gelman and Brown to discuss science fiction concepts for a card series. Gelman was an avid pulp collector who had a complete run of Hugo Gernsbach's *Amazing Stories*. Noted Brown, 'We finally came up with the idea of doing a modern *War of the Worlds*, calling the concept *Mars Attacks* after briefly considering the name *Attack from Space*. After working briefly with Wally Wood on the formative cards, we decided on the team of Bob Powell (a wonderfully talented and prolific comic book artist) and once more Norm Saunders. Bob would do the pencils and Norm would paint right over them on illustration board.

'We did 55 cards in the series and were quite proud of them. As soon as the product was printed we placed them in several test stores in Brooklyn. Sales were mixed. A couple of stores did very well, and sold the cards rapidly. A couple of other stores reported very little interest in the product.'

Topps widened the product trial and shipped the cards to other cities in the East, but began to get bad press over the cards' high quotient of blood and gore. Noted Brown, 'It was kind of shocking to top management to get this kind of attention – after all, our heritage with trading cards had previously been sets depicting *Flags of the World*, *Railroad Trains*, *U.S. Presidents*, etc. The only controversy we had encountered were with the Elvis Presley trading cards [when Elvis was thought of as a major cause of juvenile delinquency]. So, the *Mars Attacks!* series was never sold elsewhere. No further shipments were made. Only those fortunate to have seen the limited shipments remembered them decades later. The original cards became the most [valuable] non-sports collectible series that Topps ever published by the time the 1970s rolled around. We heard that individual cards were selling for $5 to $10 a card. By the late eighties, I started to hear that the original complete set was going for $1,500 to $2,000.'

Mars Attacks! *features big Hollywood names –*
many of them fried to a crisp by creatures
resembling the Mutant of Metaluna from 1955
sci-fi movie **This Island Earth.**

Brown detailed how the cards were created: 'Woody and I worked together coming up with the scenes,' he said. 'Woody, a former animator for Max Fleischer and Paramount Studios, would rough-sketch an idea. The idea was sent to Bob Powell who would dramatically redraw it as if it were the cover of a pulp magazine. When the series was painted, I wrote the descriptions on the back of the cards as well as the front captions, i.e. "Burning Flesh". Those were days that I couldn't wait to arrive at work and meet with Woody as we planned the science-fiction bubblegum cards. What a way to make a living! I thought I was pretty lucky.'

The cards emerged from limbo in the mid-1990s, after the mid-eighties pastiche *Dinosaurs Attack!* had shown that the concept, too gruesome in its own day, could now find an enthusiastic audience, eager to embrace the gory carnage. 'Probably over the years, we have received more requests for a reprint of *Mars Attacks!* than any other series we had ever published,' said Brown. 'We tested the re-issue waters about five years ago by reprinting our 1960s *Batman* trading card series. That worked out very well, and immediately we had plans to do a *Mars Attacks!* re-issue. One thing after another interfered with our plans, until we got around to doing it [in 1994].'

Brown worked with Gary Gerani at Topps in designing new cards rendered by Earl Worem in the tradition of the original series for the reissued set. 'Gary carried the ball the rest of the way with the new card art for 1994,' said Brown. 'Actually the Earl Norem paintings were done a couple of years earlier, when we first thought we would do a 66-card series.'

The success of the reissued cards has led to a line of Topps' *Mars Attacks!* comic books, with Brown writing stories for the '94 mini-series. 'The comic book seemed like a natural for Topps,' said Brown. 'While science fiction may not have a great track record in comics, we felt *Mars Attacks!* had enough of a cult following to make it work for us. I'm delighted to see it revived again this year [1996]. At Topps we believe and have proven that you don't have to be a super-hero comics publisher to he successful.'

The 1990s Mars Attacks! *trading card series, courtesy of Topps Cards, Inc. Burton's film stayed true to their pulp style, but had the Martians defeated by far sillier means.*

HIDDEN GEMS

by Anthony C. Ferrante

With the budgets of movies big and small skyrocketing well beyond that once unheard-of $100-million price tag, it's not quite unfathomable that a movie being made for $260 million isn't too far in the future. And according to screenwriter Jonathan Gems, that would have been the budget required by his first-draft script for *Mars Attacks!*.

'They told me I had to reduce the budget,' recalls Gems. 'Warner Bros. wanted to make it for no more than $60 million, so I had to lose $200 million. It was actually a wonderful exercise losing $200 million but still keeping the same value in the script.'

With Tim Burton attached as director, regardless of budget, the results are always certain to be visually arresting, which is why the 42-year-old Gems had very few worries that his vision of little green Martians attacking Earth would reach the screen intact. 'When I was writing the script, I wasn't concerned with how much thing would cost,' says the screenwriter. 'I was concerned with the whole vision of the piece. Tim and I agreed that we didn't want to make a movie like *Earth vs. the Flying Saucers* or *It Came from Outer Space* where you never felt it was really happening. Usually it happens to one guy and his girlfriend. We figured that this was going to be a big-budget movie, and it was originally planned as a summer release. So we felt, "Why not try to make this feel like the entire world is really involved?"'

Working with Burton, Gems pared the film's 60 leading characters down to 23, and the world-wide destruction planned for the film was isolated to three major cities (gone are Martians attacking China, the Philippines, Japan, Europe, Africa, India and Russia). 'Keep in mind that this was way before *Independence Day* was written,' notes Gems. 'We had things like Manhattan being destroyed building by building, the White House went and so did the Empire State Building. They figured all this would be too expensive, so we cut most of that out to reduce the cost. However, we managed to keep the feeling of global destruction by showing little details rather than the whole panoramic vision.'

Mars Attacks! may be derived from a trading card set, but Gems points out that Burton's creative methods are certainly on par with the film's offbeat perspectives. After all, where most directors have visions, Tim Burton has dreams. 'One time he told me he had a really terrible dream,' Gem recalls. 'He said he was being chased along a beach by a giant doughnut. There were a couple more that he told me about, and I realised that they're a lot like things in his movies. I really believe he gets some of his ideas from dreams.'

While *Mars Attacks!* marks their first official collaboration to go before the cameras, Gems has worked with Burton since the first *Batman* of 1988 (his biggest contribution was convincing Burton to get rid of the Robin character). 'I came in to rewrite the Sam Hamm script for *Batman*, but had to drop out because of the writers strike,' he explains. 'Tim and I kept in touch and became friends, and one day he called me about writing a script for him based on Edgar Allan Poe's *House of Usher*.'

Though the classic story has been filmed several times before, Gems admits Burton's take was slightly different. 'He wanted to make a comedy set in Burbank,' he reveals. 'If you remember, the Poe story is an extremely depressing horror tale. Tim's idea was to give it a certain twist, make it funny and contemporary by setting it in the suburbs. It was such a brilliant approach.' While both Warner Bros. and Burton both wanted to make the film, the timing always seemed to be off, though Gems notes it's the one film Burton has always kept in his back pocket. 'It's probably the best unproduced script I've written so far,' he says. 'Tim loves it and eventually we will make it.'

With that collaboration a success, Gems found his short visit from London to write *House of Usher* turning into a permanent LA residency as he took on Burton's next assignment of coming up with a *Beetlejuice* sequel. Trying to avoid rehashing the original, Burton suggested that Gems use an idea about a legendary surfing story of a 'girl who calls a wave' as the starting point for what eventually became known as *Beetlejuice Goes Hawaiian*. 'Tim thought it would be funny to match the surfing backdrop of a beach movie with some sort of German Expressionism, because they're totally wrong together,' explains Gems.

The story followed the Jeffrey Jones family to Hawaii, where he's developing a new resort. They soon discover that they're building on the burial ground of an ancient Hawaiian kahuna. The spirit comes back from the afterlife to cause trouble, and there's only one person to call – Betelgeuse. 'In order to engage Betelgeuse's services, Jeffrey Jones and Catherine O'Hara have to more or less sell their daughter Winona Ryder to him, and then all sorts of crazy stuff happens, including a surfing tournament Betelgeuse has to win by using magic.'

Michael Keaton and Ryder agreed to do the film, but would only do so if Burton directed. Then Warners offered Burton the choice of either *Batman Returns* or *Beetlejuice Goes Hawaiian,* and he naturally chose the former. 'It was a difficult choice but Warners really wanted him to do *Batman Returns*, but they made him such an incredible offer that he couldn't turn it down,' says Gems. 'It basically gave him *carte blanche* – $80 million and final cut. I remember someone saying that that movie was "the most expensive art film ever made", and only Tim could get away with doing that.'

While the *Beetlejuice Goes Hawaiian* script is still owned by Geffen Pictures, Gems feels that since none of the actors will return without Burton, the film will likely never get made. 'You really couldn't do it now anyway,' says Gems. 'Winona is too old for the role, and the only way they could make it would be to totally recast it.'

Another project Gems worked on for Burton was an adaptation of Richard Brautigan's novel *The Hawkline Monster*, about a couple of Old West gunslingers who are preparing to retire and decide to do one last job. 'Basically, they're hired by these twin sisters who want them to kill a monster that lives in their basement,' explains Gems. 'The two cowboys realise they've had to kill desperados and all kinds of other people over the years, and even though they've never had to kill a monster before, they figure they can handle it.'

The Hawkline Monster came very close to being made by Burton when Clint Eastwod and Jack Nicholson both agreed to star in it, but eventually it fell apart when Eastwood bowed out to do another film. 'Everybody was very excited and deals were being made, but when Clint decided to leave Jack didn't want to do it, because working with Clint was what appealed to him in the first place,' says Gems, who notes that the film could eventually happen with different actors and another director.

While Burton has certainly kept Gems busy over the years, their most intriguing project to date was a script based on one of the director's infamous dreams. 'He called me up one day and said he saw a movie in a dream he had and wanted to talk to me about it,' says Gems. 'So I went over to his house, and he told me that his dream was about these three girls dancing in the Nevada desert wearing go-go suits. The only weird thing about it was that they were 300 feet tall. I thought, "How could this be an idea for a movie? This is crazy." So I went home and I thought about it, and eventually I realised a whole movie could be spun off from this.'

The result was a script called *Go Baby Go*, a sort of strange variation on *Attack of the 50-Foot Woman* which follows three go-go dancers who are contaminated by a new weapon at a military testing and grow to be 300 feet tall. 'The problem is they really love music and so all they do is look for good music and a place to dance,' says Gems. 'When they start getting bigger, the military is embarrassed by all this and wants to wipe them out and sweep it under the carpet.'

While Burton expressed an interest in the film, HBO's remake of *Attack of the 50-Foot Woman* ultimately cooled his desire. 'It was sort of fresh before that, and when the remake came along it put him off a bit,' says Gems.

While Gems began his career as a successful playwright in London, he shifted gears in the early eighties to do a rewrite of the second film version of George Orwell's *1984*. Once he had got a taste of screenwriting there was no turning back. Having worked on several pictures over the years, Gems considers the greatest heartbreak of his career to be a faithful adaptation of Mary Shelley's *Frankenstein*.

'There was a company called Spring Creek Productions that had the idea of remaking *Frankenstein* starring Arnold Schwarzenegger,' says Gems. 'I expressed an interest in writing it, but I told them they should forget about Schwarzenegger, call it *Mary Shelley's Frankenstein* and stay faithful to the book. It's not really a horror romantic tragedy. It's really the story of having a child and what happens when you abandon it; I thought it was very cinematic. So I wrote the script and we were getting ready to send it out for casting when an executive friend of mine swiped the idea and pitched it to Columbia. They liked it, and it became a race between the two companies. They ended up getting a director and a cast before they had a script and beat us to it. Somebody once told me that when you get in a race like this, it always ends up that the worst script wins, and that's exactly what happened.'

While Gems will soon be directing his first feature, a low-budget black comedy entitled *The Treat,* the screenwriter feels his experience working with Burton has been by far the most rewarding, entertaining and enjoyable. 'Tim lives in his imagination,' concludes Gems. 'There's no one else in this town who can get away with that, and that's why I feel very fortunate to have been able to work with him.'

MEN ARE FROM MARS, WOMEN ARE FROM VENUS

by Christine Spines

Tim Burton is taking sweet refuge in the neck of a Martian. His nose is firmly planted in that warm, safe area where shoulder meets neck. Just above this cozy love zone rests the delicate face of Lisa Marie, the alien in question and his girlfriend of four years. She's sporting a beehive that would make any astronaut's wife jealous – a masterpiece of Aqua Net engineering. Her gown, a floor-length web of red spirals, is an alluring combination of Madonna-meets-Morticia-meets-the-B52's.

Amid a spread of coffee urns, cheese logs, Wheat Thins, and a big pile of doughnuts, the two engage in an intimate public display of affection sidled up against the craft-services table. They haven't said a word to each other for nearly ten minutes. They're just holding hands, gazing into each other's eyes, rubbing noses. No one dares go near them. It is one of the few breaks Burton takes during a long day of shooting *Mars Attacks!*, his wacko Martians-invade-Earth comedy adapted from the ultraviolent 1960s trading cards of the same name. No *Independence Day* this; Burton's movie is a patently low-concept, low-tech story of what happens when an army of little green men fly their saucers to Vegas, the White House, and Grandma's house, aiming their ray guns at everything that moves.

Mars Attacks! *was originally intended to feature stop-motion animation. Instead, it used state-of-the-art computer effects to replicate 1950s 'cheesiness'.*

Lisa Marie has the honour of being the only flesh-and-blood Martian in the movie. Her towering coif is more than a fetching tribute to sixties cheesecake – it's hiding her hideous, big-brained Martian skull. In a Tim Burton movie, the alien, monster, outsider, or freak is always the plum role.

If Burton took his mind off Mars for a nanosecond, he might notice it's Oscar day in Hollywood. The day the phones stop ringing after four o'clock, the streets empty, and an almost religious silence descends upon the city. It's like Jerusalem on a Friday. But here on the Warner Bros. lot, a pleasant lack of concern for the whole affair has shrouded the set. Only the teamsters seem to be aware that they're missing out on a big-money night.

'Cheese!' yells Martin Short from across the cavernous soundstage. 'I need more *cheese.*' The word in its adjectival form is used frequently by cast and crew to describe *Mars Attacks!*: *cheesy* as in good cheesy, like the old Vegas casinos they have yet to demolish, like lava lamps, like Tom Jones – basically, all the elements that compose this film.

The next scene is ready to be shot. The set is all you'd expect from Burton: the Kennedy Room, an imagined secret love pad in the White House where the president and friends can conveniently conduct their domestic affairs. It is a lavish, otherworldly spectacle of naughty and nice: a round, womblike space lined in ladyfinger couches with a circular bed sunk into the middle of the room like a Jacuzzi. If the Trump Taj Mahal has a honeymoon suite, this is what it must look like.

His seven minutes in heaven are up, and Burton and Lisa Marie disengage. Burton clomps across the soundstage with an uncanny forward motion. His long, spindly legs and combat boots propel him instead of weigh him down. For all the cool style in his movies, Burton himself is endearingly passé. He would fit right in at a New Jersey mall food court circa 1988: black jeans, untucked black oxford, his face sweet with innocence, his large hair a Medusa-like tangle of black curls. If he looks like he still listens to the Cure, he does.

The scene he's about to shoot is one in which Short, who's playing a lusty presidential press secretary cut from the Dick Morris mould, invites Lisa Marie's mysterious, mute bombshell into the president's love lounge for a little hanky-panky, unknowingly giving a Martian access to the executive suite.

Burton has his face pressed up to a giant tropical fish tank that makes up one wall of the set. The idea is to get alternating shots of Short and Lisa Marie looking at each other through the aquarium, as if their heads were actually inside. But the fish aren't co-operating. Each time the cameras roll, Short says his line ('Pretty nifty, huh?') and they mysteriously vanish into the bottom of the tank.

A crew of fish wranglers, bearing long poles with nets at the end, try to coax these Greta Garbo extras out of hiding by stirring up the bottom of the aquarium. The fish reluctantly start swimming, Burton yells action, Short says his line, and the fish disappear. Again. And again. And again. This quick-and-easy scene is suddenly taking an inordinate amount of time. Lisa Marie has gone offstage to hang out with two set visitors – her yoga teacher, who is wearing a big turban on her head, and a person called Cherry Vanilla. Somehow, Burton keeps smiling.

Between takes, Short whistles 'Disco Baby' and dances around the set. Burton is forever giggling. If he's feeling any pressure at the moment, he isn't letting on. It seems odd that the guy responsible for this $80 million sci-fi extravaganza with a galaxy full of stars – Jack Nicholson, Annette Bening, Danny DiVito, Glenn Close, Pierce Brosnan – is sporting a Teflon demeanour as the meter tick, tick, ticks with take after take of one line. It's getting late. Dinner is ordered.

Meanwhile, a small group of people has given in to Oscar day, gathering around a TV offstage to watch the awards. Theme music blares as Susan Sarandon accepts her Best Actress trophy for *Dead Man Walking*. She's crying. The camera keeps cutting to Tim Robbins. He's so proud of her! Lisa Marie and her hairdresser mosey up to the TV. Sarandon thanks a nun. Burton wanders up and watches for a moment and slyly wonders aloud, 'Hey, guys, what's on?'

The gifted and oblivious *wunderkind* – it's a role Burton has down pat. To studio executives searching for that elusive hit-movie X factor, Burton is a creative genius who makes weird flicks they don't understand, but the kids just love 'em. Ever since his 1985 feature debut, *Pee-wee's Big Adventure*, turned into a runaway box office success, Burton has managed to give his quirky and bizarre sensibility a phenomenally commercial spin, making hits out of *Beetlejuice* and *Edward Scissorhands* and a mega-megafranchise out of the *Batman* movies. It's an enviable record, but one that gives Burton the artist the unwelcome responsibility of also being Burton the hit machine.

During the production of *Batman Returns*, the burden of that responsibility started to get to Burton. Though the movie ended up grossing $163 million in the US, many were put off by its grim tone, and it was widely seen as a disappointment, costing much more than the original and making much less. Burton started to question whether he should remain in Hollywood. He sank into a deep depression and became ever more aloof and non-communicative, alienating many friends and colleagues. 'Tim was nice and great while he needed you,' says his college chum director Henry Selick. 'And then he would just stop calling.'

Mars Attacks! marks a significant leap of faith for Burton. He has made a concerted effort to mend fences and, after a four-year absence, make up with a fickle old friend: big-budget movies. Most people close to Burton say that falling in love with Lisa Marie is what pulled him out of the abyss. In the carnival of the absurd that is Hollywood, Lisa Marie seems to have given him a grounded focus outside his job – or, at the very least, a warm neck to retreat to from the pressure-packed world of aliens, cheese, and prima-donna fish.

When screenwriter Jonathan Gems stepped into a Melrose junk shop and picked up two packs of trading cards – one featuring incredibly gory images of suburbia being torn to shreds by dinosaurs, and another depicting a troop of crafty Martians firing their ray guns at scantily clad blondes – he immediately knew their kitschy, anarchic sensibility would appeal to Burton. Initially, Burton loved the idea of making a dinosaurs-on-tract-homes epic, but he was concerned about its similarity to Spielberg's *Jurassic Park*, and as for the *Mars Attacks!* cards, he wasn't sure whether anyone still cared about invaders from outer space.

What ultimately won him over was the idea of making an Irwin Allen-style disaster movie with aliens, a cast of thousands, and a groovy, subversive message. 'It was during the Gulf War,' says Burton, 'when the media seemed to have taken it to another level – wars having titles and theme music – and I found it kind of disturbing. I felt like these characters were just a good cathartic shakeup of that kind of thing. There are things you recognise about these Martians, but at the same time you can't understand them.'

Gems envisioned the story as a satire of American culture. 'There's a certain kind of joy in the way that the Martians just come and smash everything up,' says Gems. 'I was a punk in London and we always used to do pranks. So here you get the Martians taking the piss out of society.'

Which is classic Burton. 'I just thought it would be fun to see big stars getting blown away,' he says. 'It's like all those movies that they used to make where you never know who's going to make it. I remember seeing Robert Wagner on fire in *The Towering Inferno*. I didn't expect Robert Wagner to be on fire. It's kind of cathartic in a way.'

Cathartic, perhaps, but a bit of a handicap when it comes to casting. 'Agents didn't want to see their star clients play loser roles, and a lot of big actors passed on the project,' says Gems. 'At one point we actually thought we were going to have to cancel the film. The guy who saved our butt was Jack Nicholson.'

Burton had cut his teeth on big-budget movies working with Nicholson on *Batman*. But when Burton sent Nicholson the *Mars Attacks!* script, Nicholson one-upped him in out-there sensibility. 'I was location scouting,' recalls Burton, 'and I phoned Jack from the plane and asked him, "Which part would you like to do?" He answered, "How about *all* of them?" He was joking, but it was perfect.' Burton cast him as both president of the United States and a sleazy Vegas land developer.

Pumping up the movie's star wattage was tricky, but creating its walking, talking, five-foot-tall, giant-brained Martians was like triple-bypass surgery. Unlike the aliens in *Independence Day*, the Martians in *Mars Attacks!* go *mano a mano* with the film's characters. They run, they fight, they drink martinis, they speak to Congress. Burton wanted these brothers from another planet to resemble the elegant, hobbling stop-motion-animated skeletons that special-effects whiz Ray Harryhausen created for *Jason and the Argonauts*.

At first he approached Selick, a stop-motion guru and the director of *Tim Burton's The Nightmare Before Christmas*. But Selick was still in the throes of directing his own stop-motion feature, *James and the Giant Peach*, and didn't have time to create what Burton needed. Though *Mars Attacks!* had yet to be green-lighted, Burton imported an international troupe of about 70 animators headed up by Barry Purves, whose English stop-motion art films caught Burton's eye.

'The success of the film depended on the Martians' acting,' says Purves, 'so I kept renting *Sunset Boulevard*, because I thought Norma Desmond with her big eyes and wild movements was an absolutely perfect role model.' Unfortunately, even though both Burton and the studio adored what Purves's crew was coming up with, the arduous stop-motion process was taking longer and costing more than Burton had anticipated. 'The movie was being budgeted at a little over $100 million, and Warner's wanted to do it for under $70 million,' says producer Larry Franco, who tried to persuade Burton to use computer animation.

Burton, ever the purist, had said no to computers twice before, but the advantages were increasingly compelling: Computer-generated imagery is cheaper and faster than stop-motion and provides options at the flick of a finger. As Purves and crew toiled away, Franco, fresh off of the CGI-laden *Jumanji*, went to Industrial Light and Magic and requested a test reel. The results looked enough like the stop-motion footage to convince Burton, and the animators were history.

'We were green British people working without contracts,' says Purves. 'The same day big knobs at the studio had been applauding our rushes, they came in two hours later, while I had my hand up a Martian, and said, "Sorry, folks."' Without severance or official credit, Purves's entire crew was sent packing (and as they exited the studio lot, they were searched). 'I was there for eight months,' laments Purves. 'And now it's as though we've been swept under the carpet.'

While all this creature discomfort was being ironed out, the rest of the production was left in limbo. 'There was a period, maybe about five weeks, we had to lay off our crews because of script changes and budget things we couldn't carry – like a construction crew, our decorator – and then we started back up again,' says art director James Hegedus.

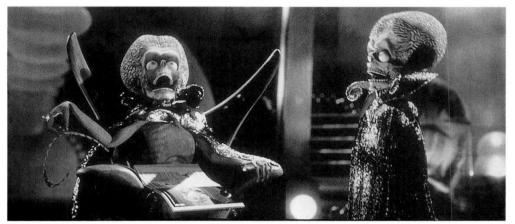

In contrast to the earnestness of its counterpart, Independence Day, Mars Attacks! *has fun with playful destructiveness and the animated aliens' belligerence.*

Missteps in preproduction – and the consequent bitterness – are par for the big-budget course. But it's a credit to Burton's unlikely finesse with executives that, throughout it all, he was still able to get his unique vision through the bottom-line studio brass. 'Tim's amazing because he really does protect the film, and he really does have a strong vision of the film and how it should be,' says Gems. 'But he does it in a way that's extremely subtle, so that he outwits the studio some of the time. He doesn't confront. He doesn't do it by yelling and screaming. He does it by diplomacy. Tactical diplomacy.'

Burton also put himself on the line to cast lesser-knowns in heroic roles and give a second shot to people whose careers were on ice. 'He went against everything and said, "I want you,"' says Jim Brown, the ex-football legend and one-time blaxploitation star. Burton cast him as an ex-boxer cum Vegas greeter, the film's only true martyr. 'There weren't any screen tests,' says Brown. 'He was interested in my mind, in the things I thought.'

Which the big stars appreciate as well. 'Tim laughs harder than anyone else when you're doing something,' says Bening, who plays a UFO-obsessed ex-stripper whom she modeled after Ann-

Tim Burton — A Child's Garden of Nightmares

Margaret in *Viva Las Vegas*. 'He's a wonderful audience, which is a terrific quality in a director.'

'He assumes you're going to do what he wants – you never feel intimidated by him,' says Sarah Jessica Parker, who worked with Burton in *Ed Wood* and plays a talk-show host in *Mars Attacks!* 'You want to make him happy. If he asked you to stand on your head and shoot flames out of your heels, you would just do it, and you wouldn't even ask why.'

While Burton's distanced, easygoing personality keeps the cast happy, it can also make a crew person's hair fall out. 'You can sit in meetings [with Tim] for months and not get anything,' says Hegedus. 'The communication isn't there for you to understand what the parameters are. Somebody would want a decision and he wouldn't give a decision – repeatedly. But I think when you realise what Tim brings to the table, you leave him alone.'

A small, black portable telephone is ringing, and it's causing Burton great pain. He looks around helplessly with each successive ring. He is sitting on the back porch of his mission-style retreat in the mountains an hour north of Los Angeles. The decorations from his 38th birthday party still adorn the otherwise barren yard: An Indian-style harem tent with giant, red-and-gold batik throw pillows beside his kidney-shaped pool.

'I *hate* the phone,' he says, absentmindedly getting up and going over to some bushes with the phone in hand, as if to chuck it into the shrubs. Then he reconsiders, turns around, and brings it back to the table. 'Every time it rings, I feel like I'm about to have a heart attack.'

It's Friday the 13th, and Burton looks stricken and pained when asked to describe the look of his not-yet-completed movie. Still, he's doing his best to communicate, which he does with images and feelings. His hands are in a constant state of motion, as if he were speaking in sign language.

The reindeer from *Edward Scissorhands* sits atop a green mound at the centre of a circular driveway in front of the house. Just beyond is a large crop of six-foot-tall sunflowers just past their bloom. Their heads slump downward atop their emaciated bodies, like Jack Skellington from *The Nightmare Before Christmas*. Filled with random objects that seem loaded with sentimental value – an upright piano, some Indian antiques, a few leopard-skin chairs – the décor is a cross between a Luis Bunuel and a *Brady Bunch* dream sequence.

Indeed, Burton frequently brings up dreams in reference to the things that make him feel safe and good in an otherwise hostile world. 'Seeing *Invaders From Mars* when you were young,' he says, explaining the origins of his B-movie fetish, 'you never knew if you really saw the movie or you dreamt it. It had that stylised symbolic power.'

When Burton was growing up in Burbank, monster movies and sci-fi creep shows provided a necessary injection of passion into his stifled suburban boyhood. He spent countless hours devouring Godzilla movies, Ray Harryhausen, sci-fi and anything starring or narrated by Vincent Price. Both making and watching movies have been Burton's ways of dealing with the alienation he's always felt. 'A lot of why you make movies is 'cause you couldn't get dates in high school,' says Burton matter-of-factly. 'A lot of emotion gets welled up and you put it into this.'

As a child, Burton spent his time hanging out in the cemetery down the street from his parents' home. His room was a dizzying splash of sixties bad taste ('bright red shag carpet and this black-and-white psychedelic-pattern quilt – where the hell I got that, I don't know') and it was his refuge from the world. At twelve, he decided not to live with his parents – Mom owned a cat-accessory store; Dad was a former minor-league baseball player – and moved in with his grandmother. He doesn't much like to talk about this period of his life, except as it applies to his movies and artwork. 'By the time kids are, like, ten years old, they think they can't draw or something,' he says. 'But you go through school and people get it beaten out of them.'

In high school, Burton had an art teacher who saw something in him and encouraged him to keep drawing his strange, quirky sketches. 'She let you kind of do what you wanted to do,' he says. 'She got you excited about doing something, as opposed to saying "No, no, you draw houses exactly like so."' But in college, at the prestigious California Institute of the Arts animation program, he still felt a lot of pressure to conform and draw by numbers. 'I remember sketching in Farmer's Market in L.A.,' he recalls, 'and I had this – I never had this happen before – mind-blowing experience. My mind felt as if some weird drug was kicking in. I went, "I can't draw, and I'm just going to draw how I want to draw." And then I was able to draw. Maybe not great, maybe not the way anybody else liked, but it really did something to me. I can still feel that feeling.'

When Burton left CalArts to become an animator at Disney, he was lucky enough to find some executives who understood his talent, principally Julie Hickson, who set him up with the means to make his short film, *Frankenweenie*, a sweetly macabre *Frankenstein*-meets-*Leave It To Beaver* story about a kid who revives his dead dog. 'I remember a test screening for *Frankenweenie* where kids started crying,' says Burton. 'Parents forget that for some kids, being scared isn't a bad thing. It's actually helpful in your life.'

Not surprisingly, some of Burton's best work has arisen from terror. 'Without the struggle, Tim's movies wouldn't turn out as good,' says Selick, who has often seen Burton trying to convince the studios that people will 'get' his movies. 'If he had unlimited budget and free rein . . . who knows?'

With nearly every film he's made, Burton has had to fight against a lack of confidence in his work. But he's been on the side of the majority almost every time. Paul Reubens hired him to direct *Peewee's* . . . after seeing *Frankenweenie*, and the critics, for the most part, trashed it. On *Beetlejuice*, Warner's fought with Burton over the low test-screening results, but then the film surprised everyone with its mass appeal. (He does have the studio to thank, however, for nixing his desire to cast Sammy Davis, Jr., in the title role.)

The immense popularity of *Batman* gave him more freedom to make *Batman Returns* in the manner he pleased. He decided to make this one reflect his sensibility – tormented, conflicted, filled with psychosexual energy and dreamlike violence – and was devastated by its negative reception by critics and the industry. 'It made me realise that I shouldn't do sequels,' says Burton, insisting that he still feels the film is funnier and closer to his heart than the original. 'It was hard. I was going through a lot of stuff that affected me more than I realised. I think, even though I blamed it on the pressure, it was much more what was going on with me personally.'

His aloofness at that time struck people as inconsiderate, and they were wounded by it. 'What makes it so difficult with Tim is that he's not like Pablo Picasso, who was just a genuinely talented asshole,' says Selick. 'Tim is so charming and childlike that people end up falling in love with him.'

Then came some bad press. *Vanity Fair* ran a venomous piece cataloguing Burton's sins – he's fired assistants and alienated collaborators – and implying, without evidence, that Burton's not returning calls was a contributing factor to *Batman* production designer Anton Furst's suicide.

Everything seemed to be crumbling under Burton's feet. The sudden shift from public acclaim to criticism was devastating; his marriage, to German painter Lena Gieseke, was breaking up, and he was still reeling from Furst's death. 'After *Batman Returns*,' recalls Gems, 'he was very depressed about the possibility of making films in Hollywood. I remember him saying that he wanted to give it up. He wanted to just be a painter.'

It was during this dark period, on Christmas of 1992, that Gems introduced Burton to an old friend, a former Calvin Klein model named Lisa Marie. The three of them went out with a group of friends to a yuppie-friendly New York go-go bar. Burton and Lisa Marie were left at a small table talking long after the others had left. 'Tim wasn't looking for a girlfriend at the time,' says Gems, 'but they just fell for each other the first time they met. I think she saved his life.'

As Lisa Marie tells it, the lifesaving was mutual. This was a girl who left her New Jersey home at the age of sixteen and headed for Manhattan, did some modelling, and basically made a profession out of hanging out with cool people. Then she got serious about acting and her life hit the skids. 'I was really a blue girl,' she recalls. 'Things were not happening for me at that time.'

From the beginning, holidays have been very significant in their relationship, as they are in Burton's movies. They fell in love on New Year's Eve, but they didn't consummate until Valentine's Day. 'An old-fashioned courting thing,' says Lisa Marie. 'Tim was really glad he waited. At the beginning he wasn't but he realised it later.'

Others were realising that all of a sudden Burton was a lot more focused, well adjusted, and easier to deal with. 'Tim was very successful very young, and he was surrounded by gold diggers who would betray and lie a lot,' says Gems. 'He just lost his faith in people. Then Lisa Marie comes along and she's like a child – very loving and generous and giving. And gradually, over the past few years he has healed up to the point where he has lost his distrust of people.'

Burton's friends agree that love has changed him. 'Tim has started to make a big effort to make amends for mistakes he's made in the past,' says Selick. 'I think Lisa Marie has had a huge impact on his life. I've seen him eating vegetarian, he dresses better, and his personal hygiene has definitely seen a dramatic improvement.'

Before Lisa Marie met Burton, she says his friends told her that 'he wouldn't be able to hold a conversation, he would hide in his hair and he could barely speak. But what he is today was always there. When you have love, you gain confidence. I don't think anyone ever loved Tim – really loved him – in his life.'

So the misfit redeems himself with love, makes up with his old friends, charms the pants off the studio again, and rides off into the sunset. Close, but not quite. The real Burton is no fairy tale. He describes *Mars Attacks!* in sarcastic sound bites – 'On the depth chart, it's like a *Love Boat* episode' – and then sloughs off a probe for specifics: 'Just make it up, it's more interesting that way.'

More interesting or less threatening? 'Up until a few years ago, I never spoke very much,' he says, a vague sense of tranquility settling over his distant and distracted eyes. 'You always feel like you're on borrowed time to some degree, but you just keep on truckin'. I'm just having some fun watching great actors acting to imaginary Martians. It's just so beautiful and funny, and I laugh at it every day.' Burton's face lights up as a blanket of grey storm clouds descends upon the canyon where his house sits. It's a welcome break from the persistent sunny glare.

PAX AMERICANA

by J. Hoberman

If the mission of the movies is, as Siegfried Kracauer wrote in his *Nature of Film: The Redemption of Physical Reality*, to preserve that which is transitory, to monumentalise the ephemeral and to celebrate the poetry of trash, then *Mars Attacks!* is pure cinema. Tim Burton's latest opus may not be the first mega-million dollar Hollywood blockbuster based on a bunch of 35-year-old bubblegum cards, but it's surely the standard against which all such subsequent efforts will be judged. Certainly, no one will ever accuse Burton – among the few Hollywood filmmakers with a modicum of aesthetic integrity – of betraying his supremely cheesy source. (Having previously worked from the compost heap of comic books, Grade Z sci-fi cheapsters, and television kiddie shows, the director is practically the Merchant-Ivory of American idiot culture.) Like Burton's *Ed Wood* (1994), *Mars Attacks!* is rooted in what the horror-film historian David J. Skal calls 'Monster Culture'. A form of (mainly) male adolescent humour inspired by the campy telecasts of old horror movies that began in the late fifties, Monster Culture was big on the Universal stable of Mittel-European bogeymen. In addition to reading the pun-ridden fan magazine *Famous Monsters of Filmland* (an utterly disreputable publication whose adolescent devotees included Joey Dante and Stevie Spielberg), Monster Cultists might construct moulded-plastic models of the Wolf Man, the Frankenstein Monster, and Dracula, some of which glowed in the dark. 'Perfectly Detailed Down to the Smallest Fang,' the comic book ads promised: 'Decorate Your Room! Surprise Your Mother!'

Monster Culture coincided roughly with the Khrushchev Era (sputnik, missile gap, ban-the-bomb), reaching its mainstream apotheosis with such sitcoms as *The Munsters* and *The Addams Family*, both of which had their premieres during the pre-Vietnam 1964-65 television season. As obviously counterphobic as grown-up 'sick' humour, the craze peaked in the autumn of 1962 to merge with the imagined apocalypse of the Cuban Missile Crisis – the period during which the sepulchral tones of Bobby 'Boris' Pickett's novelty hit 'The Monster Mash' actually reigned as the number one single on the Billboard Chart. Joe Dante's amiable and underrated *Matinee* (1993) provided a reasonably valid high-school view of the Missile Crisis by entwining the most angst-ridden week of the Cold War with a satire of the schlock apocalyptic radioactive mutation movies that everyone, even then, recognised as a primitive manifestation of nuclear terror.

In his design sketches, Burton christened Lisa Marie's alien girl 'Queen of Outer Space' – in tribute to another piece of trash sci-fi, a 1958 flick starring Zsa Zsa Gabor.

It was during that same season that the original *Mars Attacks!* made its sensational debut as a series of 55 trading cards, conceived by the Topps bubblegum company in the wake of a successfully scurrilous series of centennial American Civil War cards depicting all manner of gross, bloody, *imaginary* battles. Despite their fictional details, the *Civil War* cards were praised by the nation's educators. Not so the *Mars Attacks!* series which, in showing scenes like a pet dog being vapourised, were deemed too lurid for kids. It was attacked in the press, as well as by a Connecticut district attorney, and effectively driven from the nation's candystores and hence into the realm of mass-cultural legend.

Like any self-respecting Monster Culture product, the movie *Mars Attacks!* has provoked grown-up disapproval. The sternly celebrity-driven *New Yorker* scolded irresponsible Burton for squandering the capital of his success ('There's a strong whiff of self-destructiveness in this picture . . . *Mars Attacks!* is *meant* to be a kind of anti-entertainment'), while, validating Burton in another way, *The New York Times* advised anxious parents that, like *The Cable Guy* (the year's prize *film maudit*), *Mars Attacks!* might be too dark for their children.

'More weird than funny' according to the *Times, Mars Attacks!* is also less camp than hyperreal in adapting the Topps series – to which it is surprisingly faithful in representing the green-faced, bug-eyed, ecto-skulled Martians and their flesh-burning raygun violence. Given the potential to make *any* sort of alien creature, there is something irresistibly perverse in Burton's using state-of-the-art computer animation to produce this simulation of supreme tackiness.

The theremins wail overtime as a flotilla of rotating saucers clutters up space, like so many hubcaps on the cosmic junk heap. *Mars Attacks!* offers a sentimental taxonomy of Cold War extraterrestrial-invasion cliches, from the official all-purpose scientific expert and the bellicose military commander to an anachronistic reel-to-reel 'translation machine' used to convert alien babble into English. That the movie is set in a nominal future, resembling a more fabulous version of the High Fifties, further suggests a particular form of cultural nostalgia (Washington DC never more resembled Imperial Rome than during the prolonged saucer attack at the climax of the didactic 1956 'semi-documentary' *Earth vs. the Flying Saucers*). Infused with the Populux Jetsonism of the early sixties, *Mars Attacks!* draws on the entire 1948 to 1973 'Golden Age' of Eric Hobsbawm's Short Twentieth Century, including the cycle of Disaster Films that marks the Golden Age's end.

No less than the lugubrious *Independence Day*, but to far more desecratory effect, *Mars Attacks!* celebrates the Pax Americana. Although *Mars Attacks!* often seems to parody *Independence Day*, it was actually longer in the production pipeline. The *War of the Worlds* paradigm notwithstanding, the films' similarities are very probably a function of market-testing. Both use the crowd-pleasing convention of a righteous black man (essential America) punching out an alien's lights. And both propel their narratives by channel-surfing the Land of the Free – but where *Independence Day* concentrates on the power citadels of LA, New York and Washington DC, *Mars Attacks!* replaces the coastal Sodom and Gomorrah with the fantasy heartland realms of rural Kansas and downtown Las Vegas. Where *Independence Day* revels in the survivalist scenario of public order breaking down, the more honestly 'what-me-worry?' *Mars Attacks!* shows that hope springs eternal for the television-blitzed populace.

While *Independence Day* pits a gaggle of hyped-up flyboys against a horde of interplanetary locusts (the movie's rhetorical highpoint being the hitherto wimpy President's 'Let's nuke the bastards!'), *Mars Attacks!* allows Earth's marginal losers to best the juvenile pranksters from Outer Space. And as *Mars Attacks!* ridicules Las Vegas, America's fastest-growing metropolis (as well as the national Democra-city where the architecture synthesises all human history and the casino dress code encompasses everything from star-spangled tuxedos to damp swimming trunks),

Independence Day celebrates American military and cultural hegemony.

A pure cultural expression of what *The Nation* magazine has dubbed the National Entertainment State, *Independence Day* is the spectacle for which the Republican attack on the Clinton White House and the revelation that life may have once existed on Mars were but part of a three-month publicity build-up. Among other things, *Independence Day* afforded the key negative moment in America's interminable presidential campaign. Having played to the Religious Right by attacking America's foremost industry, the mired-in-the-polls Republican challenger Bob Dole created a midsummer media event out of his wife's sixtieth birthday by treating her to a box of Goobers, a basket of popcorn, and a matinee showing of America's most popular movie in a nearly empty Century City cinema.

What did the candidate see? Accurate as far as it went, Dole's thumbs-up review ('Leadership/America/Good over Evil') only underscored his cultural cluelessness. Not only had he endorsed the movie's projection of an improved Clinton, but by failing to comment on the money shot – of the White House blown to smithereens – Dole served notice that he had never even caught the most successful trailer in recent memory.

As *Independence Day* united America before one movie, so the movie showed America organising the world to establish 4 July as a global celebration of independence – from what? Surely not Rupert Murdoch, the immigrant lad whose Twentieth Century-Fox studio bankrolled the flick. Among other things, *Independence Day* was an example of shameless synergy, plugging not only Murdoch's Sky News but *The X-Files* – a Fox television show that refers regularly to the so-called Roswell Incident (in which an alien-piloted flying saucer crash-landed in the New Mexico desert in 1947, a world-historic event allegedly covered up by the US Air Force ever since).

In terrestrial terms, the confluence of these two special-effects invasion thrillers is an episode in the ongoing struggle between Murdoch and Burton's patron, the world's largest multi-media conglomerate, Time-Warner. In New York City, where Murdoch received a special waiver of the US anti-trust laws to allow him to be the only media mogul in America to own both a daily newspaper and a television station in the same marketplace, Time-Warner refused to allow Murdoch's new 24-hour news station on its cable system. As Murdoch's *New York Post* lambasted Time-Warner's latest acquisition, Ted 'CNN' Turner, the city's mayor Rudolph Giuliani attempted first to pressure Time-Warner and then to put Murdoch's news station on a city-owned cable channel as a public service. (To add to the mix, Giuliani's wife Donna Hanover – seen to splendid effect in the role of former President Jimmy Carter's evangelist sister in *The People vs. Larry Flynt* – is a newsreader on a Fox station.)

Personal and anarchic where *Independence Day* is corporate and patriarchal, *Mars Attacks!* has an even purer hatred of politicians – and of adult authority in general. 'Extraterrestrial life – the people are going to love it,' President Jack Nicholson calculatingly smirks on seeing the first images of the approaching saucer armada and, as Manohla Dargis put it in her review, 'smelling [the] supreme Photo Op'.

Playing the nation's senior star as the Hollywood king he actually is, Nicholson's performance is so layered with insincerity that he's all but lost beneath the waxy build-up (a pompously rancid blend of Reagan and Clinton, he is truly the leader we deserve). He even contributes a superfluous bonus stint as a leathery wheeler-dealer in a red-on-red cowboy suit and Stetson with attached orange wig; Burton's fondness for strapping performers into bondage drag notwithstanding, actors must enjoy working with him.

Mars Attacks! is overstuffed with cameos by Burton alumni, including Sarah Jessica Parker as a Barbara Walters-type television personality in go-go boots, Danny DeVito as a Las Vegas low-roller, octogenarian Sylvia Sidney as a nursing home diva and, topping her *Ed Wood* Vampira turn in the movie's one universally appreciated sequence, Lisa Marie as a seven-foot-tall, blankly gum chewing, bubble-coiffed, hip-swivelling, torpedo breasted, alien-designed sex doll.

The most sensitive director of live cartoons since Frank Tashlin put Jerry Lewis and Jayne Mansfield through their paces, Burton here achieves a near Preston Sturges-like density (or at least a *Hollywood Squares* form of celebrity familiarity). He casts blaxploitation superstars Pam Grier and Jim Brown as an estranged couple; gets Annette Bening to play a New Age Spielbergette; recruits Glenn Close as the fatuous First Lady and Pierce Brosnan as a suavely inane scientist with a pipe attached to his jaw; has Paul Winfield impersonate a Colin Powell-style political general; and rehabilitates Martin Short to bob and grin as the President's mutant Stephanopolous. (That some of Short's antics anticipate the over-publicised peccadilloes of another Clinton adviser, the disgraced Dick Morris, just shows that American politics and American showbiz are two hemispheres of the same galactic brain.)

All the more remarkable is that the human stars have to compete for attention with a screen full of computer-generated Martians. (In this sense at least, *Mars Attacks!* is a glimpse into the Hollywood future. Though the synthesised creatures of the 21st century are more likely to be long-dead movie stars, Burton has allowed that the chief Martian, distinguished by his plush crimson cape, is modelled on Gloria Swanson in *Sunset Boulevard*.) With oversized, iridescent heads, half skull, half lushly exposed brain, these quacking, eye-rolling little cuties are as ferociously scene-stealing as they are lethal. Indeed, half the human cast is wiped out in the spectacular first attack of these killer

Destruction on a grand scale and the assassination of the US president are laughing matters in Mars Attacks!. *Such joyful irreverence may have sabotaged it at the box office.*

toys, who (as gleeful in their destruction as Joe Dante's gremlins) pack heat-zapping rayguns that char their victims down to their green-or-orange-glowing skeletons.

In *Mars Attacks!* the narrative is so inconsistent that screenwriter Jonathan Gems, who brought the project to Burton, might have generated his script William Burroughs style, by tossing the Topps cards in the air and then tracking their random pattern. Who cares? No effect is too tacky – a herd of flaming cows (lifted from the original cards), a couple of transposed heads, flying saucers over Vegas, the notion of alien bachelor pads. *Mars Attacks!* is a form of pop surrealism. (Call it the chance meeting of Tom Jones and Godzilla in the Luxor parking lot.)

Burton is no more afraid to trash the bogus counter-culture piety of Spielberg's grotesquely revered *Close Encounters of the Third Kind* than he is to dress a set with violently polka-dot spherical chairs, to locate his trailer park in the shadow of a massive Donut World, or to set an AA meeting in a Pepto Bismol-pink prefab church. As shot by David Cronenberg's favourite cinamatographer Peter Suschitzky, the radioactive pallette seems based on mood rings, lava lamps and tropi-holic slurpies. Fittingly, the Martians are defeated not by Earth's indigenous microbes but by the endless permutations of America's native vulgarity.

Triumphantly solipsistic, *Mars Attacks!* is the sort of movie in which the resident nerd triumphant (Lukas Haas) is serenaded by a mariachi band's 'Star Spangled Banner'. So God bless America. When our maximum leader Jack Nicholson takes to the tube to tell his fellow citizens that 'a powerful memory is in the making . . . This is the perfect summation to the Twentieth Century,' he's actually providing *Mars Attacks!* with its perfect pull-quote.

MARS ATTACKS!

review by Kim Newman

USA, the present. A fleet of flying saucers from Mars nears the Earth. US President James Dale, after consulting with Professor Donald Kessler, Generals Casey and Decker and press agent Jerry Ross, cautiously extends a welcome to the Martians. In Las Vegas, real estate tycoon Art Land concentrates on a big deal while his new age wife Barbara prepares to welcome the aliens; ex-heavyweight champion Byron Williams, a casino employee, is more concerned with getting across country to reunite with his wife and children. Television newsman Jason Stone is miffed when his fashion presenter girlfriend Nathalie Lake flirts with Kessler during an interview. Doughnut shop minion Richie Norris is ignored by his parents, who proudly send their other son Billy Glenn off to the Marines.

The Martians land and exterminate the greeting party, including Jason, Billy Glenn and Casey, but they kidnap Nathalie and her chihuahua. Dale is persuaded this might have been the result of a misinterpreted gesture, so he invites the Martian Ambassador to address Congress, which he wipes out. The Martians kidnap Kessler, whose living severed head develops a relationship with fellow abductee Nathalie (whose head is now grafted onto her lapdog's body). The Martians attack in force, ravaging America. Among the dead are Art, Richie's parents, Jerry, Decker and the President and the First Lady. Byron and Barbara join forces with singer Tom Jones and escape from Las Vegas. While rescuing his Grandma, Richie discovers that her Slim Whitman records make the aliens' brains explode and Whitman's music is used to defeat the invaders. Byron bests a horde of Martians in single combat and rejoins his family. Taffy, Dale's teenage daughter, sole survivor of America's chain of command, commends Richie for his heroism.

Tim Burton — A Child's Garden of Nightmares

The US box-office disappointment of *Mars Attacks!* in the wake of the success of *Independence Day* begs the question of how Stanley Kubrick's nightmare comedy *Dr Strangelove* might have fared if it had opened *after* rather than before Sidney Lumet's similarly themed Cold War flashpoint movie *Fail-Safe*. The hit in 1964 was Kubrick's hip, cynical satire on nuclear Armageddon and the flop was Lumet's square, solemn version, in which everyone acts with stifling nobility and reason. By the mid-nineties, attitudes have reversed: the mass audience is now more prepared for a 'B' movie hymn to the American Spirit of Endurance than a *Mad* magazine grotesque vision of a country deservedly laid to waste by bug-eyed monsters.

Ironically, the Godzilla-loving Tim Burton's original interest was not in the 1962 *Mars Attacks!* bubblegum cards but in an eighties pastiche entitled *Dinosaurs Attack!*. He switched to the earlier inspiration for fear of invidious comparisons with *Jurassic Park*, and has wound up with a movie that seems doomed to be unjustly written off as a coat-tail rider. There are as many similarities between *Mars Attacks!* and *Independence Day* as there are between *Strangelove* and *Fail Safe*: indeed, all four films have their crisis-confronting presidents, conflicting military and scientific advisers, big White House sets, aerial actions and exploded cities. One or two moments even play like canny parody, though presumably this is coincidental: in place of *Independence Day*'s momentous destruction of the White House is a hilarious scene with a flying saucer nudging a monument so it leans first this way, then that in an effort to topple it perfectly onto a pack of Boy Scouts. While the Earthlings of *Independence Day* are awed and impressed by the appearance of the alien ships, the venal fools and knaves of *Mars Attacks!* barely take notice, being too caught up in petty endeavours.

Though it would be easy to read Jack Nicholson's President James Dale as a parody of Bill Pullman's President Whitmore, there is no obvious correspondence between the two, just as Peter Sellers' Adalai Stevenson-like Merkin Muffley (in *Strangelove*) is a completely different creature from Henry Fonda's dignified President (in *Fail-Safe*). The most subtle, most astonishing element of Burton's savage satire is that Dale chooses to greet the Martian Ambassador with a windy paraphrase of Rodney King's famous 'why can't we just get along?' speech. Typically, the invader then kills the President with a detachable hand that turns into an alien flag which unfurls to mark the conquest of Earth. Nicholson also takes the secondary role of the Vegas hustler Art Land (perhaps to suggest that President and con man are two sides of the same coin), but does surprisingly well toning his natural flamboyance down to play the most powerful stooge in the world. There is room for a shrug of humour (Dale's '*ca va*' when the President of France calls him up) among the frenetic mugging and world-destroying. Furthermore there are great lines such as 'you can tell the American people we still have two out of three functioning arms of government,' after the mass skeletonisation of Congress.

This is the first Burton film not to revolve around a central eponymous protagonist and the diffusion among the large and varied cast means that its storytelling seems more haphazard even than such straggling items as *Beetlejuice* and *Batman Returns*. It is clear that Burton himself invests his identification in the put-upon Richie, the lank-haired doughnut counter boy who saves the world (using a plot gimmick poached from *Attack of the Killer Tomatoes*) and the film does resolve his story with a wonderfully awkward meeting with the also convincingly adolescent Taffy. However, Burton didn't unleash these skull-headed, big-brained CGI midget monsters to express admiration for anything much. The film – following the blithely sadistic cards – is mainly concerned with blasting away at a whole parade of detestable images of American 'normality': smug President, fierce First Lady, slick estate agent, militarist goons, survivalist trailer trash, lecherous Washington aides, dim-bulb scientific expert, tabloid television hacks, lawyers ('you're taking over the Earth, you're gonna need a lawyer,' Danny DeVito pleads), yapping dogs, even a symbolic hippie dove of peace. All are reduced to smoking coloured skeletons, and one can sense the natural born anarchist's joy in blasting out of hand an assortment of A-list players from mainstream Hollywood, while the survivors are a lovably eccentric parade of exploitation names (Pam Grier, Jim Brown), mixed-up kids, a feisty old-timer (Sylvia Sidney) and the self-parodying Tom Jones.

With Danny Elfman's humming theremin score to accompany the delightfully retro flying saucers, this expertly evokes the fifties feel of *Earth vs. the Flying Saucers* or *The Man from Planet X*, or the more colourful sixties look of *The First Men in the Moon* or *Daleks' Invasion Earth 2150 AD*. There are a few genuinely surreal images (some from the cards) like the herd of burning cows, but this is mostly a delight for its pulp sci-fi magazine cover one-offs: the flying saucer ramp unrolling precisely to match the red carpet waiting for it, the giant Martian walking machine, green brainbursts spattering the inside of the aliens' helmets when Slim Whitman hits the high notes. The most sustainedly eerie (and funny) sequence casts Lisa Marie – Vampira in *Ed Wood* – as a voluptuous temptress whose beehive hairdo conceals her Martian brainpan: chewing gum and wobbling in a tight dress as she invades the White House, the actress achieves the remarkable, disturbing feat of being at once a demonstrably real person and moving as if she were as computer-generated as the remainder of the alien horde.

Less focused than *Dr Strangelove*, and as interested in childish 'B' picture homages as in lampooning contemporary America, *Mars Attacks!* is as much in the spirit of *It's a Mad, Mad, Mad, Mad World* or *1941* as it is an attempt at a big-budget science fiction blockbuster. It has its moments of quiet humanity – Richie interprets a Martian's circle-in-the-air greeting with 'he's made the universal sign of the doughnut' – and flat-out sickness (Martian communication machines barking 'we are your friends' as their owners gleefully raygun fleeing humans), but its main commitment is to chaos. Like *Batman Returns* it's the sort of thing that alienates far more people than it converts, but it has so much sheer verve packed into its admittedly incoherent frame that it's hard not to take something cherishable away from it, whether it be the severed heads of Pierce Brosnan and Sarah Jessica Parker shyly kissing as their flying saucer crashes, or the chortling Martians erecting a mammoth and complicated ray-cannon to point at one little old lady's head.

HEADS WILL ROLL

A TIM BURTON FILM

Sleepy Hollow

JOHNNY DEPP   CHRISTINA RICCI

ONE ON ONE — TIM BURTON

by David Mills

The first thing people usually ask when you mention you've met Tim Burton is, 'Is he weird?' He must be, the reasoning goes. Just look at his movies: *Beetlejuice* (1987), *Batman* (1989), *Edward Scissorhands* (1990), *Ed Wood* (1994), *Mars Attacks!* (1997). All weird, they say. And yes, he is what some might call slightly eccentric, what with his wild, wild hair, a mass of unruly black curls that would terrify the strongest of combs. And yes, he has a propensity to gesticulate a great deal, grabbing, jutting, helicoptering his hands before him, chopping through the air, Bruce Lee-stylee, in an effort to illustrate some point when words are not enough. And yes, the man likes to wear shirts with little skeletons imprinted upon them. But spend some time in Burton's company and you can't quite shake the feeling that maybe, just maybe, it's the rest of us who are weird, and he's the perfectly sane one.

Having begun his career as an animator at Disney, Burton has, some say, continued to turn out animated movies ever since – only his films feature animated human beings rather than cute cut-outs. The Disney thing is, in retrospect, hard to fathom. The idea of Burton sitting down and drawing furry little animals, when inside his head raged stories of scissorhanded boys and invaders from Mars, is an amusing one – although it was not long before his own peculiar vision was given vent. From *Pee-wee's Big Adventure* (1985) to *Beetlejuice*, *Batman* and *Edward Scissorhands*, Burton was Hollywood's darling. Eccentric? Possibly. But, by God, his films did boffo box office. So that was okay, then.

By the time *Batman Returns* (1992) came around, people had started calling his stuff too dark, and while that film made a fortune at the box office, it wasn't perceived to be enough. Then came *Ed Wood*, arguably his best film. It won Martin Landau an Oscar for Best Supporting Actor as long forgotten horror icon Bela Lugosi, and Burton the best reviews of his career. But no one came. Ditto *Mars Attacks!*.

After a year working on the aborted *Superman* movie, Burton was spent. Until producer Scott Rudin presented him with a script called *Sleepy Hollow*.

Sleepy Hollow *marks the third time you've worked with Johnny Depp. There were rumours that the studio originally wanted other people, such as Brad Pitt, for the role of Ichabod Crane. Was Depp your first choice?*
This is what happens. It's like on *Edward Scissorhands*, yes he is the first choice, then you kind of go through this little song and dance with the studio. Not that they don't like him. You're making a movie, and as soon as it's going to cost a certain amount they go, 'What about . . . ?' and you go through the list that everybody goes through and it's just like you play this little game and what you hope for is the right thing comes out of it, which is sort of the way it was in this case as well. It's normal Hollywood procedure. They have their list . . . 'What's Mel Gibson doing?'

Sleepy Hollow *was the first gothic horror movie in Tim Burton's career. Its tacky promotional tagline aside, the film is a strangely dignified essay in* Grand Guignol.

Tim Burton — A Child's Garden of Nightmares

You and Depp do seem to bring out the best in one another.
Johnny is so great to work with and he's willing to do anything. That's what I love about him. I like chameleons, I like people who like to do different things. It's great too, because it's collaborative. If you work with a scenic painter and they paint a beautiful sky, it gives me something. Same thing with an actor – you have a feeling about something and they do it, and yet it's also their own thing, so it creates a positive momentum. I can see similarities in the characters Johnny's played, yet they're all different.

Much has been made of Depp being your on-screen alter-ego ...
It's for other people to make those conclusions. I've always felt it's best when things come from an emotional point, rather than if I think too much about something. I'm not so much of an intellectual that I can handle that. I get myself into trouble. I feel much more secure doing things coming from a subconscious point of view. But anybody who contributes to something, you put some of yourself into it, because that's how you make it resonant. That's what I try to do with any character and most of the actors I work with.

Depp described [main character Ichabod] Crane as so tight he couldn't fit a pin up his ass. I always like characters who think they know things, but don't. We all kind of go out on a limb. You're in these meetings in Hollywood and halfway through the meeting you hear yourself talking and realise you don't know what the fuck you're talking about and yet you're pretending like you do. That's part of what the whole trip is about in a way.

It's a wonder you've not used Christina Ricci before ...
She's like a silent movie actor and I went for that with this. You're talking about this place Sleepy Hollow and you think about people from upstate New York and the kind of weird inbreeding that goes on, and you just think about these weird looking people and she just seemed to be appropriate.

So what interested you in the script?
I had been working on *Superman* for about a year and I didn't know what to do. Then they sent me this script and I really liked it. I had never really done something that was more of a horror film and it's funny because those are the kind of movie I liked probably more than any other growing up. And it's a fascinating story. There's something strong about a headless character – and being able to do it when you're not having to do this routine [he lifts his shirt up to cover his head] – which was the technology up until fairly recently. Also I wanted to get back to making a movie where you're building sets and you're doing things where it's less manufactured. We're using the technology more to take something away than to add characters, more like an old-fashioned movie.

Why did you bring in Shakespeare in Love's *Tom Stoppard to rewrite the script?*
That was producer Scott [Rudin]'s suggestion and it was good. The spirit of the script was Andy [Walker]'s – that's why I got into it and wanted to do it, and I worked a lot with him and I think what ended up happening is he took it as far as he could and it did need something else. Even just getting a different perspective on it can be good, just a little bit of a different flavour. He's very talented, but also cool. He's open, he's not, 'Whatever I write is gold . . .' He was just really fun to talk to and he's smart.

Sleepy Hollow *performed fantastically in the US, making up for the turn-out for* **Mars Attacks!**. *Why do you think America stayed away from that film?*
It kind of confused people I think, because I was looking at it from all different kinds of points of

Johnny Depp and Christina Ricci consolidate their gothic credentials in Sleepy Hollow. *Ms Ricci previously appeared as little Wednesday Addams in the* Addams Family *films.*

view, all at once. People didn't know how to take it. I enjoy it. I get something different out of each movie and that was a fun one to make. When I was making it, I kept thinking of it as an animated film in a sense, like it was about a bunch of different ideas that don't necessarily link up, thrown together. You get so close you don't really know. European audiences seemed to get it better.

The film's writer, Jonathan Gems, called it a 'politically incorrect' movie. Do you agree with that assessment?

I can never tell. That was part of what the energy of the film was. Often what I think is funny, other people don't find funny; or what I think is scary or disturbing, other people don't. It's like I have trouble identifying what's correct or incorrect. For instance, when we were working on the trailer for *Sleepy Hollow* and you saw the Headless Horseman with a blue ski mask [worn to enable his head to be removed by computer] and then you saw him without his head, it's like a completely different energy. Without a head, it's, like, great and kind of almost funny. To me, I have no problem showing this movie to kids. And of course the ratings board comes back and thinks the opposite of what I see, they think that without his head he's scarier. To me, you see someone without a head, you start to laugh and you kinda get excited and it becomes a fantasy character.

You've cast your girlfriend Lisa Marie once again in Sleepy Hollow, *this time as Ichabod's mother. She appears in your artwork and photographs, too. What is it about her that inspires you?*
It's just nice to do this stuff and have somebody that you love around – as opposed to my whole life, pretty much doing it on my own. I remember on *Mars Attacks!*, we were in New York and we bought a cheap wig and went to Washington and took some Polaroids. It's a process I really like.

A theme that's been present in your work since the beginning is duality. Was that one of the things that attracted you to Superman?
We thought of the idea of focusing more on the fact that he's an alien, and maybe for the first time feel what it's like to be Superman. The duality, what's shown, what's hidden, had never, in my mind, been explored deeply with that character. Here's this guy who's from another planet and he's really strong, and he's got to hide it. What if he gets angry? How does he have to hide that? You would have to be careful. And Nic Cage is the kind of actor who could pull that off.

So what happened, then? Why, after a year, did Warner Bros. pull the plug?
The combination of Warner Bros., me, and [*Batman* producer] Jon Peters was not good at all. I basically wasted a year. I shouldn't be saying this, but it's not really bad-mouthing per se. A year is a long time to be working with somebody that you don't really want to be working with. It's fine if you get something done, but to go that hard and that long and not get something done is devastating, because really I'm in it to make things, I'm not in it to have these bullshit meetings.

So other than Nicolas Cage, who else had you cast?
Nobody. We were talking to Kevin Spacey for Lex Luthor. If we could have just cut through some of the bullshit and done it, it would have been interesting.

You once said your parents bricked up your bedroom window when you were a kid, though you didn't know why. Have you ever asked them?
At one point I did, and they did say it had something to do with keeping the heat in. And then I thought, 'Well, we fucking live in California; it's not like we're in Alaska.' So I did ask, but I'm not sure I got the answer I was after . . .

GRAVEYARD SHIFT

by Mark Salisbury

The Headless Horseman isn't looking himself today. For starters, there's a head resting on his inordinately broad shoulders where normally there'd be none. And it's his own head at that – not one he'd decapitated earlier and brought along as a gruesome joke. Even stranger, he's wearing a bright blue ski mask that makes him look like . . . well . . . 'He looks like something out of one of those Santo wrestling movies,' says director Tim Burton, referring to the Mexican panto-style superhero series. 'We're trying to make the most expensive Mexican horror movie ever made.'

It's close to midnight on a cold, damp March evening, midway through Burton's $60-plus million adaptation of Washington Irving's classic tale. They're preparing a pivotal fight scene between Johnny Depp's Ichabod Crane, Casper Van Dien's Brom Van Brunt and the aforementioned Headless Horseman. Van Dien and Depp, armed with suitably bonce-toppling scythes and sickles, practice their moves against the sword and axe-wielding blue-masked stuntman. Even clad in his silly blue mask (put there so that effects geniuses Industrial Light and Magic can digitally erase it later), the Still Headed Horseman looks pretty damn scary as he impressively whirrs through his moves. It later turns out that he's Ray Park, although this is still months before he became known to audiences worldwide as horny-headed evil Jedi Darth Maul. Watching this unlikely trio walk through their moves around a canopied wooden bridge in the heart of this small, eighteenth-century Dutch-immigrant farming community is like watching a curious, gothic puppet show – only with life-size puppets.

They repeat the sequence a few more times before going for a take, at the end of which the actors move out of frame and the camera continues to roll, shooting background footage for the visual effects department. When Burton is happy with each take, an SFX supervisor brings a floating silver sphere about the size of a football into shot which, once again, is used for the people back at ILM to judge lighting levels and shadows. 'The sphere of destiny!' Van Dien booms when he sees it. It's enough to spook the dead. Tonight is Van Dien's last day on set and, despite his sadness to be leaving, the *Starship Troopers* star is in high spirits. 'I can say I worked with Tim Burton,' he beams, 'which is kinda cool.'

This particular town of Sleepy Hollow is, in reality, an enormous, purpose-built set created on the Hambledern Estate near Marlow in Buckinghamshire, west of London. There are about a dozen wooden buildings in total – including a church, livery stables, a pub and some houses – constructed around a small duck pond in a style the film's production designer, Rick Heinrichs, terms 'colonial expressionism' by way of Dr Seuss. The mud is real, as is the horse shit, and that really is smoke puffing from the chimney tops. But there's also a studied sense of artifice to the place that makes the town feel like a model.

Dangling high above the set on 150-foot-tall cranes is a series of what can best be described as massive Chinese lanterns, bathing the area in an eerie, off-white glow which enhances the town's otherworldly atmosphere. The illusion is complete. 'I love upstate New York. It's such a haunted place,' Burton says. 'The story, the placement of it is so important, and that's why it's so funny to be here in Britain. But this location, it's weird . . . The first moment I came here I felt the terrain was so like upstate New York.'

While Irving's story has been filmed previously on a handful of occasions (notably Disney's very scary 1949 cartoon adaptation and a 1979 TV movie starring Jeff Goldblum as Ichabod Crane), Burton's version is the first to play up the horror and dream-like quality. The impetus behind the project came, initially, from make-up FX-artist-turned-director Kevin Yagher (*Tales from the Crypt*) who, back in the mid-nineties, was introduced to screenwriter Andrew Kevin Walker while Walker's then-unmade script for *Se7en* was winning him powerful friends in Hollywood.

Together Walker and Yagher cooked up a movie plot, using the novella as a starting point, and transforming the bumbling schoolteacher of Irving's tale into a New York policeman with a notable interest in forensic science and a disbelief in the supernatural. Sent by his superiors to investigate a series of brutal slayings in the tiny hamlet of Sleepy Hollow, the eighteenth-century Fox Mulder believes that his scientific methods will blow apart any notions of ghostly goings-on. Instead, he's forced to concede the existence of, and do battle with, the legendary Headless Horseman. It was at that stage, as Walker has noted, a hardcore horror story. Walker and Yagher pitched the idea to producer Scott (*The Addams Family*) Rudin, who bought into their more youthful and horrific take on the tale. The script was commissioned and Paramount were sold on the project, but, as co-producer Adam Schroeder explains, 'They never really saw it as a commercial movie. The studio thinks "old literary classic" and they think *The Crucible*. There was a fear about that. So everybody saw this as a bit of a labour of love.' Indeed, at one stage there was even talk about making the film very low-budget. 'When we started developing it, it was before horror movies came back,' Schroeder notes.

'Certainly this is no *Scream*,' he continues, 'but the fact is, people think Ichabod Crane is Jeff Goldblum or John Malkovich. We never had that in mind. It was always going to be a young, sexy Ichabod, very different from what people think of from the Disney cartoon or some of the descriptions of him in the novella.'

The project spent five years in development hell, before Rudin pitched the script to Burton. At the time, Burton was reeling from the tepid reception he'd received for *Mars Attacks!*, and from having the plug pulled on his *Superman* project, which had been developed for more than a year as a Nic Cage vehicle. Locations for Metropolis had been scouted, the original script (by Kevin Smith) rewritten out of existence and an art department hired, before Warner Bros. decided to axe it. Burton blames a combination of factors, including 'creative differences' with *Superman Lives'* producer, Jon Peters.

Burton – in skeleton-pattern shirt – directs Johnny Depp as Ichabod Crane. No longer Washington Irving's nerdish teacher, Depp's Ichabod is an early forensic detective.

'I love the process of making films, and that whole year of not working after *Mars Attacks!* affected me deeply,' he says. 'I don't think I've ever been quite so affected that way.' When Rudin approached him with Andrew Kevin Walker's version (Yagher became a co-producer), he was eager to get behind the camera again. While Burton never read Irving's tale until he was on the production, he was familiar with Disney's animated version, which he says had a profound effect on him as a child, with its painfully gangly rendering of Ichabod Crane and berserk camera angles.

'That's one of the reasons why I wanted to work at Disney in the first place,' says Burton, whose first job after graduating from the California Institute of Arts was as an animator on *The Fox and the Hound*, definitely one of the House of Mouse's lesser efforts and a bizarre match if ever there was one. Burton would have been far happier if Disney had stuck him on a movie like the one that terrified him so much growing up. 'They created a wonderful sense of the story being funny, scary and visceral, all at the same time,' Burton recalls. 'The layout and the colour and the design was so beautiful. I remember the feeling of seeing it; it tapped into lots of different things. It had a great energy all the way through.'

Born in Burbank, California, Burton is, quite literally, a child of Hollywood – albeit a child who was considered by those around him, not least himself, to be a gawky misfit, a non-conformist who spent his days feeding on a steady diet of horror and science fiction. It's this eccentric outsider quality that has percolated through all of Burton's work, from *Pee-wee's Big Adventure* to *Ed Wood*, and can now be found again in *Sleepy Hollow*'s Ichabod Crane. 'What I liked about the Ichabod character was it was very much a character inside his own head,' explains the 41-year-old director, who hired *Shakespeare in Love*'s Oscar-winning screenwriter Tom Stoppard to polish up Walker's script. 'That, juxtaposed against a character with no head, was a really good dynamic. I've always responded to characters who have conflicts of interest within themselves. Ichabod's a character who's pretty fucked up in the sense that he's smart, but sometimes you can think yourself into a corner.'

Although various 'star' names – Brad Pitt and Liam Neeson among them – cropped up in connection with Ichabod, in Burton's mind there was only ever one person for the part: Johnny Depp, who he'd previously cast as the lead in both *Edward Scissorhands* and *Ed Wood*. 'He's perfect for this,' says Burton. 'And it's easier when you work with somebody more than once, because you don't have to verbalise, you don't have to talk about every single thing you're doing.'

Once Depp signed on, finding the right actress to play Ichabod's paramour, Katrina Van Tassel, became that much easier. Burton found his feisty, sexy heroine in Christina Ricci, an actress who, despite her tender years, has already amassed an enviably varied resume (including Rudin's *Addams Family* films), and whose unorthodox beauty and aloofness marked her out as a perfect foil for Depp. 'I was a little bit afraid that Tim was going to be really pretentious and, like, a "genius",' recalls Ricci. 'He *is* a genius, but he doesn't act like that. He just really loves doing it and he's so enthusiastic and mouths your dialogue along with you while he's watching the monitor. It definitely made me appreciate him a little bit more. He's just like a child. He's got a child-like awe when it comes to films.'

The original plan was to shoot the movie predominantly using existing locations. With the story set in upstate New York, the filmmakers began their search for a town to use there, but were disappointed to find that the real village of Sleepy Hollow didn't live up to expectations. 'It's this very commercial town where everything's very polished and manicured,' says Adam Schroeder. 'They actually had a whole insignia of the Headless Horseman on all the police cars and taxis; it was very commercial. They had a Headless Horseman gift shop. We realised we couldn't shoot there.'

Tim Burton – A Child's Garden of Nightmares

Since the initial idea was to film *Sleepy Hollow* predominantly using existing locations with some studio work, alternatives were sought throughout upstate New York and the Hudson Valley, and reaching as far north as Sturbridge, Massachussetts, with the filmmakers even considering using a number of Dutch colonial villages and period recreations. When no town proved suitable, that, coupled with a lack of studio space in New York, forced the filmmakers to look further afield. It was Rudin's idea to try England. 'We came here figuring we would find the perfect little town,' laughs Schroeder, 'and then, of course, we had to build it anyway.'

Which, as it turned out, suited Burton just fine. His vision for *Sleepy Hollow* was influenced by his love for Hammer films, as well as *Black Sunday*, Mario Bava's 1960 Italian horror movie about a witch seeking revenge on her persecutors – in particular the otherworldly feel they evoked as a result of being filmed primarily on sound stages.

Charged with facilitating this enormous task was production designer Rick Heinrichs, whose long-term collaboration with Burton dates back to the 1982 stop-motion short *Vincent*. The duo made the film while working in the animation department at Disney, and Heinrichs has worked with Burton in varying capacities (including visual FX consultant and art director) ever since, most recently as production designer on the ill-fated *Superman Lives*.

'Part of the character of the narrative is about the feeling you get from this town,' says Heinrichs, 'in the same way you would get it from *Frankenstein* or Hammer horror. Those designers understood about setting the mood and saying something about what the characters are like by showing, not telling, which is a big thing in animation.'

While Schroeder says they were always going to build a fair number of sets, it was decided to shoot the movie in a totally controlled environment to best fulfil Burton's concept. It effectively meant that all *Sleepy Hollow*'s interiors, as well as the majority of its exteriors (other than those in Buckinghamshire), would be shot at Leavesden Studios. By applying techniques they'd used in both traditional and stop-motion animation – such as false perspective sets – to live action, Burton and Heinrichs ended up creating a set-bound world for *Sleepy Hollow* that today's audiences aren't used to seeing.

'You don't see them doing many exteriors on stage anymore, because it doesn't really fit the overall look of films, the naturalism that movies tend to gravitate toward,' explains Heinrichs, who estimates that 99 per cent of *Sleepy Hollow* was filmed on sets. 'We're not going for naturalism, we're going for a kind of natural expressionism. It's not as hard-edged or graphic as stop-motion animation, like *Nightmare [Before Christmas]* or something like that. It's a bit softer.'

Heinrichs says that Burton told him to watch *Dracula Has Risen from the Grave*, as well as sundry other Christopher Lee Hammer films, as reference for the atmosphere and feeling he was after in *Sleepy Hollow*. 'I didn't want it to be a hardcore period piece and go in that direction,' explains Burton. 'I could never tell what time it was in those Hammer movies. They had to put in "1892: London" or whatever to let you know, because you could never guess from the costumes. I wanted to go for more simplicity and try to make it a real place.'

After the special-effects meltdown of *Mars Attacks!*, with its multitude of CG aliens and Earth-threatening spaceships, Burton was determined to make *Sleepy Hollow* as conventionally as possible. 'I know the way forward seems to be the digital backdrop, as in the new *Star Wars* film,' says Burton. 'But in films like *Black Sunday*, where you feel you are there, that's what's important to me. There are certain shots, like looking down on Sleepy Hollow the town, that people might think looks like a model. It doesn't look real but it is, and that's the wonderful thing about it.'

Working on these shores also gave Burton the opportunity to populate *Sleepy Hollow* with a *Who's Who* of English character actors, including Hammer veterans Christopher Lee, in the small but significant role of the burgomaster who sends Ichabod to Sleepy Hollow, and Michael Gough

The Headless Horseman, a figure of pseudo-folklore, originated in 'The Legend of Sleepy Hollow'. In Burton's version he is no longer a macabre hoax.

(*Batman*'s butler Alfred), as Hardenbrook, the town lawyer, Michael Gambon as Baltus Van Tassel and Miranda Richardson as his wife Lady Van Tassel, along with Ian McDiarmid and Richard Griffiths. They joined an American cast, many of who, like Gough, had worked with Gambon before, such as Jeffrey Jones (*Beetlejuice*), Christopher Walken (*Batman Returns*) and Burton's girlfriend Lisa Marie.

'We were able to cast the best actors in the world,' raves Schroeder. 'I remember the first time we shot the scene where the elders [Gambon, Gough, Griffiths, McDiarmid and Jones] take Ichabod into a room to tell him the legend of the Headless Horseman. You saw these five amazing faces, all in period, looking like a painting from the time, with Johnny Depp, who is ageless but contemporary. It was this great soup.'

'We wanted to have a mix,' explains Burton of *Sleepy Hollow*'s eccentric cast. 'Michael Gough, he's just so great. I was watching him work on set a few nights ago and then I went home and saw him in *The Legend of Hell House*. He plays a corpse. A great job – he didn't move much.'

If *Sleepy Hollow* is everything Tim Burton wants it to be, then the resultant dreamy, macabre, gothic atmosphere will be redolent of the best Hammer films, down to the copious blood and gore. 'I've tried to inject the joy I got from watching those films into this,' he reflects, before adding: 'We wanted to keep the spirit of the horror movie but be fun with it. I wouldn't say we lightened it up – but this is not a Merchant-Ivory horror film.'

THE CAGE OF REASON

by Kim Newman

'The dominant spirit, however, that haunts this enchanted region and seems to be commander-in-chief of all the powers of the air is the apparition of a figure on horseback without a head. It is said by some to be the ghost of a Hessian trooper, whose head has been carried away by a cannon ball, in some nameless battle during the Revolutionary War, and who is ever and anon seen by the country folk, hurrying along in the gloom of night, as if on the wings of the wind.'

Originally published in *The Sketch-Book of Geoffrey Crayon* (1819-20), Washington Irving's short story 'The Legend of Sleepy Hollow' is a humorous character study, holding up schoolmaster Ichabod Crane as an example of ludicrous superstition, rather than a true horror tale. The spook which pursues Ichabod through the woods is unmasked, *Scooby-Doo* style, as the ungainly scholar's romantic rival Brom Van Brunt, intent on scaring him away from pretty heiress Katrina van Tassel. Establishing the American order of lusty jock above too-thoughtful nerd, Brom gets the girl and Ichabod is persecuted into fleeing the town. 'As he was a bachelor and in nobody's debt, nobody troubled his head any more about him,' concludes Irving, never guessing that this confident preference for the muscular bully would eventually lead to *Revenge of the Nerds* and even the tragic shootings at Columbine High School. The bluff callousness strikes modern readers as rather chilling; we are now used to stories of worms who turn, sandy-faced weaklings who take Charles Atlas courses and speccy nerds who win the prom queen. The casual dismissal of Ichabod – first archetype of America's nightmare self-image, the loser – is as conceptually frightening to us as a real spectre was to him and would be to later ghost-story writers.

The Headless Horseman is the first truly American addition to the gallery of horror figures which evolved, over 100 years later, into the monster-movie pantheon. Like such comparable British characters as Frankenstein's monster and Dracula, the Horseman is a foreigner, an invader of sacred soil; like that other great bogus ghost the Hound of the Baskervilles, he is such a potent image that many later readers, and all film versions, have regretted he turns out to be a fake. Until Tim Burton's new film *Sleepy Hollow*, the most familiar version of the tale was a Disney cartoon narrated by Bing Crosby, *The Adventures of Ichabod and Mr Toad* (1949), which boasts a flamboyantly animated ghost on a rearing steed, though dotty old Mrs Farren (Julia Dean) effectively retells the story, with only sound effects, as an aside in *The Curse of the Cat People* (1944) and there is a bland 1979 made-for-TV movie with Jeff Goldblum and Meg Foster well cast as Ichabod and Katrina.

All film and television versions of 'The Legend of Sleepy Hollow' are torn between Irving's smug, rational puncturing of superstition – which he links to Puritan America's witchcraft panic, noting Ichabod's devotion to the works of minister Cotton Mather – and the thrilling visual and dramatic possibilities of the ghost itself. Burton's *Sleepy Hollow* is not merely torn between rationality and superstition, but torn apart by the dichotomy, with each of the film's several significant creators drawing subtly different, mutually exclusive readings from the material. The project was originally developed by Kevin Yagher, the make-up effects man most famous for the animatronicidal doll Chucky in the *Child's Play* films and the Crypt Keeper in the *Tales from the Crypt* television series, as a follow-up to his inauspicious directorial debut *Hellraiser: Bloodline* (1996), 'un film de Alan Smithee'. Working with Andrew Kevin Walker, a specialist in exploring more modern American horrors in *Se7en*(1995) and *8MM* (1999), Yagher plotted *Sleepy Hollow* as a low-budget effects showcase with a spectacular murder every five minutes or so and a delight in the process of creating fake monsters that might have led him to sympathise with Irving's Brom – who is, after all, the first special make-up effects man in literature.

In the event the film was scaled up to a major big-budget release with several other visionaries involved – though like *Se7en* it remains at heart what Walker once characterised as 'a pretentious slasher movie'. Among the executive producers is Francis Ford Coppola, continuing an attachment to the genre begun with *Bram Stoker's Dracula* (1992) and developed in *Mary Shelley's Frankenstein* (1994). Coppola has been working up a secondary career, restoring to the horror genre the literary weight it once had, all the while trying to find ways of retelling old, old stories in new emotional-romantic lights, which may strike unusual chords with temporary audiences but also work against what we may take as the primary purpose of the horror movie – to be scary. With Walker and Coppola on board, it should be no surprise that *Sleepy Hollow*, though shot in the English countryside, addresses the American roots of Irving's tale.

With the action laid in 1799, and Ichabod Crane (Johnny Depp) raising groans with a speech about how the millennium draws near and a new modern era is to begin, we are only a generation removed from the War of Independence, which created both the US and the Headless Horseman. The Crane who sets out from New York City to the upstate hamlet of Sleepy Hollow is explicitly an American who will interrogate transplanted Dutch and British old folks (the young principles are American actors, the character players almost all British). The hero's commitment to reason is born out of the tension between his Puritan father and witch mother, whose violent clash of beliefs has left him with memory blanks gradually filled in by bad dreams. His reaction has been to reject both their faiths in favour of a scientific method epitomised by Cronenbergian surgical implements and complex optical devices that never enable him to see anything,

This Ichabod is no mere pedagogue but a scientific policeman whose overconcern with matters of detection prompts his superiors to pack him off to Sleepy Hollow to enquire into a series of decapitations that has a symbolic as well as a literal gruesomeness, as the heads of the community are being lopped off. This is the sort of puzzle Walker has specialised in, and Depp's Ichabod merely follows the sleuths of *Se7en* and *8MM* who crack the case but find out more than they want to know about themselves and the nature of the world in the process. There is a flaw in this conception, best understood by looking at *The Hound of the Baskervilles*: though Arthur Conan Doyle was a firm believer in ghosts, he knew the character of Sherlock Holmes could not co-exist in a universe with a genuine supernatural creature and therefore unmasked his hound as a mastiff coated in phosphorus. *Sleepy Hollow* establishes Crane if not as a Holmesian figure then as a clear predecessor of Edgar Allan Poe's ratiocinator Dupin, fussing with his crime-solving chemicals and probing always for motive and means. When faced with an actual apparition he collapses and takes to his bed to conclude his flashback memories and become reconciled to his mystic heritage, symbolised by his consultation of a wood witch and growing attraction to Katrina, who is herself magically inclined. However, there is a curtain behind the curtain, with Ichabod accepting the supernatural only to realise that the killer ghost is acting to a plan under the control of a human mystery villain straight out of Terence Fisher's Hammer film version of *The Hound of the Baskervilles* (1959).

In the end, however, *Sleepy Hollow* is a Tim Burton movie. Taken on after the commercial rejection of *Mars Attacks!* (1997) and the collapse of his long-developed *Superman* project, material that was already well formed has been thoroughly worked over into something unmistakably the director's own. Depp's Ichabod is his third role for Burton after Edward Scissorhands and Ed Wood in 1990 and 1994, and his third go as the director's alter ego, again Struwwelpeter-haired and laced into a tight black jacket that makes him scuttle rather than walk. Burton's curious ability to rethink anything from *Pee-wee's Big Adventure* (1985) through *Batman*

(1989) and *Batman Returns* (1992) to *The Nightmare Before Christmas* (1993) as an experiment in expressionist autobiography is yet again in evidence. Ichabod's dreams of his mother (Burton regular Lisa Marie) hauled off to the torture chamber allow the director of *Ed Wood* an opportunity to regenerate moments from favourite films – conflating scenes with cult actress Barbara Steele from Mario Bava's *The Mask of Satan* (1960) and Roger Corman's *The Pit and the Pendulum* (1961) – while imbuing them with an emotional resonance that is as rich and strange as Kenneth Anger's appropriation of drive-in imagery for his own magickal purposes.

Brom Van Brunt (Caspar Van Dien) is the latest in a line of bested bullies (Anthony Michael Hall in *Edward Scissorhands*, Jack Black in *Mars Attacks!*) Burton has enjoyed gruesomely killing off. It is a key to Burton's universe that only the truly terrified and alone, like Michael Keaton's Bruce Wayne in *Batman* or Winona Ryder's goth chick in *Beetlejuice* (1987), can face up to the monsters and earn the reward of romantic fulfilment. Christina Ricci's Katrina, more than answering to Irving's description ('a blooming lass of fresh eighteen, plump as a partridge, ripe and melting and rosy-cheeked as one of her father's peaches'), is as devoted to her strange beau

The legend in corporeal form: Christopher Walken as the Horseman, plus head. Sleepy Hollow *fleshes out its premise by presenting his death during the War of Independence.*

(unlike Irving's shallow coquette) as Jack Skellington's sewn-together girlfriend in *The Nightmare Before Christmas* or Ed Wood's succession of supportive helpmates. Ricci seems a natural inhabitant of Burton's world, her broad, child-woman face blank in adoration of her deeply embarrassed swain, credibly witchlike, chaste but not asexual, clearly willing to step into madness if that's what it takes to join the man she loves.

Though the addition of a genuine supernatural creature – wonderfully played, in his headed form, by a wordless Christopher Walken with teeth filed to cannibal points and a Sid Vicious hairdo – is the most striking divergence from the original story, Burton's real rebellion lies in seeing Ichabod Crane not as an awkward weirdo but as an identification figure. As in his earlier freak roles Depp remains a handsome man got up to simulate grotesquery and is never allowed to be the scarecrow geek Goldblum was ideally suited to, most faithfully translated from page to screen in the cartoon version. Given to fainting spells, several times squirted in the eye by jets of blood and thoroughly screwed up by his upbringing, Depp's Crane is a marginalised hero, but a hero nevertheless. Brom is an idiot who blunders pointlessly to his death without helping anyone, but Crane defines that type of courage which involves being genuinely terrified throughout a hideous experience but still getting the job done.

Rarely can a major studio horror film have been the product of so many people who are knowledgeable and enthusiastic about horror as a genre, who take such delight in revisiting the by-ways of its history. There's a real *frisson* to be had from the cameo casting of the likes of Christopher Lee and Michael Gough, whose genre history goes back to their co-starring roles in Fisher's *Dracula* (1958), though the script gives more weight to such occasional visitors to the genre as Miranda Richardson, Michael Gambon and Richard Griffiths, while finding significant moments for Burton regulars Jeffrey Jones and Martin Landau (decapitated before the credits). The woods through which this Horseman rides look exactly like those stretches of the New Forest Hammer liked to pass off as Transylvania, though there's a tangled CGI hell-tree that evokes Oz and *The Company of Wolves* (1984), and the finale takes place in a burning windmill which is ostensibly a faithful recreation of a set from James Whale's *Frankenstein* (1931) – already homaged as a miniature golf course in Burton's short *Frankenweenie*, (1984) – though it might also be a nod towards the more highly coloured locale of Fisher's *Brides of Dracula* (1960). It's fairly easy to cast a familiar face or drop in a plot reference to a Hammer film, but this is a movie that knows exactly the colour palette of Arthur Grant's cinematography for Hammer or Floyd Crosby's for Corman and works hard to get the mist swirling in the right direction and the precise shade of red for a startling door in an all-white dream church.

Despite Burton's fondness for character comedy and the prevailing Hollywood notion that nobody could possibly take horror seriously, the pleasure of *Sleepy Hollow* come from high style rather than high camp: a scarecrow (another American horror icon, from Nathaniel Hawthorne to the *Batman* villain) which whirls whenever the monster brushes; an animated tendril of ghostly mist snuffing out a row of burning torches before the spectre comes for its next victim; the Hessian motioning two angelic little girls not to give away his hiding place, only to have one calculatedly snap a twig to summon the mob who hack off his head; Richard Griffiths' head spinning on his neck after the fatal slice then tumbling to the ground between Depp's legs to be speared and carried off by the Horseman with a circus-style flourish; the Horseman finally regaining his skull and reattaching it to be covered by sinew and skin in a reversal of the usual monster-movie ending that allows for a wild display of *Evil Dead*-ish effects; the bustle of a 1799 New York street scene in which we see the outlines of the city to come.

Given the nature of the monster's favourite mode of transport, this is a film that has to keep on the move, with thundering hooves and careening carriages. And despite its sometimes mechanical and often broken-down storyline *Sleepy Hollow* is never less than ravishing to look at – courtesy of cinematographer Emmanuel Lubezki and production designer Rick Heinrichs, though Burton's eye is evident in every composition – and manages, when it gets its speed up, to come across as terribly exciting.

What it isn't, and this may be a failing of Irving's conception, is very frightening. Heads are lopped off regularly (the inevitable poster line is 'Heads will roll') and human corruption is everywhere. But Ichabod Crane is terrified for intellectual and psychological reasons we can't really share and Burton has his hero overcome all his fears so he can come up trumps in the extended finale, which combines chase, deduction, confrontation and revelation into one big ball of plot string.

HEADS OR TAILS

by J. Hoberman

Tim Burton has yet to tackle an 'adult' theme but there isn't a bankable Hollywood director with a flintier sense of aesthetic integrity. More insolently pop than David Lynch and less eager for approval than Steven Spielberg, Burton has repeatedly twisted studio resources to his own dank and gibbering expressionistic purposes.

Burton's *Sleepy Hollow* is by no means as radical an anti-entertainment as his ill-starred *Mars Attacks!* but this splendid, shuddering contraption has a dazzling purity of vision. It's a Halloween spookarama in which the falling leaves hit their marks, the shutters rattle on cue, and the goblin entrances are lit by lightning. Although populated by flesh-and-blood actors, Burton's fun house is as ruthlessly stylised as the Disney animation that, half a century ago, breathed a comic chill (not to mention Bing Crosby's narration) into Washington Irving's ghostly yarn.

The most literary of Burton films, *Sleepy Hollow* opens in a dark and smoky 1799 New York City and, humorously *fin de siecle*, drifts rhapsodically to a foggy fairy-tale village in the sumptuously autumnal Hudson River valley. Elevated from Irving's gawky schoolteacher, Ichabod Crane is not only played by the beautiful Johnny Depp but transformed into a self-consciously modern and amusingly timorous police officer, sent upstate to meet a comic gaggle of well-upholstered British actors (notably Michael Gambon and Miranda Richardson), all bewigged and befuddled to grotesque effect.

Officially, Ichabod has come to solve a series of mysterious decapitations. Screenwriter Andrew Kevin Walker, who wrote *Seven* and *8MM*, has reworked Irving's classic American fake-lore as (what else?) the story of a serial killer. The Horseman, a hoax in Irving's tale as well as in the scary old Disney cartoon, is literal enough here – a monstrous Hessian mercenary forever searching for his lost head (Christopher Walken with filed teeth). Burton scarcely strays from the screenwriter's well-trodden path but, like all of his films, *Sleepy Hollow* is not so much a narrative as it is a place. The mood isn't grim but Grimm. Burton directs the grisly action as though it were a jolly puppet show, another *Nightmare Before Christmas*.

Prissy and pedantic, Ichabod is an inventor of elaborate detection devices. He's an artist *manque* who, supremely rational, doesn't flinch from the occasional ghoulish operation. (There's a bit too much Dudley Do-Right to Depp's delivery but – as in *Edward Scissorhands*, if not *Ed Wood* – he's at the service of his director's spectacular *mise-en-scene*.) A typically traumatised Burton hero, Ichabod has mysteriously-punctured palms and revisits his childhood throughout the movie with regular trips to dreamland. There, his witchy mother (played – significantly? – by Burton's significant other, Lisa Marie) presents him with the proto-cinematic optical toy, known as a thaumatrope, which serves as his talisman.

Ichabod shows the illusion-producing thaumatrope to Katrina Van Tassel (Christina Ricci), the most innocent of the movie's several witches, explaining to her that 'truth is not always appearances'. You may not believe your eyes either, each time the Headless Horseman emerges from between the roots of a bleeding, twisted tree – less sleepy hollow than a vaginal passage to hell. Rampant castration anxiety notwithstanding, *Sleepy Hollow* is essentially comic – although perhaps a bit gory for small children, most especially in the savage punishment visited upon the village midwife and her little boy. (Like young Ichabod, he was partial to optical amusements.)

Although Walker's script is both overcomplicated and underwritten, *Sleepy Hollow* gallops along at a goodly clip, offering a number of breathless (or should we say, headlong) thrill rides. The main attraction in this magic kingdom is Burton's gorgeous production design. The images are as rich as compost; every clammy detail is subordinate to the whole. Still, Burton and Walker have done yeoman service in creating an indigenous gothic, mixing fear of the primeval woods with the guilt arising from colonial rebellion.

The Horseman serves as an all-purpose return of the patriarchal repressed – a mutilated, yet potent, remnant of the American Revolution. (It's as though the statue of George III that New Yorkers pulled down at the Battery came back as a living thing.) But the movie itself is an act of historical hubris and symbolic regicide. Disneyland is revised as rampantly Freudian – and historically resonant – Grand Guignol.

07·27·01
RULE THE PLANET.

THIS FILM IS NOT YET RATED

REMAKING, NOT APING, AN ORIGINAL

by Richard Natale

Even the devilish Tim Burton couldn't have come up with a more amusingly incongruous anthropomorphic image for his upcoming remake of *Planet of the Apes* than the sight of British actress Helena Bonham Carter, in full primate face, a cigarette dangling from her lips as she picks her nose.

It is mid-afternoon and Bonham Carter is on a break, sitting on a stoop outside a sound stage in downtown Los Angeles indulging her nicotine habit and delicately trying to scratch her real nose through the left nostril of her simian prosthesis without creasing or tearing the many folds of rubber, glue and hair that obscure her naturally porcelain skin.

Bonham Carter, famous for her many roles in British costume dramas such as *A Room with a View* and *Howards End* (she's been described as pre-Raphaelite so often that it's practically part of her name), has spent so much screen time in ornate, constricting costumes that she once swore she would never accept another role that required wearing a corset. Now she finds herself trapped behind an ape mask that requires four-and-a-half hours to apply every morning and almost two hours to remove. With her shooting schedule drawing to a close, Bonham Carter confesses that impatience sometimes gets the best of her, and 'I tend to tear off my face.' Master makeup artist Rick Baker's aesthetic design is so lifelike that Bonham Carter ably conveys a pang of guilt through its many layers.

'I must be a bit of a masochist,' she says, trying to laugh. If so, she is not alone. The on-again, off-again *Planet* remake is one of the most anticipated films of the summer. It has a great deal to live up to, including the 1968 original starring Charlton Heston and its four sequels, as well as what-might-have-been ruminations if the new movie had been directed by James Cameron, Chris Columbus or Oliver Stone, who at various points had signed on. After almost a decade of false starts, *Planet* finally came together last fall and is rushing toward a July 2001 opening, less than three months after the completion of principal photography.

'People keep thinking it's coming out *next* summer,' says Burton, who is holed up in an editing room in New York, where he lives. 'It's a ridiculous kind of schedule. It took longer to greenlight than to make, but that's the way things happen on movies like this. They're such big monsters that it takes an unnatural act to get them going and keep them moving.'

Producer Richard Zanuck's involvement in the new *Planet of the Apes* is one of those 'only in Hollywood' stories. Without him, there would never have been an original *Planet of the Apes*. In 1967, when he was running Twentieth Century Fox, Zanuck was approached by a former publicist turned producer, Arthur Jacobs, with Rod Serling's screenplay adaptation of Pierre Boulle's novel. The project had been put in turnaround by Warner Bros., who he said 'got scared of the idea' of a dominant ape culture with enslaved humans.

'When he [Jacobs] presented it to me, I didn't take it seriously,' Zanuck remembers. 'I only read it because of Serling [the mastermind of the classic *Twilight Zone* TV series] and because the writer

Planet of the Apes, *the most hyped Burton project since* Batman. *Referring to the legend, 'This film has not yet been rated,' the director retorted, 'This film has not yet been shot.'*

of the book had also written *Bridge on the River Kwai*. Even then I read it with scepticism.'

But he became intrigued by the idea of an upside-down world. When Charlton Heston agreed to play the lead and Roddy McDowall, Kim Hunter and Edward G. Robinson accepted the prominent ape roles, Zanuck tentatively moved ahead. 'I wasn't going to commit until we'd done makeup tests.'

After the tests were satisfactorily completed, Robinson dropped out. 'He said, "I'm getting way too old to be getting into heavy makeup and eating through straws,"' Zanuck explains. (Robinson was replaced by Shakespearean actor Maurice Evans.)

Director Franklin Schaffner was signed to direct, despite misgivings that he might not be able to handle a 'big' movie. At the time, Schaffner had worked mostly in television. Ironically, after *Planet of the Apes*, Schaffner directed nothing *but* big movies, including the Oscar-winning *Patton*.

That was just one of the many pleasant surprises in the history of *Planet of the Apes*. Still not sure of what he had, Zanuck previewed the film for the first time in Phoenix. 'If we could get by the first scene of talking apes and the audience didn't laugh hysterically, I knew we'd be OK,' he recalls. The moment passed without incident and by the end of the preview the audience was applauding wildly and hanging around to discuss the film in the lobby afterward for the better part of an hour.

'I'd never seen anything like it before,' Zanuck said.

Planet became one of Fox's biggest hits of the decade, grossing $34 million (on a $6 million budget) and spawning four sequels of decreasing quality and appeal, as well as two short-lived TV series in the mid-seventies. In addition to its trendy anti-nuke message, which played into the late sixties counterculture movement, the film arrived around the same time as *2001: A Space Odyssey*, helping fuel a science-fiction movie craze, spawning other films such as *The Omega Man* and *Soylent Green*.

Zanuck, who left the studio ranks soon thereafter to become a producer (including the Oscar-winning *Driving Miss Daisy*), had kept tabs on Fox's intention to remake the film. When he read last year that it was going ahead with Tim Burton as director, he thought about calling Fox studio head Tom Rothman to tell him what a good selection he'd made, but never did. A few weeks later, Rothman phoned Zanuck and asked if he wanted to produce the film.

The intention from the start was to make a remake that wasn't a remake, says Burton. 'You can't really remake *Planet of the Apes*, because the whole vibe and feeling of the original movie was very sixties. You have to look at it from a different perspective, and I saw something oddly compelling about the concept of talking apes. When you do primate research, you start thinking about how weird our perception of apes is, that they're kind of close to us, yet they can rip you to shreds. That's kind of frightening. Even when they smile at you, they don't really mean it in the way humans do.'

'You mean they smile the way Hollywood executives do?' Burton is asked.

The director begins to laugh until he comes close to choking. 'Anyway,' he continues, 'you put all that into the mix and sometimes things that don't seem like a good idea become exciting because there's something risky about it.

'And besides,' he adds, '*The Beverley Hillbillies* had already been remade and the *Gilligan's Island* script wasn't ready.' From anyone else that would obviously be a joke, but with Burton you wonder. This is the man who brought *Batman* to the big screen, and, earlier, *Pee-wee's Big Adventure*. Think of it. Johnny Depp as Gilligan and Jack Nicholson as the Skipper. The mind reels.

'Tom [Rothman] told me to start with a blank page,' says William Broyles Jr. (*Apollo 13* and *Cast Away*), who shares screenwriting credit. 'And I thought it would be very intriguing to create this movie from scratch.'

Since Boulle's book had been heavily mined for the 1968 original, Broyles kept only the premise. He never read any of the various remake scripts and only heard about them vaguely (one reportedly involved a virus that drives humans underground). The new version does not take place on Earth, which provided the surprise ending of the first film, and the characters and locations are all new. Broyles presented Fox with an outline based on his research of Roman history. 'What I described was a structure and class system on the ape planet, how its economy worked, what their religion was like, and how humans fit in as the slave culture. I had a great deal of fun with it.'

The subtext, which Broyles said became less 'sub' as the project moved along, was the whole issue of consciousness. 'If someone believes that creatures have a soul and spirit that is uniquely theirs, that can hold true across religious and racial lines – and in this case across species – and that's what we all have in common.'

Which is not to say that the new *Planet of the Apes* has become an existential art film. Broyles brought spectacle to the project – elaborate, primitive battle sequences (there is no gunpowder in the ape culture), giving the film an epic sweep.

The biggest battle over *Planet of the Apes*, however, took place before filming. 'Big, bloody budget battles,' Broyles laughs.

At the ShoWest convention in March 2000, then-Fox studio head Bill Mechanic announced that after almost a decade of talking about it, *Planet of the Apes* would finally be released in July of the following year. But Mechanic left Fox early last summer with the studio in a bit of a slump and reluctant to undertake a project that could potentially spiral out of control.

As Burton and Broyles continued refining the script, it became apparent that efficiency was crucial. 'It would have cost us $200 million if we'd done half of what was in that script,' says Burton. Fox was thinking about spending half that. Before production began, Broyles agreed to leave the project rather than make Fox's budget-minded revisions, and the team of Lawrence Konner and Mark Rosenthal (*Mighty Joe Young*) were brought on to fine-tune and simplify the script.

'These movies get made in prep,' says *Apes* executive producer Ralph Winter (*X-Men*),

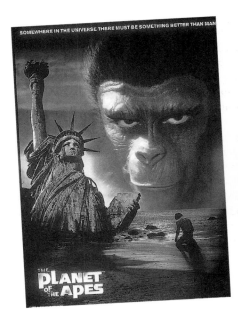

Posters for the 1968 Planet of the Apes. *The power of the original film derived from the novel ape make-ups, and the conflict between ape culture and the last intelligent man.*

describing its production schedule as a 'logistical nightmare' involving constant changes and compromises in order to adhere to the parameters of the film's budget – a 24-hour schedule beginning at two in the morning for the 80 days of principal photography, as well as a separate crew for second-unit work.

For those who are curious about some of the ways $100 million can be spent on a single motion picture, Winter cites the preparations for the battle sequence filmed at Lake Powell in Arizona. The dozens of horses that appeared in the sequence had to be cared for and fed for a month before the scene was shot. By mid-winter, the water level of the lake was dangerously low, so a million gallons were pumped in. The sections where the filming took place also had to be heated. 'The Humane Society won't let horses in the water if it's too cold,' explains Winter, 'not to mention the actors.'

The film's main set, Ape City, was constructed on a rented sound stage at Sony Pictures Studios, since all the Fox stages were occupied. Construction began July 2000 and took four months. 'Then we have a week after we wrap to tear it down, since *Spider-Man* is due to come right after us,' Winter says.

The Ape City set resembles a giant pop-up jungle storybook, with every alcove holding another, more compact location. 'The great challenge with Ape City,' says production designer Rick Heinrichs, who is a veteran Burton collaborator, 'was not only that it serve the action, but that it say something about the apes, their dual nature. Aspects of their culture and civilisation had to be intertwined with their natural animal habitat.'

More creative differences saw the departure of the film's original makeup artist, Stan Winston. He was replaced by Oscar perennial Baker, who considered using animatronic apes, but was more excited by the challenge of 'actor driven' gorillas, chimps and orangutans, with movable faces (unlike the stolid masks in the original film).

As astronaut Captain Leo Davidson, who lands on the simian-run planet, Mark Wahlberg is sleekly and simply clad throughout the film. 'I'm basically just there to get my ass kicked by guys in gorilla suits,' he says. Wahlberg sheds his blue-collar screen persona in *Planet of the Apes*, taking his first step toward playing a more sophisticated leading man. He's currently in Paris shooting Jonathan Demme's remake of *Charade*, in which he plays the Cary Grant role.

But, he says, 'I'm still having dreams about gorillas – that I'm in prison with a bunch of apes.'

Last August, all the actors playing simians enrolled in 'ape school' under the tutelage of Terry Notary, a former UCLA gymnast turned Cirque du Soleil performer. 'Tim wanted the apes to be realistic, about twenty per cent ape, 80 per cent human, since they were fairly developed,' Notary explains. Most of the six weeks of training was in ape movement – shoulders down, knees bowed, arms swinging like independent appendages. 'The walk took a long time,' says Notary. 'Once they got it, we started to develop how they would sit, eat, pick up something, throw a sword. Every little thing had to be learned. Nothing was formal. And there was a lot of maintenance.'

Some of the actors, like Tim Roth and Paul Giametti (who plays an orangutan), took to it quickly. Notary, who also plays Roth's stunt double in the movie, says that 'Tim did so well that, after a while, he was correcting me.' Bonham Carter, however, had to take remedial courses. 'I failed ape school,' she laments. But, Notary points out, she made up for it by remaining in character even while off-stage and hanging out with some of the real live chimps who appear in the film, 'so lovable and affectionate one moment, and if you don't do what they want, they practically rip your arms out of their sockets,' Bonham Carter says.

The method to all this madness is Burton. 'When you have a guy like Tim Burton, people come,' says Wahlberg. 'Everything he did was spot on.'

On the set, Burton is a dervish, climbing into nooks with his viewfinder (he rarely storyboards anymore, he says, preferring not to limit his options) to assess new angles, different shots, completely absorbed and utterly unflappable. He is the calm in the centre of this storm. In person, Burton, who resembles his own Hirschfeld drawing, is anything but disheveled and lax – he's completely focused, never wasting a moment, never losing his inimitable sense of humour.

Planet of the Apes is being marketed as a giant action film. But everyone involved is there for the bizarre wit he brings to every project. 'Tim comes at everything that way,' says Zanuck. 'He's always surprising us. The other day there was a scene that called for Helena's character to be brushing her hair. Tim started the shot from the waist up and we notice that she's writing something. But the quill seems to be moving by itself. Then we pan down and we see she's writing with her foot. It's a fun moment. And those things happen every day. It's part of his magic.'

Still, as with his *Batman* movies and *Sleepy Hollow*, Burton says he is being careful to delicately sculpt the humour into the film and not lay it on with a trowel. 'Each project has its own nature. You don't want to interject too much humour into a story about talking apes, because it can quickly turn into "The Chimp Channel". It's a tricky balance. It remains to be seen how much humour there will be [in the final cut]. It's definitely not going to be campy.'

Plot specifics are a closely held secret, as is the surprise ending. Those script pages were given only to the people who participate in the final scenes. Zanuck promises it will be as big a doozy as the original's and will explain why apes on a distant planet speak English.

PLANET OF THE APES

review by Owen Gleiberman

The 1968 *Planet of the Apes* is fondly remembered for a great many reasons. The humanoid gorilla makeup was, at the time, unprecedented in its elastic expansiveness, and the story, taken from Pierre Boulle's novel, had a fearful sci-fi charge that was thrilling in its very blatancy. The film's comic book racial overtones, crude as they may look now, carried a bold symbolic immediacy amid the heat and tumult of the civil rights era, and the whole production was staged with an irresistable end of the empire vastness, even if it all looks far cheesier than the way you remember it. (Viewed today, that 'spectacular' white boulder ape city might be a shopping centre patronised by the Flintstones.)

I doubt, however, that *Planet of the Apes* would ever have hooked so powerfully into its era, spawning four sequels, had it not been for the grizzled self-righteousness, the nearly totemic overacting, of Charlton Heston. Caged, stripped, mocked, led around in dirty rags by his ape tormentors, his noble airman wasn't just oppressed, he was all but violated. When he finally let loose with 'Take your stinkin' paws off me, you damn dirty ape!' Heston was the very image of Hollywood – of America – fighting to retain its virility in a world that had seized the power to lay the establishment low.

Mark Wahlberg, his physical bravura rippled by undercurrents of moody protest, can be an actor of quiet charisma, but in Tim Burton's *Planet of the Apes* he's a blank; he comes as close as possible to being a generic hero. In the midst of chimp research at an outer space station, his Captain Davidson straps himself into a pod that looks like a giant electric razor and ends up having a close shave with an electromagnetic storm, crash-landing on the ape planet. Imprisoned, he leads a handful of slaves on what is essentially a protracted great escape, but there's precious little urgency to the flight.

The simian army of Burton's 're-imagined' planet. Revising the premise of the original film, gorillas and chimpanzees fight side-by-side, without firearms, in heavy armour.

Burton, abandoning any pretence of Gothic poetic style, shoots most of the movie in monotonous woodland darkness, and Wahlberg has been given virtually nothing to do except react to immediate physical ordeals. The script is a busy, sometimes amusing babble of ape-human double entendres and tidbit tolerance lessons (an ape forces Davidson's mouth open and rasps, 'Is there a soul in there?'), most of it draped over a routine action skeleton. Since all of the humans talk this time, the notion that they're just regarded as 'lowly', while certainly unjust, isn't resonant enough to stir audience outrage.

Besides, with Kris Kristofferson coming on like Nick Nolte in Neptune curls and Estella Warren scampering around in a pointlessly conservative version of Raquel Welch prehistoric wear, what the human race in this movie seems most in need of being saved from is the perils of threadbare screenwriting.

Are there surprises? A couple of big money ones, notably the ludicrous would-be jaw-dropper of a finale. Yet *Planet of the Apes*, whose makers have claimed that it is less a remake than a reimagining, features backlot spectacle, a cast of hundreds battle, a weak whisper of gladiatorial vengeance – everything, in fact, but imagination. Following *Sleepy Hollow*, with 'ye olde slasher' repetitiveness camouflaged by virtuoso displays of ground fog, the movie is all but destined to become Burton's second hit in a row. Let's hope that he uses his newly restored power in Hollywood to become an artist again.

DON'T MONKEY WITH A GREAT APE

by Jonathan Romney

According to one definition, a myth is a narrative so powerful and coherent that not even the worst translation can spoil it. In that case, cinema myths should be doubly impervious to damage; for in film, it can take just one strong image to colonise our consciousness, regardless of narrative execution. It doesn't matter much whether the 1967 sci-fi fantasy *Planet of the Apes* was a great film, or even a good one. The important thing is that its premise was a dream of comic-book simplicity – a world ruled by apes, with humans as the shambling underclass. And the visual hook was unforgettable – suave gibbons in futuristic safari suits, Charlton Heston in all his chest-baring agony.

Still, there's no image in the world that a literal-minded remake can't drain of its mythic power. In many ways, Tim Burton's new *Planet of the Apes* is more visually striking than Franklin J Schaffner's original: Helena Bonham Carter as a chichi chimp, with shaggy chops and silky bob, made one of the more engaging *Premiere* covers of recent times. Yet Burton has little to offer but a refinement of the first film's imagery. He may have Industrial Light and Magic and make-up wizard Rick Baker on his side, but what's missing is a single sharp new idea or a searching critical angle on the original. No-one involved seems to have thought much about what the story meant in the decade of civil rights, Vietnam and rising environmental awareness, and what new meanings it might possibly acquire today.

This remake shows that middle-budget Hollywood sci-fi in the sixties was more alert and more *zeitgeist*-attuned than today's blockbusters, which inhabit only their own numbed void of opening-weekend grosses. The rhetorical point of Schaffner's original, a pop-Swiftian cartoon about racial intolerance and oppression, is taken pretty much as read here, and handled with the ironic subtlety of a fifth-form debating match: 'You can't tell them apart,' growls one simian bigot, eyeing up the humans. But however explicitly spelled out in the script, the allegory is effectively sabotaged by species stereotyping among the primates: while the enlightened chimps, led by Bonham Carter's liberal aristo, are characterised as sophisticated white Europeans, Michael Clarke Duncan's laconic warrior gorilla is cast as a black henchman with barely any narrative function.

There's a strange inconsistency in the playing too. Both Bonham Carter and David Warner are uncannily recognisable, and surprisingly expressive, under their four hours' application of make-up – Bonham Carter with a pert, flirtatious repertoire of pouts, sniffs and knowing eye signals, and a distinct touch of Katharine Hepburn in her delivery. Paul Giamatti too works his elastic features to droll effect, as a sleazy slave-trader gibbon. But if they can emote through all that latex, why does Tim Roth's chimpanzee general have the same expression of curled-lip rage throughout, like Klaus Kinski with lockjaw? It could be anyone behind those flared nostrils: you wonder whether Gary Oldman didn't pop in as substitute on Roth's days off.

There's one neat in-joke, Heston himself as a primate doyen, explaining human firepower. One gun, says the figurehead of the National Rifle Association, has 'the power of a thousand spears'. But it's a mistake to give Heston's original role to the clod-hopping Mark Wahlberg, whose entirely unfazed astronaut hero, trying to rouse the humans to insurgency, is like a high-school football captain pep-talking a losing team. And Estella Warren is a pure waste of space, pouting vacantly in the skimpy buckskin last modelled by Raquel Welch in *One Million Years BC*.

It all finally goes off the rails when Wahlberg is saved at the height of battle by a scandalously silly *deus ex machina*. The lazy premise of the conclusion relies on our willingness to accept that if

Burton with Mark Wahlberg, generic hero of Planet of the Apes. *The confused climax spells 'sequel', but Tim Burton's next film would be a more personal vision.*

it's sci-fi, then there's probably a time-warp involved somewhere and no questions asked. As for the new surprise ending, it's not quite the original's Statue of Liberty revelation but a variation on that, and based, I suspect, on an excruciating unspoken pun: it feels like the product of a panicky brainstorming session just as the coffee was running out.

This extremely mainstream effort clearly isn't giving Burton anything like the good time he had with *Ed Wood* or *Mars Attacks!*. There's only a smattering of characteristic touches: some eerie scarecrows, an ape child frilled up like a Victorian moppet, Lisa Marie's larky turn as an orangutan's simpering trophy wife, and a passing moment of ape jazz, bass fiddle plucked with the feet (tree-bop, I guess).

There are other impressive design touches – the apes' helmets with their bizarre scimitar curves, and the army's scarlet tents, which seem like a terrific merchandising opportunity, just the thing for avant-garde camping holidays. A lot of thought has also been given to making the apes actually move like apes, leaping and swinging, or charging into battle on all fours. Their marching formation, though, lurches along in a way that made me think they were going to strike up the 'Oh-ee-oh-ohhh-oh!' chorus of the flying monkeys in *The Wizard of Oz*.

As for subtext, forget it. The hovering spectre of miscegenation is summarily dispelled – despite their coy glances, there's no chance of a truly hairy moment between Wahlberg and Bonham Carter. Who'd have imagined that Burton, Hollywood's pet maladjusted adolescent, would play it so straight or so impersonally opulent? You wish he'd followed in the spirit of his erstwhile role model Ed Wood, and kept it chimp and cheerful.

BIG FISH IN HIS OWN POND

by Josh Tyrangiel

Because he tends to dress like a mortician and has made a fair number of films that romanticise gloom, Tim Burton has emerged as one of those directors who are not just makers of myths but subjects of them too. The most prevalent Burton myth is that he is dark and possibly a little disturbed. In addition to his clothes and movies, there are eerie bits of biography to support this view, like the fact that Burton's parents blacked out the windows of his childhood bedroom, apparently to save on heating bills. (Burton grew up in Burbank, California, not a notoriously difficult place to heat a home.) The second Burton myth is that his mind is still trapped in the eremitic universe of that darkened bedroom. Evidence includes his lavish recreations of sixties pop trifles (*Batman, Mars Attacks!* and *Planet of the Apes*) as well as more personal films (*Edward Scissorhands, Ed Wood*) that centre on misunderstood emotional savants with a likeness to a certain director.

Cross the wires of the Burton myths, as Hollywood studios often do, and – it's alive! – you get Frankenstein's multiplex monster, a developmentally arrested auteur capable of turning out an almost consistently profitable brand of kooky horror. Naturally, Burton loathes these myths. 'You get pigeonholed very easily in Hollywood,' he says, 'even if you do something they were leery of to begin with. I try not to think about it, but, oh, it kind of drives me out of my mind.'

Burton, 45, has no desire to be understood outside of his movies, but he wouldn't mind being, as he puts it, 'un-Burtonized'. His new movie, *Big Fish*, will probably help matters. *Big Fish* has chimerical elements, but they're in the service of a life-affirming story about fathers and sons, the kind of thing Steven Spielberg keeps returning to. (Spielberg was at one point attached to direct the film, as was *The Hours'* Stephen Daldry.) The movie stars Albert Finney as a man on his deathbed who recalls his younger self, played by Ewan McGregor, as a force of indefatigable buoyancy; Finney's son, played by Billy Crudup, believes his father is just an indefatigable liar. *Big Fish* is rooted in a conflicted adult world, and for the first time in a Tim Burton film, it is the parent – not the child – who is whimsical and misunderstood.

On one count, the un-Burtonizing process turns out to be fairly easy. Burton's home in north London (he has lived off and on in London for several years) is neither a cave nor a haunted mansion but a series of four cottages in a sylvan courtyard that he and actress Helena Bonham Carter, his girlfriend and the mother of their new son, lovingly renovated into a single cosy home. It is the kind of place Hansel and Gretel would run to. Inside, a coal fire hisses softly, and Burton, in clothes of muted colour, but colour nonetheless, sock-slides his way across the wood floor and into his study, where he flops with charming gracelessness onto a red velvet couch. He is as brooding as a Muppet. 'People who really know me know that I'm not dark at all,' he says. 'I mean, at all. Like, yeah, I like monster movies, but it's cathartic. I don't even . . . I don't know where . . . I don't know.'

Burton is warm, funny and optimistic. He is also incapable of finishing a thought. He begins conversations with a symphony of dancing hands and flopping hair, only to end up drifting in deep verbal space. Even simple topics can be tough for him. When he mentions that he used to live around the corner, Burton scans the ceiling and the words emerge warily, as if he were debuting a shiny new piece of vocabulary but were unsure of its pronunciation. 'I had a flat on . . . Belsize . . .

Edward Bloom (Ewan McGregor) encounters a giant
on his American odyssey. 7'6" actor Matthew McGrory
was blown up to twice his size for Big Fish *(2003).*

Park . . . Gardens?' Later he acknowledges, 'I didn't leave the house very much.'

Which brings us to Burton myth Number Two, that of the sealed adolescent universe. This one is a bit more difficult to dismiss. When he's not making a movie, Burton doodles a lot (he usually has at least two pens tucked into his shirt pocket). Otherwise, he says, 'I can't really account for my time. It kind of spooks me out because I don't really know how I spend it. I'm a little scattered. I think about things and do things, but I don't seem to have a specific thing that I do. Somehow the day goes by.'

Burton needs movies not just as an excuse to get up in the morning but also as a means of exchange between himself and the real world. 'Half the things I've ever worked on are these big behemoths where there's a release date before there's a script,' he says, but the other half are abstract attempts at autobiography. 'I'm amazed at people like Robert Wise [*The Sound of Music, The Andromeda Strain*] who can go from genre to genre, and every movie seems different,' he says. 'I never felt that I could do that. I need some sort of connection. The doing of it – making a movie – is a cathartic experience, so there's got to be . . .'

A wound? Burton would prefer that no one confuse the art with the artist, but he makes it tough. Many of his earlier films are responses to growing up in a family that couldn't express itself. His father, a parks employee, and his mother, who ran a gift shop, rarely touched their two children, says Burton, and at age ten, he left his family and moved in with his grandmother. He never fully reconciled with his father before the elder Burton's death in 2000, which could be why he was driven to direct *Big Fish*. 'My father died, and my mother was ill, so I read the script,' he says, 'and I feel like it captured a thing that was always quite difficult for me to put into words. That relationship, it just, you try to talk about it, and it doesn't, it didn't . . . Well, you can never really talk about it. You know, these issues are just in you. So I thought I'd just show it.'

Burton may live in his own space, but it is not juvenile, and it is not sealed. While he refuses to attend industry events like the Oscars – 'It's a popularity contest, and based on my growing-up experiences in school, I lost' – he loves having movie people around him. 'I enjoyed working with animation a little,' he says. 'But I love actors and sets and all of that. It's just more fun. No matter what you're doing, you stand back, and it's like there are all these people standing around in funny clothes looking at you and . . . Maybe I seem to them like the most foul-tempered, sealed-off zombie creature, but I get such incredible joy. It's like a wonderful, absurd dream.' Just real.

BIG FISH

review by Manohla Dargis

Big fish often swim in small ponds, but in Tim Burton's wistful new film about a son, a father and the lies that come between them there are no small ponds – just big, bright movie sets shimmering and bubbling with the director's imagination. Based on Daniel Wallace's delicate wisp of a novel, *Big Fish* tells the story of a raconteur who, after a lifetime of spinning whoppers about lachrymose giants and two-headed women, faces the prospect of dying under the dark cloud of his son's resentment.

There are worse paternal sins than fish tales as big as Moby Dick, but you wouldn't know it from Will Bloom. As played by Billy Crudup or directed by Burton (it's hard to tell which), Will comes across as a prematurely old fogy who has spent his life stockpiling grudges against his father and the man's predilection for self-flattering exaggeration. Played in the past by an exuberant Ewan McGregor and on the deathbed by a barely restrained Albert Finney (the robust actor often looks anxious to initiate a miraculous recovery), Edward is one in a line of fictional fathers who has long tended his own garden at the expense of his family. Edward's saving grace is his imagined life, a garden as lush and wild as that in a Maurice Sendak storybook.

A fable about fathers and sons, lies and misconceptions, *Big Fish* is the straightest movie in Burton's kinky repertoire. Or, rather, Will's tale is the straightest story the director has told. Photographed in the steady, personality-free style of the studio prestige movie, Will's part of the film tells of a soul-troubled young man trying to make peace with his past. Married to a French woman (Marion Cotillard), he works as a journalist in Paris, having tried to escape his father's gaudy good humour by devoting himself to facts in a country where people take themselves even more seriously than he does. When Will receives word of his father's illness, he grimly packs up his wife and disapproval and carries both back home to small-town Alabama.

Like the novel, John August's screenplay begins with the son talking about the father, a man who would be a myth. In Wallace's *Big Fish*, that myth assumes the shape of gentle absurdity. Along with the writer's embracing soft tone, the charm of the book lies in how it fuses the quotidian with the extraordinary: Edward experiences trials fit for a classical hero except that, unlike Hercules and Ulysses, his involve scrubbing fouled dog cages and selling girdles to waddling matrons. Burton cranks up the visual comedy of the character's self-mythology and lets it rip, sometimes to joyously dizzy effect. In the director's hands, even Edward's birth becomes an occasion for comic hyperbole, as the newborn bursts from his mother like a shot, sliding down a hospital corridor like a bar of runaway soap.

Edward rarely stops moving in the years that follow, and much of what's buoyant and appealing about *Big Fish* involves his quixotic pilgrimage toward selfhood. There's delight to be had from watching Burton conjure up one fantastical Edward-inspired scenario after another, whether it's the story of a poet turned bank robber (a wonderful Steve Buscemi), a circus interlude (featuring Danny DeVito) or a surreal peek at a variety show for comrades in North Korea. It's in these stories – by turns eye-popping and expressively de-saturated of colour, tweaked and lovingly twisted – that Burton, working with the talented team of cinematographer Philippe Rousselot and production designer Dennis Gassner, allows himself to be his most Burton-like, freed from the dull restraint of everyday life and movies.

Alas, we are allowed to stay with young Edward for only a short time. Because half of *Big Fish* involves an adult son and his terminally ill father and takes place in the familiar realm of accusation, confession, turnaround and acceptance, Burton regularly – and with palpable reluctance – yanks us out of Edward's florid imagination and thrusts us back into the desert of Will's reproach. Only Jessica Lange, as Edward's wife and Will's mother, brightens this dreary return to family melodrama, whether she's crawling into a bathtub with her husband or tenderly chiding her son for his severity. Too bad that Lange, who despite her glamorous appearance has apparently reached the cinematic age wherein actresses are relegated to matron roles, isn't given more to do – she embroiders her scenes with delicate feeling.

One of the few visionaries working in Hollywood, Burton has not always had an easy time sizing his creativity to fit the studio formula, and it's noteworthy a triumph such as the delirious freak-out *Mars Attacks!* was greeted with widespread derision. Like Will Bloom, critics tend to whack away at the unknown and unfamiliar with the gusto of deranged gardeners. Since then Burton has retreated into safer territory, including a lavishly mounted if insipid remake of *Planet of the Apes*. *Big Fish* marks an improvement on that impersonal exercise, and yet there's something sad about Burton directing a movie that pleads the case for imagination. One of the filmmaker's glories is that he's always believed adults can experience the world with the infinite vision of children. I bet he still reads Dr. Seuss.

SWEET SMELL OF SUCCESS

by Rob Waugh

It's the most spectacular scene ever filmed at Britain's Pinewood Studios – a pink, sugar boat full of children sailing across a river of gooey melted chocolate, with an orchard bearing individually wrapped sweeties on either side. There's no computer trickery involved. The river's really there, 192,000 gallons of it and halfway across one of the children falls in and is coated in the sticky mess. It looks good enough to eat. It isn't, of course – this is Hollywood, so the goo is a non-toxic special-effect fluid, made for the new version of *Charlie and the Chocolate Factory* starring Johnny Depp as Willy Wonka.

It's the first from Jennifer Aniston and Brad Pitt's production company, Plan B, and it shows that while the Hollywood power couple's relationship may be on the rocks, they're still a working partnership to be reckoned with.

The film pulls no punches. With an estimated $150 million (£80 million) budget, Plan B and director Tim Burton, famed for fantasy films such as *The Nightmare Before Christmas* and *Beetlejuice*, are sparing no expense to stay true to Roald Dahl's novel.

In *Willy Wonka and the Chocolate Factory*, the low-budget 1971 version of the film, in which the chocolate river looks like muddy water, the filmmakers replaced Wonka's trained nut-sorting squirrels with a machine. Plan B refused to compromise and are using 40 real squirrels, training them how to crack walnuts and deposit them on a conveyor belt. It took ten weeks of practice to make the rodents perform the feat. 'They're not good at taking verbal commands,' says their trainer.

Burton's no-holds-barred vision will also feature a chocolate that melts live on screen and the jungles of Loompaland, plus many other parts of the story that were missed out in the earlier film. Loompaland will be populated by an entire race of Oompa Loompas, all played by one dwarf actor, Burton stalwart Deep Roy, who will be cloned on computer into crowds of himself – and is being paid $1 million (£520,000) for his pains.

'I don't want to crush people's childhood dreams,' says Burton, who cast girlfriend Helena Bonham Carter as the mother of Charlie, the child who wins a tour of Wonka's magical factory. 'But the original film is sappy.' Author Roald Dahl himself hated the 1971 film, which starred Gene Wilder as Willy Wonka, and refused the producers the rights to make a sequel, *Charlie and the Great Glass Elevator*. His widow, Liccy, turned down dozens of scripts before finally approving the one used in Burton's remake.

'I responded to *Charlie and the Chocolate Factory* because it respected the fact that children can be adults,' says Burton. 'I think adults forget that. It was one of the first times you had children's literature that was a bit more sophisticated and dealt with darker issues and feelings. It showed there can be darkness and foreboding. Very sinister things that are part of childhood.'

Johnny Depp agrees. 'Roald Dahl's novels can be fun, but they're dark at times. Some of his stuff you wouldn't want to read to your kids. In *Charlie* there are these dark, subtle messages. Tim Burton and Roald Dahl are a match made in heaven.'

Fresh from playing eccentric writer J. M. Barrie in *Finding Neverland*, Depp was determined not to let the earlier film version overshadow his interpretation of the magical chocolatier.

'Regardless of what one thinks of the 1971 film, Gene Wilder's persona stands out,' he says. 'That

Johnny Depp, centre, as the strange Willy Wonka in
Charlie and the Chocolate Factory *(2005) – a Michael Jackson-esque androgyne in a world of his own.*

scares the hell out of you. Those are big shoes. So the only thing to do is go back to the book and try to figure out what Roald Dahl had in his head.'

Doing so has not been easy. Directors as diverse as Martin Scorsese and *Stuart Little's* Rob Minkoff have been linked to the projects, and stars including Michael Keaton, Nicolas Cage and Jim Carrey had all been in talks to play Wonka. In 2001, shock-rocker Marilyn Manson claimed he had been given the part.

But with Depp sporting giant glasses, oversized dentures, and reciting one-lines such as, 'Chewing gum is really gross – chewing gum I hate the most,' his interpretation is possibly even weirder than Manson's would have been. 'I play him as a kind of game-show host cum bratty child,' says Depp.

But Burton was determined that Wonka – although weird – should be a believable character. The sweet maker's background is fleshed out far more than it is in the book, but this is the only significant change Burton has made to his source material.

In the film, we learn how Willy Wonka lured Oompa Loompas from their island home to become his helpers in the magical chocolate factory. We also discover through flashback scenes how he found his vocation as a master sweet-maker – thanks to his domineering father, dentist Dr. Wilbur Wonka, played by Christopher Lee. The child Wonka ends up with his head encased in an orthodontic cage, while Dr. Wilbur burns his bag of sweets in the fire. Naturally, as soon as he grows up, he builds a magical sweet factory.

While it's Depp's wacky turn as the magical Wonka that has been the focus of attention so far, the real star of the film could well turn out to be Freddie Highmore, the twelve-year-old British actor who also starred alongside Depp in *Finding Neverland*.

Burton had been having difficulty casting the role of Charlie Bucket, the child who wins a Golden Ticket to explore Wonka's factory, when Kate Winslet suggested to Depp that he try the 'great kid in *Neverland*'.

Depp, with whom Highmore shares a birthday, agreed, and after an audition, so did Burton.

'Freddie is something else,' says Winslet. 'I would literally get hairs up on the back of my neck watching this boy act. It's so rare that you feel that – not only with a child actor, but with any actor you work with. With this kid, it's a scary gift.'

Hollywood insiders predict that *Charlie and the Chocolate Factory* could turn Highmore into a star as big as *Harry Potter's* Daniel Radcliffe.

If all goes to plan, it will also be a fitting opening salvo for Brad and Jen's Plan B, which is currently working on another hit children's novel, 2003's *The Curious Incident of the Dog in the Night-Time*.

And even if the film doesn't generate enough momentum for a sequel, it won't be long before we see Roald Dahl on screen again. Wes Anderson, the comic behind *The Life Aquatic*, is already working on his classic *Fantastic Mr Fox*, and other novels such as *The BFG* are in production. 'It has been a long fight,' says Liccy Dahl, who is credited as one of the film's executive producers. 'But it pays to wait.'

EYE CANDY

by David Edelstein

The cloying 1971 eyesore *Willy Wonka and the Chocolate Factory* might have left you with the impression that 'the candyman can [take tomorrow, dip it in a dream, etc.] 'cause he mixes it with love and makes the world taste good.' (Sorry if I've brought back the dulcet tones of Sammy Davis Jr.) But it's not easy to sugarcoat Roald Dahl's moralism – or sadism – in the book *Charlie and the*

Depp's Wonka is supported by veterans like David Kelly and Edward Fox (back left and second). But Freddie Highmore as Charlie (front left) almost steals the show.

Chocolate Factory, in which four self-indulgent brats (but not little Charlie Bucket, the darling hero) get their just, uh, desserts. As the reclusive candy mogul, Gene Wilder used his gift for seeming insane but also a sweetheart: He twinkled as he oversaw the punishment of the spoiled snoot Veruca Salt, the gluttonous Augustus Gloop, the gum-chewing Violet Beauregarde, and the boob-tube addict Mike Teavee. In the new Tim Burton version, properly titled *Charlie and the Chocolate Factory*, Johnny Depp is not so reassuring. He's a spaced-out, whey-faced child-man with saucer eyes: a blend of Carol Channing and Michael Jackson. He also has a king-sized chocolate chip on his shoulder.

This is a dazzling movie, yet some people (not kids, but maybe their parents) will be put off by its Grand Guignol ghoulishness. And Depp does take some getting used to. He has conceived Wonka as a smiling passive-aggressive, a Mr. Freeze weighed down by emotional baggage, and he doesn't have much variety. Like the first Burton/Depp fusion, *Edward Scissorhands*, his Wonka is stunted – deformed by inept parenting. (The resemblance to Edward is pointed up with a gag: In a flashback, Wonka cuts the ribbon on his candy factory and, from behind, the shears extend from his sleeves.)

Tim Burton — A Child's Garden of Nightmares

Edward the visionary artist tended to slash himself and other people without meaning to; it was Burton's way of saying, 'I can't help my hostility, it's how I was *made*.' Wonka's dearness, on the other hand, is too creepy to fool anyone. Burton and screenwriter John August have added a psychological back story that isn't in the book: The factory is an escape from – and a retaliation against – Wonka's repressive dentist father (played by horror great Christopher Lee), who forbade his son to eat candy and imprisoned him in a variety of medieval-torturelike braces and retainers. Now, Willy is the ultimate eternal adolescent artist who shuns family (he can't even get the word 'parent' out of his mouth) and retreats into a world of his own creation.

The Neverland-as-Oedipal-revenge is very Michael Jackson, too, and I imagine that the extra bit of perversity helped to fuel Burton's already revved-up visual imagination. He and designer Alex McDowell plainly revel in the silky-chocolate waterfall, the edible brightly coloured landscape, and the Rube Goldberg-like candy machines. There's none of the dinner-theatre-*Nutcracker Suite* tackiness of the old *Willy Wonka*. In Burton's chocolate factory, the central park has a Dr. Seuss-like swirliness, but every marvel is double-edged: You can consume it, and it can consume you.

This movie is a riot of fiendish invention. The Oompa Loompas – diminutive tree people who keep the factory going in exchange for all the cacao beans they can eat – are all played, via some of the best computer trickery I've ever seen, by the vaguely malevolent Indian actor Deep Roy. Their mocking epitaphs for each gruesomely dispatched child are show-stopping production numbers, each in a different musical style: Bollywood/Busby Berkeley, disco, etc. The music is by the impishly brilliant Danny Elfman. His name fits.

Burton doesn't just savour the sets in *Charlie and the Chocolate Factory*; he lingers on the faces,

Wonka's fantasy world owes much to the production design of Alex McDowell. Burton, typically, brings it as close to a classic horror movie as a fairytale.

Wonka's lab equipment recalls Kenneth Strickfaden's classic laboratory designs for early horror classics The Bride of Frankenstein *and* The Mask of Fu Manchu.

too. Freddie Highmore's Charlie doesn't actually have much screen time (he's a remarkably passive protagonist), but every time he gets a close-up those teacup ears make you laugh, and he matches up perfectly with the gaunt Noah Taylor (as his dad) and the gaunter David Kelly (as Grandpa Joe). As Augustus Gloop, Philip Wiegratz has cheeks so round and balloon-smooth I was convinced they were a special effect, and Julia Winter's rich-girl Veruca Salt has sharp blue eyes and exaggerated English horse-teeth.

The addictions of the two other winners of the Wonka-candy-bar gold tickets have been partially updated. Mike Teavee (Jordan Fry) is now a video-game zombie – perfect. And Violet Beauregarde is a fiercely driven karate expert as well as a gum-chewer. It would have been nice if Burton and August had figured out a way to work martial arts into her finale – and do martial-arts and gum-chewing even fit together? The film is set in the present, but it's a hodgepodge of contemporary and Victorian references, and not everything gels. Candy-chemist though he is, it's odd to hear Wonka hold forth about chocolate and the release of endorphins.

Dahl wrote some great horror stories, so it's no surprise that Burton's movie often edges into the macabre. Depp's Wonka has a whiff of Lon Chaney's Phantom of the Opera – the master torturer. And every set-piece is a mini-horror movie. Veruca's comeuppance in the Nut Room is better than anything in either *Willard*. The squirrels that crack the walnuts are a mixture of the real and computer-generated, but the blending is seamless, and they seem as sly and knowing as their master. Burton's joy makes *Charlie and the Chocolate Factory* freakishly amusing from start to finish, even when those everlasting gobstoppers get stuck in our throats.

DIRECTOR OF THE LIVING DEAD

by Edward Douglas

If it seems like only a few months ago since ComingSoon.net's last interview with Tim Burton, it's only a testament to how busy the visionary director has been this past year. Mere months after having one of the summer's biggest hits with *Charlie and the Chocolate Factory*, Burton is back with his second movie of 2005, *Tim Burton's Corpse Bride*. It's the follow-up to his 1993 animated film *The Nightmare Before Christmas*, which attempted to revive the stop-motion animation of his youth. Although it wasn't a huge commercial hit at the time, it has gone on to become a cult favourite for kids and adults alike.

Burton got more involved with *Corpse Bride*, co-directing the process as well as tacking his name in front of it. The macabre family comedy, a musical no less, gave him a chance to continue his run as one of filmmaking's most eclectic and reclusive directors, as he tells the story of a shy young man named Victor – voiced by Johnny Depp, his Willy Wonka in *Charlie* – who accidentally ends up marrying a woman murdered on her wedding night. Burton's own wife Helena Bonham Carter voiced this 'corpse bride' while other recognisable voices from Burton's regular stable of talent include Christopher Lee and Albert Finney.

When ComingSoon.net spoke with Burton last, he was in the Bahamas. For *Corpse Bride*, journalists travelled to Toronto, where he held the following press conference. As always, the outspoken director's penchant for the dark and macabre, much like his movies, is counterbalanced by a wry humour and some interesting insights about his cast and his career.

How was this experience different from working on **The Nightmare Before Christmas?**
The difference on that was that one I designed it completely. It was a very completed package in my mind, so I felt like it was there, so I felt more comfortable with that. With this, it was more organic. It was based on an old folk tale, and we kept changing it. I had a great co-director with Mike Johnson, so I feel like we complimented each other quite well. It was just a different movie, a different process.

What was the thing that drove you to turn this particular idea into a movie?
The love triangle in *Corpse Bride*, they all are outcasts in their own way and that's the beauty of the story to me. That's what gave it its poignancy to me, and its bittersweet and sort of hopeful and sad quality altogether. The juxtaposition of who is going to be with who and what's going to end up happening was a very tricky balance to get, but something that was again crucial and important to who he was.

You've been dealing with the dead and undead since **Frankenweenie.** ***What's the appeal of that theme to you?***
I think dealing with the undead comes from growing up in Burbank, I think. It's sort of a suburban

In **Tim Burton's Corpse Bride** *(2005), the living Victor and living dead Emily are stop-motion caricatures of actors Johnny Depp and Helena Bonham Carter.*

Tim Burton — A Child's Garden of Nightmares

Night of the Living Dead during the day. I always liked monster movies, and I'm always fascinated by, again, growing up in a culture where death is looked upon as sort of a dark subject and then living so close to Mexico where you see the Day of the Dead skeletons and it's all humour, music and dancing and sort of a celebration of life, in a way, and that always felt more like a positive approach to things. So I think I always responded to that, more than just this sort of dark, unspoken cloud in the environment I grew up in.

Did you base a lot of your characters on those Day of the Dead figurines?
I used to have those figurines and they'd always have these nice scenes with them in clothes. There was a lot of humour and fun involved with those characters and that's what I felt was really inspiring to me.

Are you optimistic that the afterlife is as colourful as you painted it in this movie?
I have no idea what happens, but like I said, I do respond to other cultures that treat life with a much more positive approach. I think this other form, it kind of teaches, especially as a child, to almost be afraid of everything and feel like something bad is going to happen. As to where that other way, it just seems like a much more spiritual and positive approach. That's as far as I go, because I really have no idea what will happen.

What animated cartoons did you watch as a kid and did they influence your decision to do animation yourself?
The Rankin and Bass *Rudolph the Red-Nosed Reindeer*, those kinds of things that you grow up watching stay with you. They just kind of form what you like to do, but it probably had more to do with Ray Harryhausen. He was the guy. If I saw his name [on a movie], no actor meant anything but his name certainly meant something, and that's where I think the love of this type of animation came from for me, because you could see an artist at work. His monsters had more personality than most of the actors in the movies. Even the monster wasn't just a monster, the death scene was always just so beautiful and tragic. The final little twist of the tail or the one final breath or whatever. He just brought such passion into the work, so to me, he was the guy who not only inspired me, but he inspires almost any animator. In fact, several months ago, Johnny and Helena and I went to his house in London and met him for the first time and he was just such an amazing man and so generous with his time and enthusiasm. He went to the set of *Corpse Bride* and production sort of ground to a halt that day because everyone was [makes bowing motions]. He truly has inspired not just stop-motion animators, but any animator.

Were there any other pop culture references that may have influenced some of your other recent movies, like comic books?
I wasn't a big comic book fan, really. I don't know if I was dyslexic, but I always had trouble knowing which box to read first. I kept reading the wrong box and thought this is a comic book that doesn't make any sense. Do I read the one up here or the one down here? I couldn't quite deal with it.

When you were growing up, why did you ultimately gravitate to filmmaking?
I always liked to draw, as probably every kid does, and make Super 8 movies like a lot of kids did, and I never had the real goal to do that, until in school, I was such a bad student, and I remember having to do a report where you had to read a book and write a 50-page essay on it, so I made a little Super 8 film on Houdini, a book that I had to read about. I remember not reading the book,

not having to write and getting an A+ on the project and I thought, 'Oh, this might be a good living to try to do.' So I always liked making things and then I got into animation.

You've made so many movies about outcasts and outsiders. Does that become harder as things get better for you in your career, family life, etc?
Well, things aren't always happy. (laughter) The thing is that you're very affected by your early life and I think that if you ever had that feeling of being an outsider or loneliness or whatever, it just doesn't leave you. You can be happy or successful, but I think that thing still stays inside of you. It doesn't ever really leave you. You always will have that.

Do you look for 'outcast' qualities in the actors that you work with?
Yeah, of course. When I first met Johnny on *Edward Scissorhands*, he was looked upon as this handsome leading man, but I don't think in his heart he felt that way. That's why he wanted to do it because he understood being perceived as one thing and being something else. Same thing with Helena. If you read the London papers, she's one of the worst dressed people in the history of Britain, or some sort of posh aristocrat. She is completely misperceived, and it may bother her a little bit. Once you get labelled there's really not much you can do about it.

***Let's talk about your long working relationship with Johnny Depp. How was it different working together on this film than* Charlie?**
It was weird because we were doing them at the same time, so he was like Willy Wonka by day and Victor by night. It might have been a little schizophrenic for him, but he's great. It's the first animated movie he's done, so he's always into the challenge. We just treat it like fun and the creative process, and that's the joy of working with him. He's kind of up for anything. The amazing thing is that none of the actors were ever in the room together, except for Albert [Finney] and Joanna [Lumley] did a few scenes together. Everybody else was separate, so they were all kind of working in a vacuum, which was interesting. That's the thing I felt ended up so beautifully that their performances really meshed together. [Johnny] was really canny, as they all were, about trying to find the right tone and making it work while not being in the same room with each other.

Johnny mentioned that he had to scramble to get his character for* Corpse Bride *together in about fifteen minutes.
Oh, yeah. We were shooting *Charlie* one day, I think, and I said, 'Let's go over to the recording booth and let's do some recording,' and as he was walking over, he was saying to himself, 'Oh, shit. What am I doing? What is this character?' The great thing is that he likes to work spontaneously, too, so really, in that one session, he got it. I think he might have been a bit worried to begin with, but I think he kind of likes that.

Your wife told us that she had to audition for the film and then had to wait painfully for two weeks for your answer. Is that true?
No, she's an actress, so she's making it more dramatic. (laughter) It was probably a slight bit of torture, but it's a two-way street. It wasn't as dramatic as that. I think maybe because I'm with her, I probably was a little harder on her than I would be with somebody [else]. Nobody else did have to audition, that's true. (laughter) Long before I met her, she's done many movies. She's very secure with herself and what she's done. There's never really been any problems . . . yet. No, seriously, she was fine.

Tim Burton — A Child's Garden of Nightmares

Would you ever dare to not cast Helena in one of your films?
Oh, yeah, of course. I wouldn't just cast her to cast her in the same way that I wouldn't cast Johnny or anybody that I love working with just to have them in the movie. You always want it to be the right thing and the right role. I think she and most of the people I work with understand that.

Do you think that this movie is too scary for small children or do you think they'll enjoy it?
I've always had problems with that. I remember that people were saying that about *Nightmare* and tiny, tiny little kids come up and they loved the movie. I think it's more of an adult problem then it is a kid problem. Even *Corpse Bride*, I find is even softer in a certain way. It's basically an emotional love story with humour, and any kind of fairy tale or fable, there are elements that are maybe slightly unsettling, but that's part of the history of those kinds of stories.

Did you have any problems with the ratings because it's so dark and morbid?
No, PG, which I think was appropriate, because to me, the story is quite emotional and I personally don't find it dark at all, in fact I think it's almost less dark than *Nightmare* in a certain way. I also find that adults forget that kids are their own best censors. Some kids like that kind of stuff and some kids don't, and they're usually the best ones to judge it. I think it's when adults are going, 'Oh, you can't see this, can't see that,' then it creates this climate of fear, and it makes children more afraid. I have a child that's under two years old, and he's watched *When Dinosaurs Ruled the Earth* and he's watched *Viva Las Vegas*, which isn't a horror movie, but some people may find it scary. It's about how you present things, and if he got scared, he'd run away.

And what does scare your son?
Only his parents . . . at the moment . . . truthfully. (laughter) I don't know why. We don't try to scare him, but he just looks up at us like, 'Who are you?' I don't know if it's because of the way we look or the way we act. But no, it's interesting to watch. I'm not going to start showing him hardcore porn or anything, but I find it's a fascinating subject and I was talking to somebody, who's actually writing a book on it. You go into a shop and it's like here's the Teletubbies, here's the Wiggles – which some might say is scarier than most horror movies – if you show them other things and don't present it like, 'Ohhhhhhh, it's a bad thing,' I think it might be amazing what they just accept.

You've said that you probably wouldn't ever want to do a sequel to* Planet of the Apes*. Could you elaborate a bit on why you feel that way? Would you consider doing any other remakes like* Charlie*?
I like challenges like doing something that maybe you shouldn't do. There's something about taking a classic movie that people love and then doing another version of that, but you're setting yourself up for a mistake. I loved working with [Mark Wahlberg], so I'd do that again, but you know what? I try not to go back in retrospect and say, 'Oh, I shouldn't have done this or I shouldn't have done that.' You make your decisions and then you live by them. It's always a risky thing, especially if you're thinking of classic movies. I think I would try to avoid that and there are certain ones that can't be topped. For me, it's been more successful to do more personal things. With *Charlie*, some people kept thinking we were remaking the movie, but none of us ever felt like we were remaking the movie. We always felt we were trying to make the book. Even John [August], the writer, never even looked at the movie, so that was one where we didn't feel pressure to top the other movie.

As Victor is dragged to the world of the dead by Emily's skeletal arm, Burton indulges in a knowing reference to classic horror movie Carrie.

TIM BURTON'S CORPSE BRIDE

review by Stephanie Zacharek

In Michael Almereyda's funny, ardent and moving vampire picture, *Nadja*, the title character, a downtown-Manhattan descendant of Count Dracula's, sums up the exquisite suffering of her lot: 'Life is full of pain. But the pain I feel is the pain of fleeting joy.'

The visual and narrative beauty of *Tim Burton's Corpse Bride* captures the essence of that line – it hurts a little to watch the movie, not just because it's so deeply touching but because the medium itself is calling out to us from a lost world. Stop-motion animation of the sort Burton uses here – and that he and director Henry Selick also used in the glorious 1993 *The Nightmare Before Christmas* – has been virtually wiped off the filmmaking landscape in favour of CGI. So while the story that's told in *Corpse Bride* – a Victorian Gothic romance adapted from a Russian folktale – is affecting in itself, the vitality and beauty of the textures and movement on-screen have a special poignancy. *Corpse Bride* isn't the sort of thing you see every day. It's in touch with the real world, yet out of step with it. This is filmmaking straight from the land of the undead.

Corpse Bride, which Burton co-directed with Mike Johnson, begins with a wedding gone wrong. Canned-fish magnates Nell and William Van Dort (their voices belong to Tracey Ullman and Paul Whitehouse) have money but no class; and Maudeline and Finis Everglot (Joanna Lumley and Albert Finney) have aristocratic roots but no dough. The families decide to merge by arranging a marriage between their respective children, Victor (Johnny Depp) and Victoria (Emily Watson), who, as of the night before the wedding, have never even met. They fall in love, of course, at first sight. But by a curious turn of events, Victor accidentally stumbles into the world of Emily, the Corpse Bride (Helena Bonham Carter), who was killed by her intended on her wedding day. Her heart, she notes, is capable of being broken even though it has stopped beating. And she desperately wants Victor to be her husband, even though he's betrothed to someone else.

So Emily conveys Victor to the Land of the Dead, an underground world rendered in vivid jellybean colours, a far cry from the muted grey Victorian reality Victor knows. But *that* world is home to Victor, and he aches to get back to it. *Corpse Bride* was written by John August, Caroline Thompson and Pamela Pettler, and as a piece of storytelling, it holds up admirably against any live-action script. The story is beautifully worked out, and it gets most of its momentum from the feelings of the characters. There's Victor, charming but hapless at first, whose strengths are ultimately magnified by his compassion for a person in pain; the steady and true Victoria, left to believe that Victor has willingly abandoned her for someone else; and, most affecting of all, the fragile but vital Emily, who sees Victor as her last chance at happiness – the only other option for her is to face the rest of eternity alone.

The world of *Corpse Bride* is so vivid that it's hard to believe these are puppets we're talking about. Victor, with his saucer eyes and brilliantined forelock, looks more like the human Johnny Depp than Depp himself did in *Charlie and the Chocolate Factory*. And Emily, perched on matchstick ballerina legs (on one of them, her flesh has rotted away and you can see an exposed flash of bone, a disconcertingly erotic visual), is a spectre of tragic love wrapped in tattered wedding clothes. Her nose is a pert inverted 'V'; her lips have a sensual pout that suggests not even death can fully destroy the human sex drive.

Emily's world is populated by singing, dancing skeletons (they perform several songs composed by longtime Burton collaborator Danny Elfman, including a rousing Gilbert and Sullivan-style ensemble number); by beings who used to be soldiers or waiters or bakers in life and just can't break the habit even now that they're dead (some of these skills come in handy when it's time to make the couple's wedding cake, a towering creation festooned with fondant skulls and femurs); and by tiny, mischievous skeleton kiddies (they tiptoe through the movie, giggling, in their little Victorian frocks and sailor outfits). There's an ick-green talking maggot who takes after Peter Lorre (his voice actually belongs to Enn Reitel) and a dog named Scraps, Victor's beloved, deceased childhood pet – Emily presents him to Victor as a wedding present. He's now a butt-wriggling assemblage of bones, but his essential spirit of doggyness is undiminished.

It's a tossup as to what's more appealing, the rainbow-hued Land of the Dead, beneath the Earth's surface, or the greyish Land of the Living up above. There's definitely more fun going on down below, with lots of live dead entertainment and an eternally open bar. (As a wise old dead elder, voiced by Michael Gough, observes, 'Why go up there when people are dying to get down here?')

But the colours in the Land of the Living are more subtly beautiful: There are endless variations of greys, and Burton (along with his clearly hardworking technical team) uses the whole palette, tinting this allegedly boring colour with pinks and blues and violets. The delicacy of these creamy tones suits the passionate but tender nature of the story, and their earthbound beauty fits the movie's realistically romantic theme: Love isn't ownership, and it's no good unless it's freely given. *Tim Burton's Corpse Bride* is a lush, modern valentine to old-fashioned sentiment, and to old-fashioned moviemaking, too. When Victor sits down at a grand piano, we see that it features a brass plate inscribed with 'Harryhausen' in majestic letters, a tribute to special-effects genius Ray Harryhausen, whose work is so lovingly referenced here. Harryhausen is now 85, and although today's kids may not know who he is, many of yesterday's kids do, from Saturday-afternoon movie staples like *Jason and the Argonauts* and *The Golden Voyage of Sinbad*. With *Corpse Bride*, Burton and Johnson pay tribute to the people, and the techniques, that have inspired them. Their movie is a living love letter, not a memento mori.

Tim Burton Filmography

Stalk of the Celery Monster (1979)
Animated and Directed by Tim Burton

Luau (1982)
Animated and Directed by Tim Burton and Jerry Reese

Vincent (1982)
5 mins (Walt Disney Productions)
Animated by Stephen Chiodo. Production Design: Rick Heinrichs.
Director of Photography: Victor Abdalov.
Produced by Rick Heinrichs. Written and directed by Tim Burton.
Cast: Vincent Price (Narrator).

Hansel and Gretel (1982)
45mins (The Disney Channel)
Executive Producer: Julie Hickson. Produced by Rick Heinrichs.
Written by Julie Hickson. Directed by Tim Burton.
Cast: Jim Ishida (Stepmother/Witch), Michael Yama (Toymaker)

Frankenweenie (1984)
25 mins (Walt Disney Productions)
Music by David Newman and Michael Convertino. Film Editor:
Ernest Milano. Director of Photography: Thomas E. Ackerman.
Associate Producer: Rick Heinrichs. Produced by Julie Hickson.
Written by Leonard Ripps. Directed by Tim Burton.
Cast: Shelley Duvall (Susan Frankenstein), Daniel Stern (Ben
Frankenstein),Barret Oliver (Victor Frankenstein), Joseph Maher
(Mr Chambers),Roz Braverman (Mrs Epstein), Paul Bartel (Mr
Walsh), Jason Hervey (Frank Dale), Paul C. Scott (Mike Anderson),
Helen Boll (Mrs Curtis), Bob Herron (Street Player),Donna Hall
(Street Player), Sofia Coppola (Anne Chambers).

Aladdin and his Wonderful Lamp (1984)
47 mins (Showtime TV), (*Faerie Tale Theatre TV Series*)
Executive Producer: Shelley Duvall. Producers: Bridget Terry and
Fredric S. Fuchs. Written by Rod Ash and Mark Curtiss.
Directed by Tim Burton.
Cast: Valerie Bertinelli (Princess Sabrina), Robin Carradine (Aladdin),
Leonard Nimoy (Evil Magician), James Earl Jones (Genie of the
Lamp),Ray Sharkey (Grand Vizier), Rae Allen (Aladdin's Mother).

The Jar (1985)
23 mins (NBC TV), (*Alfred Hitchcock Presents TV Series*)
Written by Michael McDowell. From a short story by Ray Bradbury.
Directed by Tim Burton.
Cast: Alfred Hitchcock (Host), featuring the voices of Griffin Dunne
and Paul Bartel.

Pee Wee's Big Adventure (1985)
90 mins (Warner Bros.)
Casting by Wallis Nicita. Music by Danny Elfman.
Music Editor: Bob Badami.Costume Design by Aggie Guerard
Rodgers. Special/Visual Effects: Dreamquest Images. Animation
Effects by Rick Heinrichs. Production Design Editors: David L.
Snyder and Billy Weber. Director of Photography: Victor J. Kemper.
Executive Producer: William E. McEuen. Producers: Richard Gilbert
Abramson, Robert Shapiro and Paul Reubens. Written by Phil
Hartman, Paul Reubens, Michael Varhol. Directed by Tim Burton.
Cast: Paul Reubens (Pee-wee Herman), Elizabeth Daily (Dottie),
Mark Holton (Francis), Diane Salinger (Simone), Judd Omen
(Mickey), Irving Hellman (Neighbour), Monte Landis (Mario),
Damon Martin (Chip), David Glasser (BMX Kid), Gregory Brown
(BMX Kid), Mark Everett (BMX Kid), Daryl Roach (Chuck), Bill
Cable (Policeman #1), Peter Looney (Policeman #2), Starletta
DuPois (Sergeant Hunter).

Family Dog (1985)
(NBC TV), (*Amazing Stories TV Series*)
Animation Design by Tim Burton. Executive Producer: Steven
Spielberg. Producer: David E. Vogel. Written and Directed by Brad Bird.
Cast: Ray Walston (Fireside Storyteller).

Beetlejuice (1987)
92 mins (Geffen Film Company/Warner Bros.)
Casting by Janet Hirschman and Jay Jenkins. Music by Danny
Elfman. Special Effects by Chuck Gaspar. Visual Effects by Alan
Munro and Rick Heinrichs. Costume Design by Aggie Guerard
Rodgers. Production Design by Bo Welch. Film Editor: Jane Kurson.
Director of Photography: Thomas E. Ackerman. Producers: Eric
Angelson, Michael Bender, Richard Hashimoto, Larry Wilson.
Written by Tim Burton, Michael McDowell, Warren Skaaren, Larry
Wilson. Directed by Tim Burton.
Cast: Michael Keaton (Beetlejuice) (Betelgeuse), Geena Davis
(Barbara Maitland), Alec Baldwin (Adam Maitland), Winona Ryder
(Lydia Deitz), Catherine O'Hara (Delia Deitz), Jeffrey Jones
(Charles Deitz), Glenn Shadix (Otho Baloofer), Sylvia Sidney (Juno
DeSalva), Robert Goulet (Maxie Dean), Dick Cavett (Bernard
Grey), Annie McEnroe (Jane Butterfield), Susan Kellerman (Grace
Altieri), Adelle Lutz (Beryl), Carmen Filpi (Roadkill Man), Cynthia
Daly (3-Fingered Typist).

Beetlejuice (1989) (TV Series)
(Nelvana/NBC TV)
Executive Producers: Tim Burton and David Geffen. Developed by
Tim Burton.

Batman (1989)
126 mins (Warner Bros.)
Casting by Marion Dougherty and Owens Hill. Music by Danny
Elfman and Prince. Special Effects Supervisor: John Evans. Costume
Design by Linda Henrikson and Bob Ringwood. Production Design
by Anton Furst. Editors: Chris Lebenzon and Bob Badami. Director
of Photography: Roger Pratt. Executive Producers: Benjamin
Melniker and Michael E. Uslan. Producers: Peter Guber, Barbara
Kalish, Chris Kenny and Jon Peters. Written by Sam Hamm and
Warren Skaaren. Based upon characters created by Bob Kane.
Directed by Tim Burton.
Cast: Jack Nicholson (The Joker/Jack Napier), Michael Keaton
(Batman/Bruce Wayne), Kim Basinger (Vicki Vale), Robert Wuhl
(Alexander Knox), Pat Hingle (Police Commissioner Gordon), Billy
Dee Williams (Harvey Dent, Gotham District Attorney), Michael
Gough (Alfred Pennyworth), Jack Palance (Boss Carl Grissom),
Jerry Hall (Alicia), Tracey Walter (Bob the Goon), Lee Wallace
(Mayor Borg), William Hootkins (Lt. Eckhardt), Richard Strange
(Goon), Carl Chase (Goon), Mac McDonald (Goon).

Edward Scissorhands (1990)
105 mins (Twentieth Century Fox)
Casting by Victoria Thomas. Music by Danny Elfman. Special
Effects Supervisor: Michael Wood. Costume Design by Colleen
Atwood. Art Director: Tom Duffield. Set Designers: Rick Heinrichs
and Paul Senfish. Make-up Effects: Stan Winston.
Production Design by Bo Welch. Editors: Colleen Halsey, Richard
Halsey. Director of Photography: Stefan Czapsky. Executive
Producer: Richard Hashimoto. Producer: Denise Di Novi. Written
by Caroline Thompson. From a story by Tim Burton, Caroline
Thompson. Directed by Tim Burton.
Cast: Johnny Depp (Edward Scissorhands), Winona Ryder (Kim
Boggs), Dianne Wiest (Peg Boggs), Anthony Michael Hall (Jim,
Kim's boyfriend), Kathy Baker (Joyce Monroe, neighbour), Robert
Oliveri (Kevin Boggs), Conchata Ferrell (Helen, neighbour),
Caroline Aaron (Marge, neighbour), Dick Anthony Williams (Officer
Allen), O-Lan Jones (Esmeralda), Vincent Price (The Inventor), Alan
Arkin (Bill Boggs), Susan Blommaert (Tinka), Linda Perri (Cissy),
John Davidson (Host – TV).

Conversations with Vincent (1990)
(unreleased)
Documentary about Vincent Price. Directed by Tim Burton.
Cast: Vincent Price (Himself), Roger Corman (Himself).

Batman Returns (1992)
126 mins (Warner Bros.)
Casting by Marion Dougherty. Music by Danny Elfman. Special Effects Supervisor: Chuck Gaspar. Special Make-up Effects: Stan Winston. Costume Design by Bob Ringwood and Mary E. Vogt. Art Director: Rick Heinrichs. Production Design by Bo Welch. Editors: Bob Badami, Chris Lebenzon. Director of Photography: Stefan Czapsky. Executive Producers: Peter Guber, Benjamin Melniker, Jon Peters, Michael E. Uslan. Producers: Holly Borradaile, Ian Bryce, Tim Burton, Denise di Novi, Larry J. Franco. Written by Daniel Waters and Sam Hamm. Based upon characters created by Bob Kane. Directed by Tim Burton.
Cast: Michael Keaton (Batman/Bruce Wayne), Danny DeVito (Penguin/Oswald Chesterfield Cobblepot), Michelle Pfeiffer (Catwoman/Selina Kyle), Christopher Walken (Maximillian 'Max' Shreck), Michael Gough (Alfred Pennyworth), Michael Murphy (Mayor), Cristi Conaway (Ice Princess), Andrew Bryniarski (Charles 'Chip' Shreck), Pat Hingle (Commissioner James Gordon), Vincent Schiavelli (Organ Grinder), Steve Witting (Josh), Jan Hooks (Jen), John Strong (Sword Swallower), Rick Zumwalt (Tattooed Strongman), Anna Katerina (Poodle Lady).

Family Dog (1993) (TV series)
(NBC TV)
Executive Producer/Co-Producer: Tim Burton.

Tim Burton's The Nightmare Before Christmas (1993)
76 mins (Touchstone Pictures/Buena Vista)
Music and Songs by Danny Elfman. Special Effects (Digital FX): Ariel Velasco Shaw. Production Design by Tim Burton, Denise di Novi. Visual Consultant: Rick Heinrichs. Editor: Stan Webb. Director of Photography: Pete Kozachik. Producers: Tim Burton, Denise di Novi, Danny Elfman, Kathleen Gavin, Jill Jacobs, Jeffrey Katzenberg, Diane Minter Lewis, Philip Lofaro. Written by Michael McDowell, Caroline Thompson. From a story by Tim Burton. Directed by Henry Selick.
Featuring the voices of: Chris Sarandon (Jack Skellington), Danny Elfman (Jack Skellington/Barrel/ Clown with Tearaway Face), Catherine O'Hara (Sally/Shock), William Hickey (Dr. Finklestein), Glenn Shadix (Mayor), Paul Reubens (Lock), Ken Page (Oogie Boogie), Ed Ivory (Santa), Susan McBride (Big Witch), Debi Durst (Corpse Kid/Corpse Mother/Small Witch), Greg Proops (Harlequin Demon/Devil/Sax Player), Kerry Katz (Man Under Stairs/Vampire/Corpse Father), Randy Crenshaw (Mr. Hyde/Behemoth/Vampire), Sherwood Ball (Mummy/Vampire), Carmen Twillie (Undersea Gal/Man Under the Stairs).

Cabin Boy (1994)
(Touchstone Pictures/Buena Vista)
Produced by Tim Burton.

Ed Wood (1994)
127 mins (Touchstone Pictures/Buena Vista)
Casting by Victoria Thomas. Original Music by Howard Shore. Special Effects Supervisor: Kevin Pike. Costume Design by Colleen Atwood. Production Design by Tom Duffield. Editor: Chris Lebenzon. Director of Photography: Stefan Czapsky. Executive Producer: Michael Lehmann. Producers: Tim Burton, Denise Di Novi. Written by Scott Alexander, Larry Karaszewski. Based on the book The Nightmare of Ecstasy by Rudolph Grey. Directed by Tim Burton.
Cast: Johnny Depp (Edward D. Wood, Jr.), Martin Landau (Bela Lugosi), Sarah Jessica Parker (Dolores Fuller, Ed's Girlfriend), Patricia Arquette (Kathy O'Hara), Jeffrey Jones (Criswell), G. D. Spradlin (Reverend Lemon), Vincent D'Onofrio (Orson Welles), Bill Murray (Bunny Breckenridge), Mike Starr (Georgie Weiss, President of Screen Classics), Max Casella (Paul Marco), Brent Hinkley (Conrad Brooks), Lisa Marie (Vampira), George 'the Animal' Steele (Tor Johnson, aka 'Swedish Angel'), Juliet Landau (Loretta King).

Batman Forever (1995)
(Warner Bros.)
Produced by Tim Burton.

James and the Giant Peach (1996)
(Walt Disney Productions/Buena Vista)
Produced by Tim Burton.

Mars Attacks! (1996)
105 mins (Warner Bros.)
Casting by Matthew Barry, Jeanne McCarthy, Victoria Thomas. Music by Danny Elfman. Special Effects: Michael Lantiari. Costume Design by Colleen Atwood. Production Design by Wynn Thomas. Editor: Chris Lebenzon. Director of Photography: Peter Suschitzky. Producers: Tim Burton, Paul Deason, Larry J. Franco, Mark S. Miller. Written by Johnathan Gems. Based upon a trading card series created by Lee Brown, Woody Gelman, Wally Wood, Bob Powell, Norm Saunders. Directed by Tim Burton.
Cast: Jack Nicholson (President James Dale/Art Land), Glenn Close (First Lady Marsha Dale), Annette Bening (Barbara Land), Pierce Brosnan (Professor Donald Kessler), Danny DeVito (Rude Gambler), Martin Short (Press Secretary, Jerry Ross), Sarah Jessica Parker (Nathalie Lake), Michael J. Fox (Jason Stone), Rod Steiger (Gen. Decker), Tom Jones (Himself), Jim Brown (Byron Williams), Lukas Haas (Richie Norris), Natalie Portman (Taffy Dale), Pam Grier (Louise Williams), Lisa Marie (Martian Girl).

Hollywood Gum (1998)
(French TV commercial for chewing gum)
Directed by Tim Burton.

Sleepy Hollow (1999)
105 mins (Paramount Pictures and Mandalay Pictures present a Scott Rudin/American Zoetrope production)
Casting by Susie Figgis, Ilene Starger. Music by Danny Elfman. Costume Design by Colleen Atwood. Special Effects Supervisors: Joss Williams, Ron Ottesen. Production Design: Rick Heinrichs. Editors: Chris Lebenzon, Joel Negron. Director of Photography: Emmanuel Lubezki. Executive Producers: Francis Ford Coppola, Larry J. Franco. Producers: Scott Rudin, Mark Roydal, Adam Schroeder, Andrew Kevin Walker, Kevin Yagher. Written by Kevin Yagher, Andrew Kevin Walker. Inspired by the short story 'The Legend of Sleepy Hollow' by Washington Irving. Directed by Tim Burton.
Cast: Johnny Depp (Constable Ichabod Crane), Christina Ricci (Katrina Anne Van Tassel), Miranda Richardson (Lady Mary Van Tassel/The Western Woods Crone), Michael Gambon (Baltus Van Tassel), Casper Van Dien (Brom Van Brunt), Jeffrey Jones (Reverend Steenwyck), Christopher Lee (The Burgomeister), Richard Griffiths (Magistrate Samuel Philipse), Ian McDiarmid (Dr. Thomas Lancaster), Michael Gough (Notary James Hardenbrook), Marc Pickering (Young Masbath), Lisa Marie (Lady Crane), Steven Waddington (Mr. Killian), Christopher Walken (The Hessian Horseman), Claire Skinner (Midwife Elizabeth 'Beth' Killian).

Stainboy (2000) (Animated Internet Series)
Animation by Flinch Productions. Created by Tim Burton.

Planet of the Apes (2001)
124 mins (Twentieth Century Fox)
Casting by Denise Chamian. Music by Danny Elfman and Paul Oakenfold. Visual Effects Producer: Tom Peitzman. Special Make-up Effects: Rick Baker. Costume Design by Colleen Atwood. Make-up Supervisor: John Blake. Key Prosthetic Make-up Supervisor: Alex Proctor. Production Design: Rick Heinrichs. Editor: Chris Lebenzon. Directors of Photography: Philippe Rousselot, Paul Hughen. Executive Producer: Ralph Winter. Producers: Ross Fanger, Katterli Frauenfelder, Richard D. Zanuck. Written by William Broyles, Jr., Lawrence Konner, Mark Rosenthal. Inspired by the novel Planet of the Apes by Pierre Boulle. Directed by Tim Burton.
Cast: Mark Wahlberg (Captain Leo Davidson), Tim Roth (General Thade), Helena Bonham Carter (Ari), Michael Clarke Duncan (Captain Attar), Paul Giamatti (Limbo), Estella Warren (Daena), Cary-Hiroyuki Tagawa (Krull), David Warner (Senator Sandar), Kris Kristofferson (Karubi), Erick Avari (Tival), Luke Eberl (Birn), Evan Dexter Parke (Gunnar), Glenn Shadix (Senator Nado), Freda Foh Shen (Bon), Chris Ellis (General Vasich).

Big Fish (2003)

125 mins (Columbia Pictures Corporation)
Casting by Denise Chamian. Music by Danny Elfman. Special
Effects Directors: Stan Winston, Stan Parks. Costume Design by
Colleen Atwood, Donna O'Neal. Editor: Chris Lebenzon.
Cinematography by Philippe Rousselot. Production Design by
Dennis Gassner. Producers: Bruce Cohen, Dan Jinks, Richard D.
Zanuck. Associate Producer: Katterli Frauenfelder. Executive
Producer: Arne L. Schmidt. Written by John August. Based on the
book *Big Fish: A Novel of Mythic Proportions* by Daniel Wallace.
Directed by Tim Burton.
Cast: Ewan McGregor (Younger Ed Bloom), Albert Finney (Older
Ed Bloom), Billy Crudup (Will Bloom), Jessica Lange (Older
Sandra Bloom), Helena Bonham Carter (Younger & Older
Jenny/The Witch), Alison Lohman (Younger Sandra Bloom), Robert
Guillaume (Older Dr. Bennett), Marion Cotillard (Josephine),
Matthew McGrory (Karl the Giant), David Denman (Don Price -
Age 18-22), Missi Pyle (Mildred), Loudon Wainwright III (Beamen
(as Loudon Wainwright)), Ada Tai (Ping), Arlene Tai (Jing), Steve
Buscemi (Norther Winslow), Danny DeVito (Amos Calloway).

Charlie and the Chocolate Factory (2005)

115 mins (Warner Bros.)
Casting by Susie Figgis. Music by Danny Elfman. Special Effects
Supervisors: Alexander Gunn, Neil Davis. Costume Design by
Gabriella Pescucci. Editor: Chris Lebenzon. Cinematography by
Philippe Rousselot. Production Design by Alex McDowell.
Producers: Brad Grey, Richard D. Zanuck. Executive Producers:
Bruce Berman, Graham Burke, Felicity Dahl, Patrick McCormick,
Michael Siegel. Written by John August. Based on the book *Charlie
and the Chocolate Factory* by Roald Dahl. Directed by Tim Burton.
Cast: Johnny Depp (Willy Wonka), Freddie Highmore (Charlie
Bucket), David Kelly (Grandpa Joe), Helena Bonham Carter (Mrs
Bucket), Noah Taylor (Mr Bucket), James Fox (Mr Salt), Deep Roy
(Oompa Loompa), Christopher Lee (Dr. Wonka), Julia Winter
(Veruca Salt), Jordan Fry (Mike Teavee), AnnaSophia Robb (Violet
Beauregarde), Philip Wiegratz (Augustus Gloop).

Tim Burton's Corpse Bride (2005)

76 mins (Warner Bros.)
Casting by Michelle Guish. Music by Danny Elfman. Editors: Chris
Lebenzon, Jonathan Lucas. Cinematography by Pete Kozachik.
Production Design by Alex McDowell. Producers: Allison Abbate,
Tim Burton. Associate Producers: Derek Frey, Tracy Shaw.
Executive Producers: Jeffrey Auerbach, Joe Ranft. Written by John
August, Caroline Thompson, Pamela Pettler, Tim Burton, Carlos
Grangel. Directed by Tim Burton, Mike Johnson. *Featuring the voices
of:* Johnny Depp (Victor Van Dort), Helena Bonham Carter (Corpse
Bride), Emily Watson (Victoria Everglot), Tracey Ullman (Nell Van
Dort/Hildegarde), Paul Whitehouse (William Van
Dort/Mayhew/Paul The Head Waiter), Joanna Lumley (Maudeline
Everglot), Albert Finney (Finis Everglot), Richard E. Grant (Barkis
Bittern), Christopher Lee (Pastor Galswells), Michael Gough (Elder
Gutknecht).

Bones (2006)

(*Video for The Killers' single 'Bones'*)
Directed by Tim Burton.

Sweeney Todd (2008)

(DreamWorks SKG)
Casting by Susie Figgis. Music by Stephen Sondheim. Editor: Chris
Lebenzon. Costume Design by Colleen Atwood. Cinematography by
Dariusz Wolski. Production Design by Dante Ferretti. Producers:
John Logan, Laurie MacDonald, Walter F. Parkes, Richard D.
Zanuck. Associate Producer: Derek Frey. Executive Producer:
Patrick McCormick. Written by Christopher Bond, John Logan,
Hugh Wheeler. Based on the musical *Sweeney Todd: The Demon
Barber of Fleet Street* by Stephen Sondheim. Directed by Tim Burton.
Cast: Johnny Depp (Sweeney Todd), Helena Bonham Carter (Mrs
Lovett), Alan Rickman (Judge Turpin), Timothy Spall (Beadle
Bamford), Christopher Lee (Gentleman Ghost), Sacha Baron
Cohen (Signor Adolfo Pirelli), Jayne Wisener (Johanna).

Acknowledgements

The following articles appear by courtesy of their respective coyright holders: 'Vincent' by David Coleman, from *Cinefantastique*, April/May 1983. Reprinted by permission. 'Tim Burton and Vincent Price' interview by Graham Fuller, from *Interview*, December 1990. Reprinted by permission. 'Hansel and Gretel' by Taylor L. White, from *Cinefantastique*, November 1989. Reprinted by permission. 'Frankenweenie' by Michael Mayo, from *Cinefantastique*, May 1985. Reprinted by permission. 'Aladdin's Lamp' by Taylor L. White, from *Cinefantastique*, November 1989. Reprinted by permission. 'Other Weirdness' by Taylor L. White, from *Cinefantastique*, November 1989. Reprinted by permission. 'Pee Wee's Big Adventure' by Taylor L. White, from *Cinefantastique*, November 1989. Reprinted by permission. 'Is America Ready for a Nut Who's a Genius' by David Elliot, from *The San Diego Union-Tribune*, 18 July 1985. Reprinted by permission. 'Pee Wee's Big Adventure' review by Alan Jones, from *Starburst*, August 1987. Reprinted by permission. 'Gleeful Grand Guignol of Beetlejuice' by Kevin Thomas, from *Los Angeles Times*, 30 March 1988. Reprinted by permission. 'Beetlejuice' review by Kim Newman, from *Monthly Film Bulletin*, August 1988. Reprinted by permission. 'Beetle Mania' by Simon Garfield, from *Time Out*, 3 August 1988. Reprinted by permission. 'Babes in Cinema Land' by David Denby, from *Premiere*, July 1989. Reprinted by permission. 'Batman' by Taylor L. White, from *Cinefantastique*, July 1989. Reprinted by permission. 'Batman' by Alan Jones, from *Cinefantastique*, November 1989. Reprinted by permission. 'Batman' review by Kim Newman, from *Monthly Film Bulletin*, September 1989. 'Tim Cuts Up' by Frank Rose, from *Premiere*, January 1991. Reprinted by permission. 'Edward Scissorhands' review by Steve Biodrowski, from *Cinefantastique*, February 1991. Reprinted by permission. 'Three Go Mad in Gotham' by Jeffrey Resner, from *Empire*, August 1992. Reprinted by permission. 'Battier and Battier' by Richard Corliss, from *Time*, 22 June 1992. Reprinted by permission. 'Trouble in Gotham' from Front Desk, *Empire*, September 1992. Reprinted by permission. 'Tim Burton' by Ken Hanke, from *Films in Review*, November/ December 1992, January/February 1993. Reprinted by permission. 'Ghoul World' by Mimi Avins, from *Premiere*, November 1993. Reprinted by permission. 'Animated Dreams' by Leslie Felperin, from *Sight and Sound*, December 1994. Reprinted by permission. 'Tim Burton's The Nightmare Before Christmas' review by Kim Newman, from *Sight and Sound*, December 1994. Reprinted by permission. 'The Wood, the Bad and the Ugly' by John Clarke, from *Premiere*, October 1994. Reprinted by permission. 'Ed Wood . . . Not'

by J. Hoberman, from *Sight and Sound*, May 1995. Reprinted by permission. 'Ed Wood' review by Kim Newman, *Sight and Sound*, May 1995. Reprinted by permission. 'Martian Inspiration: the Bubblegum Cards' by Chuck Wagner, from *Cinefantastique*, January 1997. Reprinted by permission. 'Hidden Gems' by Anthony C. Ferrante, from *Fangoria*, March 1997. Reprinted by permission. 'Men Are from Mars, Women Are from Venus' by Christine Spines, from *Premiere*, January 1997. Reprinted by permission. 'Pax Americana' by J. Hoberman, from *Sight and Sound*, February 1997. Reprinted by permission. 'Mars Attacks' review by Kim Newman, from *Sight and Sound*, March 1997. Reprinted by permission. 'One on One: Tim Burton' by David Mills, from *Empire*, February 2000. Reprinted by permission. 'Graveyard Shift' by Mark Salisbury, from *Total Film/Fangoria*, February 2000/November 1999. Reprinted by permission. 'The Cage of Reason' by Kim Newman, from *Sight and Sound*, January 2000. Reprinted by permission. 'Heads or Tails' by J. Hoberman, from *Village Voice*, 24 November 1999. Reprinted by permission. 'Remaking, Not Aping, an Original' by Richard Natale, from *Los Angeles Times*, 6 May 2001. Reprinted by permission. 'Planet of the Apes' review by Owen Gleiberman, from *Entertainment Weekly*, 25th July 2001. Reprinted by permission. 'Don't Monkey with a Great Ape' by Jonathan Romney, from *Independent on Sunday*, 20 August 2001. Reprinted by permission. 'Big Fish in His Own Pond' by Josh Tyrangiel, from *Time* magazine, 1 December 2003. Reprinted by permission. 'Big Fish' by Manohla Dargis, from *Los Angeles Times*, 10 December 2003. Reprinted by permission. 'Sweet Smell of Success' by Rob Waugh, from *Mail On Sunday*, April 2005. Reprinted by permission. 'Eye Candy' by David Edelstein, from Slate.com, 14 July 2005. Reprinted by permission. 'Director of the Living Dead' by Edward Douglas, from ComingSoon.net, 13 September 2005. Reprinted by permission. 'Tim Burton's Corpse Bride' review by Stephanie Zacharek, from Salon.com, 16 September 2005. Reprinted by permission.

We would like to thank the following organisations for supplying photographs: BFI Stills, Posters and Designs, Warner Bros., Twentieth Century Fox Productions, Walt Disney Productions, Touchstone Pictures, Buena Vista, Paramount Pictures, Hollywood Book and Poster Company, Showtime TV, NBC TV.

It has not been possible in all cases to trace the copyright sources, and the publisher would be glad to hear from any such unacknowledged copyright holders.